Becoming Rasta

Becoming Rasta

Origins of Rastafari Identity in Jamaica

Charles Price

NEW YORK UNIVERSITY PRESS

New York and London

NEW YORK UNIVERSITY PRESS
New York and London
www.nyupress.org

Library of Congress Cataloging-in-Publication Data

Price, Charles, 1963–
Becoming Rasta : origins of Rastafari identity in Jamaica / Charles Price.
p. cm.
Includes bibliographical references and index.
ISBN-13: 978-0-8147-6746-7 (cloth : alk. paper)
ISBN-10: 0-8147-6746-X (cloth : alk. paper)
ISBN-13: 978-0-8147-6747-4 (pbk. : alk. paper)
ISBN-10: 0-8147-6747-8 (pbk. : alk. paper)
1. Rastafari movement—Jamaica. 2. Identification (Religion)
3. Blacks—Race identity—Jamaica. 4. Jamaica—Religion. I. Title.
BL2532.R37P75   2009
299.6'76097292—dc22   2009014684

New York University Press books are printed on acid-free paper,
and their binding materials are chosen for strength and durability.
We strive to use environmentally responsible suppliers and materials
to the greatest extent possible in publishing our books.

Manufactured in the United States of America
c   10 9 8 7 6 5 4 3 2 1
p   10 9 8 7 6 5 4 3 2

Livication

I livicate (instead of "dead-icate") this book to all of the elder Rastafari of Jamaica, and to the younger ones who will continue to carry forward the banner of Rastafari. I also livicate this book to my baby grandson, Bongo BJ, who eventually will grapple with Blackness and identity. Ras Sam Brown, Rasta Ivey, Ras Brenton, and Brother Yendis have passed away. May our memories of them live forever.

Contents

Preface   ix

Acknowledgments   xix

Introduction   1

1   Race Formation and Morally Configured Black Identities   19

2   Ethnogenesis, Surprise, and Collective Identity Formation   55

3   The Positive Power of Stigma and Black Identity   98

4   Encounters   132

5   Acts of Identity Work   166

6   Rastafari Nation on the Move: Identity and Change   201

Conclusion: Toward a More Comprehensive   223
Understanding of Racial Identity Formation

Acronyms   233

Notes   235

References   241

Index   259

About the Author   267

Preface

This book examines the historical, social, and personal sources and consolidation of Rastafari identity and experience in Jamaica. It reveals the ways in which both the ancient and modern past provide cultural resources for the present and how the Rastafari use these resources to fashion a positive Black identity in the face of discrimination.

There exists a substantial volume of work on the Rastafari, much of it published since the late 1980s. Surprisingly absent in these accounts are Rastafari testimonies about how they came to identify as Rastafari, an identity which first appeared in the early 1930s. Their accounts tell us about the paths and journeys that people have taken to become and remain Rastafari. The recollections of the Rastafari on their experience and identity also offer us much more. Their stories invite us to ask novel questions and seek answers framed by new viewpoints. Why and how are stigmatized identities like Rastafari and Blackness given positive value? What are some of the ways in which personal experience, society, and history reciprocally shape each other? We will draw valuable answers to these questions and others from the personal and social experience of the Rastafari.

On November 2, 1930, Ras Tafari, King of Ethiopia, was crowned Emperor of Ethiopia, and adopted the name Haile Selassie I, or Power of the Holy Trinity. The Emperor also identified himself as "King of Kings" and "Conquering Lion of the Tribe of Judah." These new appellations manifested biblical significance for attentive Black Jamaicans who associated the Emperor's titles with the Messiah as identified in the Old and New Testaments of the *King James* Bible, especially the Book of Revelation. International newspapers, including Jamaica's leading paper, the *Daily Gleaner*, covered the coronation. A sentence in a brief column published there on November 3, 1930, read: "The Empress and Emperor seated on golden thrones, dressed in the Abyssinian style, beneath a canopy surmounted by the Crown of Judah" (p. 18). This passage, dripping with imagery, captured the imagination of many Black Jamaicans.

Within a year, several Jamaicans had concluded that the Emperor was the Messiah described in Revelation, and they began to preach this emergent philosophy to all who would listen. They added their own twist, however: this Emperor, this Messiah, was *first* a Redeemer of Black people, and then of humankind. By 1931, the birth of a new identity and people—ethnogenesis—was set in motion. Adherents to this new worldview called themselves "Rastafari." Others would soon call them "Ras Tafarites," and later, "Rastafarians." This newly identified people privileged a positive conception of Black identity and culture, contravening the hegemony of Europe and Whiteness in Jamaica. What was good, right, worthy, and normal in Jamaica had, up to this time, been evaluated against a standard of European and White history, culture, and experience.

Whiteness had been internalized by many Black Jamaicans in the wake of colonization. By at least the mid- to late 1700s, however, a small but growing number of Black Jamaicans established what would develop into cultural alternatives to White hegemony. Race, religion, justice, and messianism played central roles in various efforts by Black Jamaicans to create cultural alternatives.

The Rastafari are a recent incarnation of these efforts to develop racially grounded cultural alternatives, and like their predecessors, they, too, suffered from suppression and rejection by their fellow citizens and kin. Yet, the Rastafari worldview, unlike that of their predecessors, developed into a durable cultural identity—the result of serendipity and Rastafari conviction—that has persisted for nearly 80 years. Rastafari shifted from being outcasts to becoming cultural exemplars of Blackness from the early 1970s into the twenty-first century.

Rastafari identity is a version of a long-standing set of racialized dialogues concerned with challenging oppression and White cultural hegemony. The stifling of Black consciousness through deracination, miseducation, and oppression has dogged Blacks in the Americas for centuries. Along with the whip, cudgel, and rope, Whites created and reinforced their authority through culture, religion, and education. There is wisdom in the adage that a people without knowledge of their culture and history are a people adrift. An active part of Rastafari identity has involved internalizing affirmative interpretations of Black history and culture—including religion—to generate a recognizable narrative grounded in the ancient past and in remembering the modern past, the injustice and trauma endured for centuries by enslaved Africans and their descendants.

The Rastafari presaged and prefigured what the Martiniquan social critic Frantz Fanon articulated as he struggled against White hegemony, miseducation, and deracination that had skewed Blacks' views of Blackness and themselves:

> What? I have barely opened eyes that had been blindfolded and someone already wants to drown me in the universal? . . . I need to lose myself in my negritude, to see the fires, the segregation, the repressions, the rapes, the discriminations, the boycotts. We need to put our fingers on every sore that mottles the black uniform. (1967:186–87)

Blackness, in Fanon's formulation, is recognized as a potential salve for treating the sores of miseducation, deracination, and oppression. For the medicine to work, Blacks had to compound it into a dose that could be applied daily. They had to absorb it into their cultural body to invigorate the memories that marked their Blackness as a healthy experience.

We will focus in these pages on how a stigmatized racial identity is recast as positive, how it is perpetuated, and, perhaps most important, why people are motivated to embrace it. The Rastafari recognize the power of "history in person" (I borrowed the phrase from Dorothy Holland and Jean Lave [2001]) and seek to feel it, wear it, and wield it. Let us use Fanon, briefly, to illuminate what we will be learning from the Rastafari themselves:

> Every colonized people—in other words, every people in whose soul an inferiority complex has been created by the death and burial of its local cultural originality—finds itself face to face with the language of the civilizing nation; that is, with the culture of the mother country. The colonized is elevated above his jungle status in proportion to his adoption of the mother country's cultural standards. He becomes whiter as he renounces his Blackness, his jungle. (Fanon, 1967:18)

Race is of human making. The effort of humans to create categories, assign relationships, attribute causes—to create identities for ourselves and things—is universal. In developing ideas of race, we humans do what we are good at (Alleyne, 2002; Holt, 2000). Yet, subversion is also something that we are good at. If category-making and identity-making can serve positive functions, there is also the potential for nefarious uses. People of Europe and the United States, in their efforts to understand and explain themselves to themselves, and to justify their acts of colonization, ordered the world with themselves as its leaders and as the epitome of humankind. In their schema there were losers. Africans and their descendants ranked at the bottom of nearly every list. Ideas of race serving as explanations for cultural and phenotypic differences associated with biology, climate, and moral history were woven into elaborate systems of privilege perpetuated across great expanses of space and time. Schools, businesses, government policies, work, residential arrangements, rules restricting interaction, and other institutions performed this work. Accompanying those institutions were theories, books, jokes, songs, cartoons, and so on. In Fanon's words: "The feeling of inferiority of the colonized is the correlative of the European's feeling of superiority. Let us have the courage to say it outright: *It is the racist who creates his inferior*" (1967:93, original italics).

But this is only a part of the story. Remember, I said that we humans are creators of categories, relationships, makers of causes and identities. We are capable of artful subversion. So, if you continually tell me that I am an animal, unintelligent, childlike, dangerous, without culture and history, perhaps I may believe you. Perhaps I will imbibe your identity and cultural imaginaries and situate myself within a Eurocentric framework, even though I know, at least to some extent, that I am not European, that I am not White. Here is where subversion becomes relevant. You can tell me that Blackness is indicative of inferiority and fallen status, but I am also able to reply, "No. It is venerable and majestic; it is only because of Whiteness that we Blacks have to make the argument. Just as you exalted yourself in your story, I can do the same, using cultural resources that make my case—maybe even taking a page from your book by declaring that God looks like me and us." Subversion, as it relates to the identity work of producing and maintaining affirmative conceptions of Blackness, entails turning things on their head. This, the Rastafari have done.

Aimé Césaire points us to some of the elementary exercises that involved racial subversion: "We adopted the word *nègre* (dare we translate it as 'nigger'?), as a term of defiance. It was a defiant name. To some extent it was a reaction of enraged youth. Since there was shame about the word *nègre*, we chose the word *nègre*" (2000:89, original italics). Subversion, of the kind practiced by the Rastafari, has a pragmatic, deliberate aspect because it requires that its practitioners attain a certain awareness, an awareness that one can only learn. As Césaire suggests:

If someone asks what my conception of Negritude is, I answer above all that it is a concrete rather than an abstract coming to consciousness. What I have been telling you about—the atmosphere in which we lived, an atmosphere of assimilation in which Negro people were ashamed of themselves—has great importance. We lived in an atmosphere of rejection, and we developed an inferiority complex. I have always thought that the black man was searching for his identity. And it seemed to me that if what we want is to establish this identity, then we must have a concrete consciousness of what we are . . . of the first fact of our lives: that we are black; that we were black and have a history, a history that Negroes were not, as you put it, born yesterday, because there have been beautiful and important black civilizations. At the time we began to write, people could write a history of world civilization without devoting a single chapter to Africa, as if Africa had made no contributions to the world. Therefore we affirmed that we were Negroes and that we were proud of it. (2000:91–92)

Fanon recounts a personal experience of a racialized encounter in which a young White girl exclaimed in fright at the sight of him, "the Negro." This event indicated to Fanon his power as a Black man to repulse, instill fear, and arouse rejection, all powers that he never desired but which were bestowed upon him by virtue of living in and circulating through societies in which race was salient. His recognition of his Blackness and its imposition upon him was a part of his reorientation and resocialization into a consciousness that dispenses positive salience to Black history and culture, a consciousness that asks to uncover explicit connections to the past: "I was responsible at the same time for my body, for my race, for my ancestors. I subjected myself to an objective examination, I discovered my blackness, my ethnic characteristics; and I was batted down by tom-toms, cannibalism, intellectual deficiency, fetishism, racial defects, slave-ships, and above all else, above all: 'Sho' good eatin'" (1967:112).

Finally, Fanon points out the tumultuous, imaginative, intellectual, empowering, historical, and social dimensions of the process of positively valuing Blackness:

I rummaged frenetically through all the antiquity of the black man. What I found there took away my breath . . . cities of more than a hundred thousand people; accounts of learned blacks (doctors of theology who went to Mecca to interpret the Koran). All of that, exhumed from the

past . . . made it possible for me to find a valid historic place. The white
man was wrong, I was not primitive, not even a half man, I belonged to a
race that had already been working in gold and silver two thousand years
ago. (1967:130)

The deracination, miseducation, and oppression that Fanon and Césaire
highlight here, that denigrate, marginalize, and destabilize Blackness, also
paradoxically provide the context for validating, historicizing, and instilling it with divine power. Barbara Hannah, reflecting on her journey
toward Rastafari, gives an example: "It was an education of Black liberation—liberation from racism, poverty, from the constant pain of ever being a stranger in strange lands, of being ever second class in a predominantly white world. . . . Rastafari enabled a positive Black consciousness
with a God of our own" (2006:2).

There are many solutions to the identity challenges posed by racism
and Whiteness. Identities must be cut from histories, relationships, cultural resources, desires, and modes of subsistence and sewn together in
an artful way to allow their bearers to shift and rearrange them as needed.
Thus, the positive valorization of Blackness as it relates to both individuals and collectivities requires that we look to the past, assess the present,
and imagine the future, just as the Rastafari, negritudists, and other exemplars of positive Black identity have done.

This book cannot claim the ultimate word about a story that continues to be created every day. I can only provide an account that we hope
takes us further toward understanding not just the Rastafari but Blackness and racial identity. This book connects some of the pieces that have
heretofore remained disarticulated: how cultural resources developed
and reworked over centuries provide material for new collectives and
identities, how "society" reacts to these identities, and what people experience as they put these resources to work generating a new way of
being in the world.

Some Background and Context

During 1995, I began thinking about collecting life stories of Rastafari elders. I knew they and Jamaica had witnessed dramatic shifts in how they
were perceived. Many of the older Rastafari were reaching an age where in-
firmities might render them unavailable to share their experience. Along-
side telling us about such changes, I knew the narratives of the Rastafari

elders who had lived through much of the history of the Rastafari would tell us much about identity, especially why and how people had become Rastafari. Their stories might also help us patch together how their collective identity evolved. Such narratives would give us a better impression of the Rastafari sense of self, especially their view of their connection to the past. After all, ordinary Black men and women were calling themselves Ethiopians, modern Israelites, and contemporary manifestations of Shadrach, Meschach, and Abednego (biblical figures who survived being cast into a burning fire by Babylonian King Nebuchadnezzar). They were singing chants about leaving for Africa, breaking chains of oppression, and remembering slavery. Through the Rastafari, Black pride has been ingrained in Jamaica's national consciousness. The society that once forced the Rastafari to hide in alleys, ghettos, and gullies, that threatened to liquidate them, that institutionalized their leaders and called their followers dirty now exhorts the richness of their culture to attract tourists seeking an exotic experience.

A Brief Note on Style

I want to alert the reader to several stylistic practices used in this book. I refer to the Rastafari whose life stories inform this work as my "interlocutors" and "narrators" to remind us of the dialogue and interaction through which we crafted the stories. Although I mainly use "Rastafari," like other writers, where I use "Rastafarian" and "Rasta," these should be understood as synonymous (e.g., Murrell, 1998:2).

Throughout this book, I capitalize race: Black, White, and Brown. C. Eric Lincoln notes the "strong resistance" to spelling black with an uppercase "B" when it is "used as a proper noun to signify identity. But there is no such resistance in the case of 'White Russian,' or 'South Dakotan,' or 'West Virginian,' 'Blackfoot Indians' . . . such inconsistent reactions to names as symbols of identity suggests that, deep in the human psyche, names may still be confused with identity, and identity with power" (1993:220). "Black," as used in this book, does involve ethnicity and refers to specific groups and a general category. Kenneth Mostern (1999:225) decided not to use an uppercase "B" for Black because it is rarely used by the African American writers that he respects, while Susan Greenbaum (2002:341) counsels against "B" regardless of whether noun or adjective because it would mean capitalizing White and Brown, thus failing to "disarm" race. These are valid reasons and so are mine. Race, as understood by my Rastafari interlocutors, carries a force deserving of capitalization, regardless of whether we embrace it as positive, focus on how it is used to debase, or fall somewhere within these poles. "Black" is more likely to remind the reader of the salience of race than "black." And certainly, if I capitalize Black, I cannot slight White or Brown, especially because in Jamaica the three rely upon each other for positioning in the world of identities.

I use pseudonyms to refer to places, people, and associations with a few exceptions. One exception includes using the actual name if it has already appeared in print or has been used in public media such as radio or television. Another exception involves Rasta Ivey and Prophetess Esther, two women who insisted that I refer to them by name and that I tell the world about them, and Ras Sam Brown, who deemed me his "agent."

The reader will see that the names of many of my interlocutors have the prefixes "Ras," "Empress," "Brother," "Sister," "Bongo," and sometimes, "Rasta." These prefixes are titles of address. The Rastafari use several titles that signify the dignity and nobility they assign to their conception of Blackness, while other titles indicate gender and communal fellowship in the faith. Ras, borrowed from the Ethiopian vocabulary, denotes royalty and also is used to mean "head." Queen and Empress (and "Princess") denote feminine royalty. Brother and Sister indicate gender and spiritual and cultural affiliation as Rastafari, evoking ideas of comradeship within the faith of Rastafari, very similar to how Christians use the terms. Bongo (and Congo) is used both as a demeaning term for Africa, Black phenotypes (broad noses, knotted hair), and stereotyping Blacks as dull-witted. The Rastafari re-defined Bongo (and Congo) to function as a positive and honorific designation of Blackness and Africa. The use of Rasta as a prefix identifies one as Rastafari when used with a person's name (e.g., Rasta Ivey); it can also be used as a term of affection.

I have refrained from completely translating Jamaican patois into American Standard English except in some of the most opaque passages and utterances. This may make the text more challenging for some readers, but I have tried to keep as much of the style and cadence of my interlocutors as possible.

I close this preface with a spiritual chant sung at Rastafari ceremonies. It conveys the elder Rastafaris' sensitivity, criticism, and sense of power and control grounded in nature, race, and redemption:

Wonder why the White man them no go [a]way
for we want go home a yard [Africa]
for we want go home a yard
Rastafari a go burn them out, burn them out,
Burn them out Ithiopia land [Africa-Ethiopia]
Hot fire burn them out, burn them out
Burn them out Ithiopia land
I say go [a]way Babylonian,
I say go [a]way Babylonian,
Babylonian you must get a great shook of lightning
Babylonian you must get a great shook of thunder,
Babylonian you must get a great shook of earthquake,
On a this fine day.

Acknowledgments

This book has gestated within me for a long time, and with the support of many people, I am glad and grateful that it is published. I cannot list everyone who, in my mind, played a part in one way or another, to my writing this book. Nonetheless, over the past decade many people have made enormous contributions to my work, thinking, and enjoyment of life, even though they might not know it. I do.

Setha Low and William Cross Jr., both of the City University of New York Graduate Center, have been exceptional and generous mentors to me since my graduate student days there and have commented on one or another part of this book. Thanks, Bill, for reading chapter 3. Arturo Escobar and Dorothy Holland, of the University of North Carolina-Chapel Hill, have proved outstanding faculty mentors. Dorothy carefully read a draft of the manuscript and offered immensely useful suggestions for revision. I thank Dorothy and Arturo for inviting me into their homes and lives; it has made sufferable for me what sometimes painfully feels like living in a giant suburban bubble, here in the Triangle Area of North Carolina. Constance Buchanan, formerly of the Ford Foundation, read four chapters of an early draft of the manuscript and offered incisive and encouraging suggestions for developing the book. My comrade, and dear friend, sociologist Robert Sauté, read the entire manuscript, and carefully and skillfully edited my prose where it was rough and befogged. Thanks, Robert.

I have been fortunate along the way to get the assistance of many other immensely competent people. UNC-Chapel Hill Ph.D. students Robert Pleasants and Samantha Abels provided editorial assistance. Leslie Calihman-Alabi's support was indispensable; she proofread, entered corrections, formatted the bibliography, and helped me track down elusive documents. Massie Minor, an undergraduate at UNC-Chapel Hill, proved himself a capable researcher, helping me find and organize hundreds of news stories about the Rastafari. Malekia Stennett, a research assistant at the *Daily Gleaner*, helped me search out early *Gleaner* articles on the Rastafari. Pam Tarlton, Jackson

Branch Library, Jackson, South Carolina, and Linda Mackey, local historian member of the Silver Bluff Baptist Church, Beech Island, South Carolina, helped me search for unpublished sources of information about George Lisle. The staff of the public library in Barnwell, South Carolina, were always accommodating when I needed space to work and think. Amanda Henley, GIS Librarian at UNC-Chapel Hill, helped me create the maps. Norris Johnson, professor of Anthropology at UNC-Chapel Hill, helped me digitally "touch up" and repair some of the images used for this book. Courtney Smith, my daughter, assisted in formatting and organizing the table of contents and illustrations. And, thanks to my dear comrade, Michael Cooke, formerly director of Museums of the Institute of Jamaica. Michael knows about his land of birth; he taught me much about Jamaica, and he provided me a comfortable place to live during my extended stays in Jamaica. Thanks, Michael. Thanks also to Valentino Ellis, Terrence Blackman, Gregory Anderson, Julie Russell, and Fire, who provided intellectual and principled encouragement, and always took good care of me whenever I was in New York City.

Jennifer Hammer, editor at New York University Press, has been supremely professional, accommodating, and patient with me, throughout the publication process. Thank you, Jennifer. This book also benefitted from some suggestions offered by anonymous reviewers.

My work for this book was greatly aided by the release time provided by fellowships from the Institute for the Arts & Humanities (UNC-Chapel Hill) and the Woodrow Wilson National Fellowship Foundation, and a University Research Council publishing grant (UNC–Chapel Hill).

Since some of the key ideas in this book, and some of the research upon which I draw, originated with my doctoral dissertation work at the City University of New York Graduate School and University Center, I want to acknowledge my dissertation committee members: Setha Low, William Cross Jr., Joan Mencher, Donald Robotham, and Colin Palmer. They gave me the appropriate doses of support, encouragement, and critique.

Because the last shall be first, I want to acknowledge the most important contributors of all: the many elder Rastafari who shared their stories with me, and with you. Ras Sydney DaSilva, Ras Historian, and Ras Toney Campbell, were central supporters and encouragers of this work. Thanks to my mother Viola, for the inestimable support, encouragement, and love you have provided me since birth.

Should any financial profits come of this work, I shall turn them over to the Rastafari Centralization Organization to support their effort to "organize and centralize for our future development." Forward Ever!

Introduction

Rasta Ivey, one of the oldest living Rastafari women, recalled defending her faith despite being ridiculed and sent to an asylum for the insane. Another elder Rastafarian described how, before her twelfth birthday, she began hearing the voices of Christ and Haile Selassie I telling her about Africa and slavery. Her mother thought she was on the verge of lunacy. Brother Yendis remembered when, as a preadolescent during the 1940s, he saw a Rastafari man accosted by a belligerent policeman for no apparent reason. This incident led him to learn more about the Rastafari, as he questioned what made them so threatening. Today, the three remain as committed as ever to their Rastafari faith and identity, even though the paths that each followed to become Rastafari and their relationships to other Rastafari vary. What led them and others to embrace a stigmatized identity and become Rastafari? Why are Africa, slavery and injustice, and a language of redemption so prominent in the Rastafari self-concept and worldview?

A small but growing number of people began to identify themselves in the 1930s as adherents of Haile Selassie I, whom they viewed as an incarnation of God. These Rastafari, however, were concerned with more than religion. They were also concerned with racial redemption and the political concerns this entailed. Thus, we can very generally describe the Rastafari as a religiously *and* racially conscious people, many of them subscribing to some strain of the protean ideologies of Black nationalism. As Rastafari poet Mutabaruka explains it, Rastafari is a Black power ideology with a "theological nucleus" (2006:27). Within two years of their emergence, the British began spying on the Rastafari because of their anticolonial talk; within 30 years, elite Jamaicans had deemed them a threat to national security; and by the early 1970s, the Rastafari had become exemplars of Black culture noted for their caustic social commentary. The Rastafari are best known in the popular mind for their dreadlocks, their use of marijuana as a sacrament, and their contributions to the Jamaican popular music, reggae. Academics and others have depicted the Rastafari as deviants, delusional, or a liberatory vanguard. I offer a different depiction and approach. One primary concern involves explaining the evolution of a positive and morally configured formulation of Blackness and Black identity and the ways it has been variously used by the Rastafari and others. Another concern involves connecting the evolution of racialized collectivities with the experience of individuals, and the cultural resources and identity work that they separately and together entail. A third concern involves racial identity generally: how it works, and how the interaction between people, social memory, and history give it life. My account of how and why people become Rastafari is also a story of how a social movement is made. This is a fainter dialogue than the other three. But, like a conversation occurring at the next table, if you focus your attention, you can make out what is going on.

Race is central to the stories my narrators told me about becoming Rastafari. Although I could also give religion the central position in the Rastafari identity complex, I believe it is reasonable to treat the two as co-dependently central because religion, too, is racialized, along with other important identity markers such as justice and righteousness. I have sought in these pages to develop a many-sided perspective on identity—historical, social, and personal—an approach attentive to the mutual influences between "biography and history," and "self and world" (Mills, 2000:4).

On the one side, there are the stories and memories that elder Rastafari tell about their personal identity. When my interlocutors told me about their pathways into Rastafari, often I could feel the past, the ill will of the malicious police officer, the smugness of colonial administrators and litigators, ridicule from associates and strangers, and their conviction that becoming Rastafari was the right thing to do. These identity stories are more than the accounts of independent individuals. They and their stories are social and historical products, portals into the past, present, and larger world. From another side, this book is a narrative of ethnogenesis, an account of the birth and evolution of a new collectivity, the Rastafari. By considering the experience of people coming to attach themselves to and identify with a collectivity, we can also gain insight into the complex and unpredictable nature of how groups and social or collective identifications form and evolve out of interactions and collisions between people and things. From yet another side, we are interested in the history and cultural resources that provide the material that people use to fashion morally configured Black identities such as Rastafari.

I suspect that some readers might be interested primarily in the Rastafari experiences and voices and others in the conceptual frameworks used to situate their voices and my analysis. I ask readers, however, to consider both to be important, and inseparable, to an understanding of racial formation, ethnogenesis, and how individuals position themselves in relation to both.

Race Formation and the Development of a Morally Configured Black Identity

> I came to see, to know, that we [Black people] have been crucified since we arrived in this land [Jamaica]. So it go. . . . We [Rastafari] are the ancients here today, to continue that trod of Isaiah, Daniel, Elijah, Jeremiah, Moses, David, Solomon . . . it is our prophets and warriors in this land who come before us and tell the people that iniquity must done [end], that our people must be free . . . it is that same Tacky and Cuffy and Nanny and Bogle [who led insurrections for liberation and justice] . . . and Rasta come take it up [and carry it forward].
>
> (Rasta Ivey)

If we want to know how and why people become Rastafari, we must search out the lineages and history of the cultural resources they use to create their identity. This requires answering a broad question: How did Blackness and its various permutations—especially the morally configured ones—develop in Jamaica and persist to the present? Chapter 1 knits together an answer to this question.

Blackness in Jamaica evolved through pan-ethnic assimilation and consolidation. A common linguistic, religious, and racial framework crystallized and became the context for socialization and identification as various African ethnic, religious, linguistic, and regional identifications faded away. Race formation—the acts though which people use institutions, history, ideas, policies, and specific practices to make race socially significant (Omi & Winant, 1986)—has been a fundamental aspect of the development of Blackness in Jamaica and elsewhere. Blackness has shown itself to be a remarkably durable and compelling source of identification in Jamaica. It is a dynamic condition, worldview, and cluster of cultural resources flexible enough to serve many purposes.

Blacks are defined here as Africans and their descendants brought to the "New World." White Europeans[1] assigned to them the racial category

"Black" (and "Ethiopian"). Assignment of an identity does not mean that people necessarily accept that identity or that, even in the case of acceptance, it will be interpreted as the inscribers intended. However, when the power to impose an identity is strong enough, and the means extensive enough, categorization can influence a person's self-concept. Prevailing White designations of Blackness often have been disparaging and vituperative, and always less than flattering. It is not surprising that many people labeled Black have sought to avoid, ignore, or reject the label.

Yet, as early as 1700, we can identify efforts to define Blackness in religious, moral, and affirmative ways, suffusing the category with a different content. A religiously inspired Congolese woman in São Salvador, Congo, claimed that Christ had appeared as a Black man, that his Apostles too were Black, and that São Salvador was Bethlehem and Congo God's new Kingdom (Spencer, 1999:3,172).

As an ascribed category, Blackness is ethnicized through people's self-identification and claim on the category. Such claims typically emphasize beliefs in a shared homeland, history, "blood," and experience (Cornell & Hartmann, 1998). What makes this real and enduring is not genes and heritance, but social memory, feelings, and self-awareness. Being and becoming Black involves mutual engagement between the ascribed category and the feeling and awareness of Blackness from a personal perspective. "You see," said 85-year-old Sister Mariam, "through the Garvey people I come to love Black people, [because] I see we inna the same lot even though some [Black people] carry on like them different." Although much emphasis is put on phenotype (e.g., skin color, facial features, and hair texture), Blackness is really a cultural phenomenon that acquires meaning through symbols, ideas, practices, and the ways in which these intersect with people's sense of shared history and experience. Music, food preferences, language, art, phenotype, beliefs about origins, kinship, and worldview, and a history of subjugation and marginalization are some of the primary themes that may define formations of Blackness.

Blackness in Jamaica has many permutations, and we will focus on one particular orientation, a morally configured and affirmative understanding of Blackness that is prone to politicization, both by those who subscribe to the identity and those who contest it. Morally configured Blackness has been profoundly informed by religious understandings, both African and Christian, and sustained by a racial moral economy that has given character to understandings of "rightness" and rights as these relate to livelihood and freedom.

Ethnogenesis and Complexity:
The Making of a People and a Collective Identification

A handful of evangelists helped catalyze what has grown into a complex identity and full-fledged people who now imagine themselves as a nation. Who would have imagined in 1941, when founding Rastafari evangelist Leonard Howell's commune was raided by police, that the Rastafari present that day, and others like them, would evolve² into a collectivity that would significantly influence how Jamaicans conceived of Blackness and the power of liberation through self-transformation?

In chapter 2, I tap theories of complexity to augment my account of the ethnogenesis of the Rastafari. By drawing our attention to the birth and evolution of a people, the ethnogenesis approach offers us the opportunity to delve into the dynamics of collective identity formation, especially the social interactions, conflict, disruptions, and unanticipated outcomes involved. I combine the focus on ethnogenesis with the concepts of "perturbation" and "self-organization," in order to emphasize the contingency, unpredictability, and increasing complexity involved in Rastafari ethnogenesis. Perturbations are not simply crises; they involve disruption of evolutionary trajectories, change business as usual, and may lead to new practices and understandings resulting from a need to adapt to new situations or challenges. Self-organization points us toward solutions to the mysterious: how did the Rastafari continue to grow in numbers and influence without a plan or some guiding force? How do the activities and experiences of individuals connect with this evolving sense of collective identity? Consider, for a moment, the connection between Ras Jayze's experience, and the larger conflict between the Rastafari and other Jamaicans during the late 1950s:

> Warriors, we had to be. A police break off him baton 'pon me head. I had no weapon. Only word, sound, and power [a Rastafari belief that words and sounds have emancipative, healing, and protective powers]. That was all we used against them Babylon. It was so powerful them had to attack we. The power and presence of the Rasta burned them. Everyone was against we. And we had to be against them. Persecution came from the state, the police, the church, the family.

Personal experience such as Ras Jayze's provided the basis for collective identity and personal perception. Persecutors, real and imagined, played an important part in the identity work of the Rastafari.

Because ethnogenesis is far more complex than the neat narratives that people create to tell their history, I focus on disruptive and watershed moments in Rastafari ethnogenesis. These moments allow us to see plainly things like contending and shifting constructions of identity, symbols and meaning, and struggles around control and power. The watershed events that are a focus of chapter 2 marked milestones in the Rastafari's sense of themselves and how they were perceived by the public, how they collectively transitioned from pariahs to exemplars of Black culture and history.

Between Peoplehood and Social Movement

The word Rastafari is often followed by "movement," and several of my Rastafari interlocutors also apply the term to themselves. If *The* Rastafari, however, remain a social movement, they must be among the most long-lived! My view is that "movement" describes only part of what some of the Rastafari are involved in. There are those working to attain recognition as a religion, those working on legalizing cannabis as a sacrament, or those working on repatriation. I cannot remember hearing the oldest Rastafari like Rasta Ivey, Brother Dee, or Sister Mariam use movement to refer to themselves. They commonly spoke of "Rasta people," not the "Rasta movement." On the other hand, "movement" is still regularly used by those who became Rastafari during the late 1950s and after. Different generations of Rastafari have developed understandings of how to think of the collectivity and its various efforts. Many of my narrators were or remain involved in activities that we could call "political," such as agitating for official recognition as "Ethiopians." However, these Rastafari represent only a part of the Rastafari, albeit a key part.

What is baffling about the Rastafari as a collectivity has been their numerical growth and appeal, which have not relied on typical methods of recruitment. Ras Sam Brown told me that "You cannot join Rastafari. It is not something you join. That is foolishness. It is something inside of you, an inspiration that come forward." A person, in most cases, makes a conscious, deliberate decision to become Rastafari and grows into the identity through a potentially challenging identity transformation process. Acquiring and internalizing the Rastafari identity is not the end of the process, since continued commitment to it is largely in the hands of the convert (not that autonomous free will is at work). So, there must be something deeply appealing and satisfying about Rastafari identity. Brother Barody, when reflecting on his journey into Rastafari, regularly recalled his memories of the Rastafari of the early 1950s: "I look at them and see how they do things. How they talk to each other, and say 'peace and love' and those things. I did notice that . . . [even though] they say the Rasta are violent and not to be trusted."

Rastafari has much in common with "prefigurative" social movements in that the Rastafari identity (and its cultural complex) provides ideas for people experimenting with different ways of relating and living: people begin trying to model personally the society that they want to live in (e.g., Cashmore, 1979; Jasper, 1997; Poletta, 2002; Graeber, 2004). Movements like Rastafari have often been tagged as escapist and politically ineffective (e.g., R. Smith, 1997:xvi). This may be true if we assess the Rastafari from the standpoint of conventional politics. But the Rastafari show us a non-conventional politics, the kind of collective power described in *Poor People's Movements*, a power that gains traction through its capacity to threaten disruption of business as usual (Piven & Cloward, 1979; Piven, 2006). However, the Rastafari use "quiet power," their alternative model of being and relating, to persuade others. They did not seek state power or largess; yet, the Jamaican government sponsored a delegation to Africa to explore repatriation, and the People's National Party (PNP) used Rastafari language and symbols to communicate with constituents, suggesting the power of the Rastafari at different times.

Many observers believe that Rastafari movements have been "disorganized" and "lacking in leadership" (e.g., Smith et al., 1960:18). This view rests upon the inappropriate assumption that decentralization and ideological diversity are signs of weakness and instability rather than a form of adaptation with particular strengths. Decentralization and diversity mitigate state suppression, creating a range of "niches" that a group can penetrate, and encourage dynamism and innovation (Gerlach & Hine, 1970; Linebaugh & Rediker, 1990; Kebede & Knottnerus, 1998; Price, Nonini, & Foxtree, 2008). They add to the survival and persistence of vulnerable groups in ways that centralization and bureaucratization impede. There is salience in the Rastafari's arguments against centralization and in favor of indigenous anarchism. Although diffuseness may protect against efforts to root out completely a movement or people, it leaves them susceptible to divide-and-conquer strategies and can lead to detrimental competition between different groups (Edmonds, 2003).

Blackness and Identity Transformation

We know that race, like other identities, is socially constructed. We must therefore explain how and why people "construct" a morally figured Black identity and how it operates as a symbol of a collectivity or a people. Through the narratives of the Rastafari we shall see why they became Rastafari and how the process of becoming—their identity transformation—works. In becoming Rastafari, my interlocutors engaged in a dialogue with past movements, martyrs, injustices, and racial understandings. Through imagination, reflection, memory, and dialogue with other people, they became living embodiments of the Black past.

The Rastafari, as a collectivity, are less than 80 years old and comprise a small percentage of the Jamaican population. Although the number may be increasing, there are only a few people of the vintage of my narrators who were raised from childhood as Rastafari. Becoming a Rastafarian is characteristically a conversion process, an identity transformation. However, it is not *only* a religious conversion; it is also a racial one, a transition of Blackness from low to high salience in a person's self-concept. This process can profitably be grasped though Black identity theories such as William Cross Jr.'s theory of nigrescence (i.e., the process of "becoming" Black). Black identity theories such as nigrescence aim to describe the paths and experiences through which people come to positively value Blackness as a salient identification within their identity repertoire. However, the religiously and morally grounded Blackness of Rastafari identity suggested to me that nigrescence theory should be extended to include the religious and moral dimensions of Black identity formation, which I do in chapter 3.

The narratives of my Rastafari interlocutors suggest that some people *do* privilege a few salient identifications such as Blackness over others and that these privileged markers frequently inform other dimensions of their identity. Cross has been the most prolific and profound contributor to our understanding of Black identity transformation, framing it as a model of identity metamorphosis in which a person moves from no or minimal engagement of Blackness to concentrated focus on it (Cross Jr., 1995; Cross Jr., & Vandiver, 2001). Sister Ecila, a former Garveyite who was in her late sixties when I first met her at the Ethiopian Orthodox Church in Kingston, told me:

Once we recognize our Black culture and history, we were no longer content with what we had been taught. . . . It was not England first [anymore].

It was Africa and Black first . . . when Garvey done [left to England] I don't give up on the Black race . . . that is why I am a member of this [Ethiopian Orthodox] Church.

Sister Ecila, after considerable reflection, resolved that her understanding of race and history was inadequate. She believed that so much of what she knew about Blackness and Black people was distorted or negative because of what she had learned in school, in church, and from friends and relatives. It is within this framework that Sister Ecila grappled with changing her worldview, gradually coming to make Blackness and allegiance to Haile Selassie I the cornerstone of her identity. However, there is far more to her story than her privileging Blackness and Rastafari. People like Sister Ecila may have experiences or reach new conclusions about themselves that give rise to their searching for new referents or experiences. The Ethiopian Orthodox Church in Jamaica, which many Rastafari in Jamaica have joined because of its connection to Emperor Selassie I and Ethiopian culture and history, provides a space for people like Sister Ecila to assert and sustain their morally configured Black identities beyond the experiences that lead to identity transformation.

Black identity theories describe the influence of society and history on Black identities without characterizing those forces as deterministic. Nigrescence theory, though, neglects the role of religiosity in Black identity formation. Religious conversion theories, however, cannot completely fill the gap because they lack an explicit focus on identity, let alone race. Thus, I draw on some of the conversion theories that speak directly to the issues raised by the narratives of my interlocutors. For example, Brother Barody and Ras Brenton were both deeply enthralled by existential questions about God, race, and justice *before* they began their journey toward Rastafari. Rastafari, in their case, offered answers to their concerns and provided a community of like-minded believers. Through biographical interviewing and field research, and by using narratives and action as proxies for how identities work, we can deepen our perspective on individual and collective identity by socializing and historicizing it. Indeed, Rambo (2003) argues that the study of conversion requires a multidisciplinary and multimethod approach.

The recurrent patterns of experience involved with my narrators becoming Rastafari were worrying existential questions about God, race, and justice, inquisitive people in search of "the truth," visions and dreams that provoke questioning and self-reflection, and experiential witnessing—having an experience that unsettles one's worldview.

Identity transformation involves identity and cultural work. Identity work entails the activities involved in creating and managing one's self-concept and its reference points. These activities are simultaneously cultural work because people use symbols and give them meaning, learn from other people, and interpret cultural materials such as texts, sermons, and speeches. Finally, they participate in ritualistic and routine interactions that fuel (but not necessarily nourish) their identities.

The introduction of new ideas does not mean people will engage these ideas if they have no way to connect it to what they know already (Strauss & Quinn, 1997:40). My interlocutors explained that becoming Rastafari involved making connections among various dimensions of their experience: an acute awareness of oppression; a recognition of belonging to a denigrated group; a realization that there exists a long-standing tradition of positive understandings of Blackness; a discovery that one's cultural heritage has been hidden; that White cultural hegemony has distorted one's self-understanding. These are only a few examples of the connections my Rastafari interlocutors made and internalized through the interior and interpersonal dialogues that they engaged in as they reworked their self-concept. These details of personal identity transformation are taken up in chapters 4 and 5.

Life Stories: Pathways to Identity and History

Life stories are an empirical entry point to understanding how racial and religious identities form, are maintained, and how people experience them. I have considered both the "story" and "history" dimensions of my interlocutors' narratives (and lives), acknowledging the dynamic and contingent aspects of both (Peacock & Holland, 1993). To focus on the story aspect acknowledges the incompleteness, variability, and contingency of any narrative that a person tells about himself. This by no means discounts the veracity or the "history" part, but it recognizes the imperfectness of human memory and the complexities of telling a story. Some of my Rastafari interlocutors, like Ras Sam Brown and Prophetess, could precisely and accurately remember minute details of things that happened decades ago, such as the date, time, and even what a person was wearing. Brother Dee, on the other hand, regularly got dates wildly wrong. Rasta Ivey was very methodical in her talk; she was careful to say what she knew and what she didn't, and she regularly recalled pertinent details and memories after we had finished a particular conversation. I define the life story as those memories that a person determines to tell about his or her life in the context of a "guided interview" (Atkinson, 1998:8). Although I ask questions, the narrator chooses what to tell and how. To the extent that the interviewees are honest and their memory adequate, we can expect that their story will involve things salient to their identity, regardless of how many versions one could tell.

Life stories are inescapably retrospective, which poses the challenge of a person coloring their recollection with the hues of the present or elaborating on the past given accumulated experience. Some of my Rastafari interlocutors, for example, took the interview as a moment to examine their own path toward Rastafari. However, this was not an insurmountable impediment to gaining insight into important identity-relevant experiences. Indeed, identity and conversion narratives may tell us as much about the present as the past (Hobson, 1999:6; Robbins, 1988:66; Snow & Machalek, 1984:177).

Revisiting the "Native" Researcher Question

Audience is another important concern in life story interviewing. The "teller" may relate different versions of their life according to with whom they are talking and how they perceive that person. Race, gender, class, and occupation are only a few of the identifications that may influence how a narrator tells a story. Being a Black man and a fellow Rastafari surely influenced the stories told to me. Therefore, my identity is relevant to the stories told me, as well as my interpretation of the stories. However, being Rastafari myself did not mean that I did not have to grapple with the challenges that all field researchers face. For example, William Lewis (1993) and Joseph Owens (1976), both White priests, had to prove their "heart" (their ethics, intentions) to gain the confidence of their Rastafari interviewees. I, too, had to gain the confidence of my interlocutors, and race and identity were notable points of negotiation.

When my interlocutors looked at me, I was almost always certain that they saw a Black man and a Rastafari, even though I came from the United States and spoke with an accent (to their ears). That I hailed from the United States offered me neither advantage nor hindrance; that was at least apparent to me. I had to create relationships and build trust. Perhaps with the exception of Prophetess and Ras Brenton, I had to first gain the confidence of my interlocutors before they agreed to talk about their lives. The Rastafari are known for being wary of researchers and using various means to expose their motives (Yawney, 1999:162). Coming from a powerful and wealthy nation, or being a scholar and researcher, did not impress my narrators. I had no money to pay interviewees, and no connections to help people travel to the States. That I wanted to collect interviews did require repeated explanation and justification. However, research is no longer an unusual activity for the Rastafari, and neither is having a college degree extraordinary. Rastafari such as Maureen Rowe, E.S.P. McPherson, Imani Tafari-Ama, Douglas Mack, Ikeal Tafari, Dennis Forsythe, Barbara Makeda Black Hannah, Mutabaruka, and many others, are researching and writing about Rastafari from experiential and scholarly standpoints (e.g., Forsythe, 1983; Rowe, 1985, 1998; McPherson, 1996; Tafari-Ama, 1998; Mack, 1999; Tafari, 2001; Hannah, 2006; Mutabaruka, 2006). I did notice, though, that my narrators sometimes used me as proof of the international presence of Rastafari people, and the need for Rastafari people in general to become more active in documenting and representing the Rastafari to the world.

The common concern expressed by all of my Rastafari interlocutors was that I share the stories of elders and of Rastafari. This consent came with responsibilities and expectations. My interlocutors expected me, as a Rastafari, to privilege the needs and concerns of the Rastafari as a whole. I did not feel this was an undesirable imposition. It was an obligation that had to be reconciled with the work that I wanted to carry out.

Two effects that my research had on some of my narrators were that it caused them to recall things that they had all but forgotten, and it led them to connect memories in a way that they had never done. One day while I was driving, Rasta Ivey suddenly became excited, squirming in her seat and clapping her hands. She had remembered an almost forgotten Rastafari chant, taught to her by a Bedwardite. She began singing, while swaying and clapping her hands, sitting in the passenger seat:

Oh Israel stand, the lion appear
He soon begins to rule
The world get fear
great Kingdom fall
At the sound of his voice
Down in Abyssinia
All people of the world going down before him to bow
Great Ras Tafari, King of Kings who come to reign . . .

"Where the tape [recorder]?" Rasta Ivey asked me. I had not brought it with me. She had come to realize how important it was to record information that might forever be lost and wanted it saved for others to hear. Indeed, it was an opportunity we regretfully missed. Rasta Ivey knew one of the founding Rastafari, Robert Hinds, himself a devotee of self-proclaimed Prophet Alexander Bedward, whom we will meet in the next chapter. Brother Woks, once active in the Ethiopian World Federation, saw me on the street one day and said he remembered some things after we had conducted a formal interview that he wanted to add and clarify. These and other elders recognized the importance of their personal experience to, as Rasta Ivey put it, "Get the world to know of Rastafari!"

The "native" researcher question is an enduring concern of anthropologists and social scientists in general. Delmos Jones (1973) was one of the key initiators of the debate; 20 years later writers such as Kirin Narayan (1993) were still working through the arguments set forth by Jones. Jones pointed out that there was value in carrying out research on a group "of which he himself is a member" (1973:449) and contested the view that the ideal position was that of an outsider seeking to learn the ways of "natives." Indeed, researchers of Rastafari grapple with these issues of positionality—"insider" and "outsider"—and what it means to "representing" the Rastafari (e.g., Yawney, 1994, 1999). There are advantages to both positions. However, for groups who have been represented by people different from them, the "native" position offers the possibility of a different perspective, a different reading of the data: "There is no escape from the idea that outsiders and insiders view social reality from different points of view and that no matter how hard each tries, neither can completely discard his preconceptions . . . " (1973:455). From my standpoint, the questions of why and how people become Rastafari, and why and how people valorize Blackness, were questions of interest to scholars, Rastafari, and non-Rastafari alike.

To look like a member of a group or to identify with them is, of course, insufficient because it does not mean that members will see it that way. Groups and communities are diverse, and difference will always manifest in some way. Class, education, language, geographical distance, may, for example, create gulfs between people who share an identity. Some have argued, in effect, that the idea of a native researcher is too complex to really render it a valid standpoint (e.g., Narayan, 1993). We must not neglect, though, that sometimes those people who are "studied" like or want to see people like themselves conducting the research.

The idea of the researcher who can plumb the ways of a people because of their "outsider" status, because they must learn their ways and meanings, and then report this with authority by virtue of having lived that life by briefly getting close to it, is crumbling. I found this notion problematic because it implied that "insiders" or "natives" could not do the job because of their proximity—emotional and cultural—to their people. They would be unable to figure out what was important, blinded by their inside knowledge, unable to separate that from what must be learned. Outsiders could have compassion for and attachment to subjects of study, but not insiders or natives. The double standard is obvious. There is no good reason why researchers studying their own communities and people cannot do research of the same caliber as outsiders (Jones, 1994; Carnegie, 1992; Fahim & Helmer, 1982; Gwaltney, 1993). Indeed, in my case I was an outsider because I had to gain entrée into a community; I had to win hearts and did not know what my interlocutors knew. I had to learn, and in effect, they had to teach. I learned a great deal through their sharing their life experiences. I asked Brother Yendis what he thought about "foreign" researchers, and he replied by saying that there is a role for them to play: they help to spread the "news" of Rastafari. And this was what I found, in many ways: most of my interlocutors desired for other people to "hear" and learn about Rastafari—they literally wanted me to spread the word. For many Rastafari, even academic works served this purpose. I saw quite a few Rastafari—young and old—with tattered copies of the *Report* (Smith, Augier, & Nettleford, 1960) or Joseph Owens' *Dread* (1976) stuffed in a back pants pocket or rolled up in a hand. There were questions that I almost invariably had to answer, and they were the same as those posed to Barry Chevannes, a Jamaican scholar who has written extensively about Rastafari: "And one of the questions with which I most frequently have to deal with is this: 'What good will come from your research?' 'Exactly how will it benefit me and others like me?' Often, potential respondents will not co-operate unless this question is satisfactorily answered" (1978:250). Such questions attest to the intelligence of the interlocutors, their concern with how they will be represented, and how the research will be used.

Research and Data

Beginning in early 1998, I spent several months-long stretches living first in Kingston on the edge of the gulley that divided Grants Pen and Drumblair and then in the Rivoli section of Spanish Town. I spent time visiting the homes and settlements where many of the elder Rastafari live. My travels were limited primarily to the area between Greater Kingston and Spanish Town, with regular visits into rural St. Catherine and St. Thomas parishes. My interlocutors constitute a convenience sample because I met most of them through Rastafari associated with the Rastafari Federation (RF), an umbrella organization of Rastafari groups (only a handful were members of the Federation). The staff and membership offered me access to a network of Rastafari, most of whom would fit a broad definition of what a non-Rastafari would call activists. I met a few of my narrators through my own travels and effort. I would approach older Rastafari, introduce myself, and explain my interest in recording their story of becoming Rastafari. Not all of the Rastafari I approached were interested in participating in the project, but all of them shared with me something about their experience of becoming Rastafari. I spent time with many of those elders who did not "formally" participate, and thus learned much through our dialogue. The primary Rastafari affiliation of most of my narrators is the Nyabinghi Order (one of the major "sects" of Rastafari) or the Ethiopian Orthodox Church, or both. During 1998, I tape-recorded 26 life story interviews of Jamaicans who became Rastafari between 1931 and 1978. Many other Rastafari, as I noted above, shared parts of their becoming Rastafari stories with me, although I did not tape-record these; some were impromptu. Nearly all of my narrators lived in Kingston and the parishes of St. Andrew and St. Catherine, although a few lived in the parishes Clarendon and St. Thomas, and Westmoreland. With a few exceptions, these Rastafari would locally be construed as "elders," and I refer to them as such. Some of the elders are considered "matriarchs," "patriarchs," or "ancients," given their age and longevity as Rastafari. Of the first 26 Rastafari whose stories I taped, five were women (another life story told to me by an elder woman Rastafari had to be recalled from my memory and jotted down hours after we talked).

I used a life story interview strategy that drew on a small number of broad, open-ended questions. The taped interviews lasted between 90 minutes and 3 hours, focused on before-becoming Rastafari memories, race and identity, and when and how each interviewee became aware of Rastafari and moved to adopt the faith. As I saw the pattern of the "encounter" (explained in chapter 3) emerging as a recurring theme in people's stories of how they became Rastafari, I began to focus more intently on this as a part of the interviewing. I had ongoing conversations and interactions with nearly all of my narrators; these conversations provided further opportunities to learn more. Since the original interviews, I have continued collecting elder life stories, and I extended the relationships and obligations I had already developed and created new ones, as well.

Most of my narrators were self-employed as artists, vendors, higglers, and tradespeople such as cobbler, drum-maker, and wood-worker. A few, such as Brother Yendis and Empress Dinah, have worked for "Babylon." Brother Yendis worked for the sanitation department and Empress Dinah calls herself a "businesswoman." Their work, though, did not affect their commitment to their identity as Rastafari. Perhaps it bolstered it because they were regularly reminded of their identity by the discrimination and insults directed at them.

Most of my narrators' children were adults. Some raised their children to be Rastafari, but many did not. I could discern no logic in this pattern other than personal decisions about how to raise and socialize children. Ras Tee told me that you must let children "choose the path to walk," meaning that he believed they must not be forced into the faith: "They will rebel if you force them. Look 'pon the Christian them when the parent too strict 'pon them. Them go wild first chance them get." Many Rastafari shared his view. Implied in Ras Tee's view is that if parents set a good model, their children will become Rastafari. On the other hand, Ras Chronicle and Sister Sersi believed that children should be raised as Rastafari. Both had young children, boys and girls, who wore dreadlocks. "You must raise them right, that mean they must be Rasta from start. Rasta is discipline and love. Children need that," said Sister Sersi. However, as I have implied, the growth in Rastafari has not been the result of people being born as Rastafari, but becoming Rastafari at some point in the life course. This suggests that the continued vitality of Rastafari does not depend only on their raising their children to be Rastafari.

Another important point to address is the patchy presence of gender in the stories my narrators related to me. Only occasionally did some of my narrators mention gender in their "becoming" stories. This does not mean gender is unimportant, or that gender inequities do not exist. The stories related to me, especially the transformation parts, were typically self-focused. This was interesting to me given the significance many Rastafari males ascribe to themselves in relation to women Rastafari, and the general consensus that the Rastafari are a male-dominated people. For example, some Rastafari argue that a woman can become

Rastafari only through the guidance of a man. However, only one of my elder woman narrators, Sister Coromantee, made this point: "The King man should be in front, the Queen behind him. . . . He must instruct her in the proper ways." However, her story of her path into Rastafari had no man in it other than Christ. Sister Coromantee said she "crossed over to Rastafari in 1956," but she dreamed a few years earlier that she went to heaven with Christ and that this dream led her to pay more attention to "God talk" such as that spoken in the street meetings of the Rastafari. Men, especially her partner, occupy other stories that Sister Coromantee told me, but her initial move toward Rastafari was the result of her own effort.

My convenience sample of Rastafari suggests no gender-based difference in how my narrators began their journey toward becoming Rastafari. Both men and women had dreams and visions involving religious and racial symbols, burning curiosity about existential questions, and jarring personal experiences, all of which disturbed their present worldview. My inference is suggestive, but limited by whom I talked to. When I did ask questions about gender, double standards favoring men were sometimes acknowledged, but framed as behavior that was increasingly contested by both men and women Rastafari. Many of the women and men that I interviewed, especially those sympathetic to the aims of the Federation, were among the vanguard of older Rastafari promoting gender equity, recognizing that the Rastafari concern for liberation and justice must not be contradicted by their practicing oppression (we will return to this issue in chapter 6).

Much has changed during the lives of my narrators, most notably the transition of the Rastafari from pariahs to exemplars of Black culture and history. The Rastafari have a global presence, constituting what some call a "traveling culture" (e.g., Homiak, 1999). However, popularity and diffusion have roused new challenges for the Rastafari in Jamaica, in a new terrain for identity formation. The new terrain involves internationalization of Rastafari identity, new technologies, changes in social class, demographics, and attitude among the Rastafari as women, youth, and well-off people participate in shaping the personal and collective representations of Rastafari. All of this is occurring as older Rastafari like my narrators grow infirm and "drop off" (pass on). How or will the Rastafari persist into the twenty-first century? These questions and others are addressed in chapter 6.

Warriors and Saints on the "Battlefield"

"I have been fighting on this battlefield for a long time," Rasta Ivey said to me. "Which battlefield is that?" I asked. Stretching her eyes and raising her voice, the rail-thin octogenarian replied to me in a very defiant and indignant tone:

> The battlefield of righteousness, Black liberation, and Conquering Lion [of Judah] is what I am talking. From we stand up for Black people and say King Rasta come to redeem we, people start to fight against we. But we a people who don't bow [practice immorality]! I was on a mission for King Rasta. So, I don't fear police, politician, bad man, no one at all! Because I have the power in me, that is Rastafari.

Nearly all of the Rastafari whose stories inform this book are activists in that they have been consistently involved in promoting and defending their faith and identity. These Rastafari represent a limited—but significant—orientation among the Rastafari, one highly deserving of attention. These aging Rastafari have participated in chapters of the Ethiopian World Federation (EWF), the United Negro Improvement Association (UNIA), the Rastafari Movement Association (RMA), and associations of their own making, such as the Brothers Solidarity of United Ethiopia (BSUE). They have petitioned government to promote their agenda; and several of them have served as representatives of Rastafari in Jamaica and abroad. As such, we have a particular perspective shaped by the experience and standpoint of my interlocutors. In the following pages we will gain some sense of the social and personal origins of Rastafari identity as it has developed from its origins and, in doing so, witness how a morally configured conception of Blackness has been incorporated into struggles for freedom, justice, and for a positive Black identity.

1

Race Formation and Morally Configured Black Identities

We the Rastafarians who are the true prophets of this age, the re-incarnated Moseses, Joshuas, Isaiahs, Jeremiahs . . . we are those who are destined to free not only the scattered Ethiopians (Black men) but all people, animals, herbs and all life forms. . . . We are those who shall fight all wrongs and bring ease to the suffering bodies, and peace to all people.

(Ras Sam Brown, "Treatise on the Rastafarian Movement," 1966)[1]

One March afternoon in 1998, while sitting in a meeting convened by the Rastafari Federation in Kingston, Jamaica, I reflected on how the Rastafari use their identity to embody and engage the past while living in the present. Empress Dinah, a pecan-brown-skinned Rastafari woman in her late forties, sporting a steep, tightly wrapped crown of dreadlocks, stood in front of the audience on a low stage, with a microphone in one hand and notes in the other, addressing an attentive and largely male audience of approximately 70 Rastafari and a dozen non-Rastafari. Empress Dinah spoke about Blackness, injustice, and organizing the Rastafari into a confederation able to actualize their collective desires. What led me to reflect on the event were the opening lines of the Empress's speech:

Greetings to our race and the people of Rastafari. . . . Rastafari must live the words and teaching and orders of His Imperial Majesty Haile I Selassie I. . . . Rastafari must fight against colonialism, imperialism, capitalism, ignorance, poverty. . . . [Rastafari must] Think and work I-electively [collectively] for all Rasta people.

A Rastafari elder, Ras Sam Brown, spoke after Empress Dinah. He delivered a critical and rousing speech that used the European Union as a trope for declaring the utter necessity of Rastafari people to come together as "one nation"—Europe should not, he suggested, set the example for "coming together." Black people—Rastafari—should set the example. Ras Sam Brown was urging a Rastafari union. Like Empress Dinah, he used a language of defiance that drew on the rhetoric of fight and race: "Rastafari [is] forever fighting for Black liberation. . . . There is no higher reward than for a people to be called by their God to serve in the cause of Black liberation."

Predominant themes in the talk of the Rastafari I met in Jamaica were race loyalty and disloyalty, allegiance to a Black King, hostility toward oppression and subjugation, the unceasing importance of liberation, the danger of miseducation, and issues of morality inseparable from race and religion. As I listened to them speak in the meeting, I thought about the lineage of their rhetoric and practice, the varied routes they traveled in becoming who they are, and how on the eve of the twenty-first century, a people who only four decades earlier were feared and despised, had become cultural exemplars of Blackness. In this meeting off the beaten path, held at a comprehensive school located in a chancy ghetto off Spanish Town Road, were a group of people engaged in conversations about race, justice, and identity that have their source in a past that is remembered and embodied in these and other Rastafari.

Blackness as a Durable Cultural Resource

To grasp the evolving identity and rhetoric of the Rastafari, we must look to the historical and social bases of the ideas and practices they use to define themselves and the cultural worlds they have forged. We must determine how and why ideas about race, God, deracination, oppression, and miseducation are so salient, and how such ideas have endured, spanning generations. Indeed, we must reveal the emergence of Blackness itself, how out of many African ethnicities, languages, and differences a "generic" Black identity supersedes these particularities. Ethnogenesis is about the emergence and development of new groups, and to fathom this process, we must identify the cultural resources that people draw upon as a part of identifying with a particular collectivity (I expand on ethnogenesis in the next chapter). We must simultaneously consider Jamaica's distant and not-so-distant past, identify key actors and moments involved in the forging of cultural resources, and consider the ways in which those actors used resources to express their identity.

In Jamaica, morally configured Black identities like Rastafari draw deeply upon the cultural resources of racialized moral economies. These are cultural artifacts created and reinforced through Black people's experience of uprisings, reprisals, dashed hopes, marginalization, and a strong desire for better and for building genuine communitas. As we shall see, Jamaican moral economies of Blackness are informed by a racialized set of themes and values I call *justice motifs*: truth, righteousness, freedom, liberation, autonomy, and self-reliance. These justice motifs are used to articulate grievances and alternative visions of their world. People racialize these motifs through enculturation—personal experience, stories, observation, instruction, collective memories and representations, and through interaction with other people. Race—Blackness in this case—can be put to many uses; it can provide a sense of affinity and security, and furnish a framework for interpreting the past, present, and future. Indeed, the identity work of the Rastafari will illustrate how ideas of race endure and why it is so salient to some people.

To describe cultural resources as artifacts does not limit them to material element; they include ideas as well. We make cultural artifacts in practice—in doing, generating cultural and social worlds (Bartlett & Holland, 2002; Holland & Lave, 2001; Holland, Lachicotte, Skinner, & Cain, 1998). In a given cultural world some images, people, stories, concerns, and memories are more salient and more meaningful than in other cultural worlds. The sentiments and emotions that things in a figured world evoke are important in the motivation they provide and the contribution they make to remembering (Strauss & Quinn, 1997:118; Cattell & Climo, 2002). Slavery and acts of injustice, for example, are important emotive images in the formulation of Blackness that I explore in this book and that infuse Rastafari identity. Not every Black Jamaican is influenced by, interested in, or aware of these concerns regarding Blackness, or even race in general. However, as cultural forms, they are there for people to discover and embrace, accidentally or purposefully.

As my narrative unfolds, I ask the reader to keep in mind *oppression, deracination, and miseducation,* because these create the context for the need and desire to create positive and historicized affirmations of Blackness. My voice will dominate the first part of this chapter as I frame the history that is a part of the Rastafari. My narrators will enter the story later in the chapter.

The Morant Bay Rebellion: Blackness and the Moral Economy

How did Blackness become a salient identity in Jamaica by the 1860s? And how did it become intertwined with religion and morality?

We begin in a contentious moment and place—1865 and Morant Bay—where Jamaicans unambiguously displayed a rebellious and morally configured form of Blackness. We shall then determine important antecedents to the Morant Bay outburst before moving to identify important episodes and contributions that together provide a well of cultural resources that the earliest Rastafari draw from as they begin their work of building a collective identity.

On October 11, 1865, Paul Bogle, a Black Native Baptist preacher, led two, maybe three, clamorous groups of several hundred men and women into the town of Morant Bay. They marched in formation, armed with sharp implements, beating drums and blowing conch horns. Their attention was fixed on the courthouse where the parish Vestry, the local political body, was holding its regular meeting. The urgent concern of the insurgents, however, was disabling the local police, which they did handily (Heuman, 1994). The insurgents were willing to risk violent confrontation with the towns-people because of the accumulated grievances they held against the planters, the Vestry, magistrates, debt and tax collectors, and the police. The insurgents, mostly agricultural laborers and small farmers, knew they could not obtain a fair hearing in the courts; they feared they were about to lose possession of their provision grounds; and they were onerously taxed to offset the losses of the planters. There were other concerns, too, such as frightful rumors that they were going to be re-enslaved. The insurgents identified powerholders and elites—mostly Whites—as threats to their livelihood and well-being, and as violators of what they interpreted as a right to use land, make a living, and get a fair hearing in the courts. These were some of the primary causes leading to the rebellion.

Consider some of the racial rhetoric observers of the event claimed to have overheard the insurrectionists use: "We will kill every white and Mulatto man in the Bay"; "It is your colour [Black]; don't kill him. You are not to kill your colour"; "So help me God after this day I must cleave from the whites and cleave to the blacks" (Heuman, 1994:4–5). A vivid sense of justice animated their racial awareness. The rebellion epitomized the capacity of race and a moral economy of Blackness to mobilize people who otherwise might not have challenged an oppressive social order, an order that they might have considered hopeless or preordained.

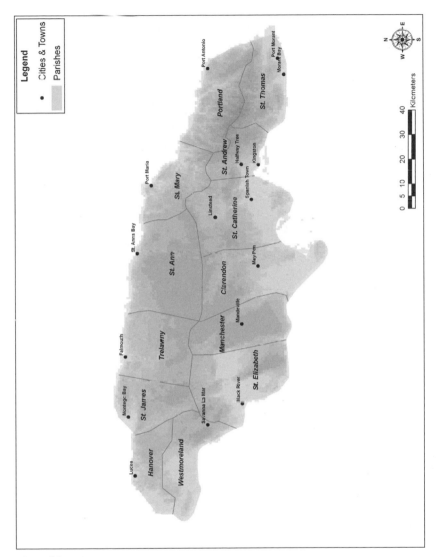

Map of Jamaica

Considerable diversity in experience and social position characterized Black Jamaicans of the 1860s. Charles Price (no relation to me as far as I know), for example, was a well-known and well-off Black Jamaican who apparently identified firmly with Jamaica's White ruling class. Indeed, his advantageous position was based on his connections to Whites and Browns and the continuation of the social order that benefited Whites. Price's complicity with the oppressive order was already understood by the Morant Bay insurrectionists. During the fray, Price harbored some of the Whites who were the targets of the crowd, and his assistance cost him his life. Nonetheless, the decision to kill Price illustrates the complexities involved in understandings of Blackness. On the one side, the crowd noted Price's multifaceted identity: "Price, don't you know that you are a black nigger and married to a nigger? . . . Don't you know, because you got into the Vestry, you don't count yourself a nigger?" Price, perhaps seeking to save his Black skin, agreed that he was indeed a "nigger" and offered £200 to save his life. But then a woman pointed out Price's support for the White racial order and how he had worked Blacks without paying them. She recommended a death sentence. Another member of the crowd pointed out that Price had "black skin and a white heart" (Heuman, 1994:9, 10). Price was beaten to death.

More than a century after the Morant Bay rebellion, metaphors of heart and race loyalty continue to serve as cultural resources. The idea remains that a person's "heart" can describe their moral and racial commitment. For example, many Rastafari use the heart as a metaphor for discerning a person's deepest values and commitments; to be "heartical" is to be morally upright, respected, and perhaps even racially conscious. There is also the mythical "Blackheart man," a shadowy and dangerous bearded figure believed to eat living human hearts and abduct children by enticing them with sweets. The modern Blackheart man drove around in a black car. Mere mention of "Blackheart man" could make the knees of children knock, and adults might suspiciously eye any lone or unfamiliar bearded man. The Blackheart man was evil, and he was Black. The Rastafari were called Blackhearted, signaling danger and depravity. Bongo J said, "In them times [the late 1930s] there was no Rastaman deh [there] 'bout . . . when you see one man is a Rasta man you run." "Why would you run?" I asked. Bongo J's face frowned, his eyebrows arched, and his voice rose: "How you mean? Intimidation! Them say him blackheart and a kill pickney [children] . . . listen to me . . . if I a pass through right now, pickney a run from me, man!" (Bongo J).

The two main instigators at Morant Bay were George William Gordon, a Brown minister who was a radical politician and wealthy landowner, and the Black minister, Paul Bogle. Both were affiliated with the Native Baptist Church, an important site for the construction and dissemination of morally configured Black identification. George Gordon was born around 1820 to a slave mother and White attorney father. Although Gordon was born a slave, his father granted him freedom and paid for his early education

Bongo J, born in rural St. Catherine in 1931. Introduced to Garveyites during the late 1930s. Began conversion to Rastafari in the late 1950s and grew out his beard in 1961.

(Hult, 1992:292; Henman, 1994:63). Gordon became a self styled defender of the poor, and converted to the Native Baptist faith in December 1861. As a politician he put himself out on a limb among his White colleagues because of his candid arguments against the racial practices of the Colonial government.[2] Because Gordon so closely participated in Blacks' lives, elites viewed all his activities with great suspicion and doubted his loyalty to "his kind." His racial identity—Brown—complicated matters because he had an opportunity to distance himself from the majority, poor Black Jamaicans. Browns, during Gordon's lifetime, were almost always the offspring of a White man and a Black woman.[3] They have constituted a significant presence in Jamaica for most of its history, even though they have always been a small racial minority.[4] Even though Browns could be born into bondage, they often received preferential treatment in the form of lighter workloads and access to education and trade training. Within Jamaica's racial landscape, both White and Brown were understood as superior to, and the antithesis of, Black (Alleyne, 2002). Not all Black Jamaicans accepted this hierarchy that debased them. By the time of the Morant Bay rebellion there were competing views of Blackness—a valued and a devalued identity—and over time the esteem given to Blackness has increased to where today its positive valences are so widely acknowledged that it seems Jamaicans have always appreciated it.

We know little about the early life of Paul Bogle. He lived in the Stony Gut community, not far from Morant Bay, and it appears that Gordon baptized and ordained him as a Native Baptist minister (or a deacon) in 1865 (Barrett, 1988:58). Like Gordon, Bogle acted as an advocate for the Black poor. Indeed, Bogle was involved in a range of alternative racial institutions, such as Black courts. These courts were extra-legal institutions that handled disputes between Black citizens because they could not expect justice within the formal legal system.

The day after insurgents marched on Morant Bay, October 12, soldiers seized the nearby town of Bath, and Maroons entered the fray on the side of the Whites (more on the Maroons below), turning the tide against the Black insurgents. The White local militias, vigilantes, and British soldiers did not stop at neutralizing the insurgents. They initiated a massacre against local Blacks, slaughtering hundreds and burning more than a thousand homes. The insurrection and the White response to it led Britain to re-take control of the island, making it a Crown Colony government.[5]

Moral Economy of Blackness

At the time of the Morant Bay rebellion, there were Black Jamaicans whose sense of moral righteousness and justice had found validation in the Bible story of the journey of the Hebrews out of bondage in Egypt and into the Promised Land. As it has done for many oppressed people (Walzer, 1985; Wilmore, 1998), the story of Exodus caught and held the attention of Jamaican slaves. Other biblical passages spoke forcibly. Psalms 68:31, "Princes shall come out of Egypt; Ethiopia shall soon stretch out her hands unto God," no doubt offered consolation and hope with its promise to redeem God's Black children. James Phillippo, a White Baptist missionary active in Jamaica during the early to mid-1800s, wrote that it was not uncommon at the time to find Black slaves identifying with Ethiopians and Israelite captivity in Egypt (1971:143, 148).

During the Morant Bay rebellion there was almost no looting. The "mob" attacked the symbols and embodiments of oppression: the police station, the Vestry, the courthouse, the Custos, tax collectors, and exploitative planters. By 1865, there had developed a moral economy that valued racial solidarity. During the week of rebellion the insurrectionists defended and asserted a moral economy of Blackness.

As James Scott (1976) has argued, a moral economy describes people's beliefs that they have a "right to subsistence." Because a moral economy involves cultural ideas, participants may not privilege it as a distinctive feature of their lives, or they may take it for granted as a part of "who we are." Outsiders might remain oblivious to its presence, but by identifying what constitutes local norms of social justice and what is considered injustice and exploitation, we can make out the contours of a moral economy (Scott, 1976:11, 32, 41). Thus, rebellion and protest can signal more than mere reaction; they are ways in which collectivities demonstrate their rights, especially to livelihood and identity. The moral economy of Blackness points us toward racialized and valued ways of life that include ideas about social welfare, tradition, community, and identity.

For the Morant Bay rebels, injustice was located in the hands of White planters and administrators and the Blacks who supported and emulated them. Land policies figured prominently in the insurrectionists' moral economy. Many Blacks in the parish had inadequate or no access to land, no avenue to move from abject poverty. Taxes, too, affected subsistence. Whenever market shifts or policy change in Britain (in this case, the end of protection for Jamaican sugar) negatively affected planters and other members of the dominant groups, they recouped some of their losses by taxing the predominantly Black and poor citizenry and by reducing wages. From the perspective of many rural Blacks, these practices were unfair and raised the specter of a slide back toward slavery. Thus, by 1865 there had evolved a racialized cluster of ideas about justice, righteousness, freedom, liberation, and truth that were connected to concerns involving land, work, livelihood, subsistence, and identity. We must add redemption—deliverance from bondage and oppression—to our cluster of justice motifs. The justice motifs and the moral economy of Blackness were more than abstractions; they found their motivating power and appeal in lived experience, memories, cultural resources, and the sentiments connected with these. Their resonance, if anything, increased over time. Sixty-five years after the Morant Bay rebellion, Leonard Howell, a founding evangelist of the Rastafari, would preach his message of the arrival of the Black Messiah and looming Black redemption to threadbare peasants in the St. Thomas districts of Golden Grove, Trinityville, Leith Hall, and Pear Tree Grove.

Elements of Moral Economy

E. P. Thompson, analyzing English riots and insurrections of the eighteenth century, argued that understanding manifestations of a moral economy requires identifying patterns and their antecedents: insurrections, for instance, "exhibit a pattern of behavior for whose origin we must look back several hundreds of years." (1971:108). The bases of a moral economy are grounded in people's sense of justice, a common notion of what is good, norms of reciprocity, and beliefs about customary rights with respect to others (Thompson, 1971; Scott, 1976; Gosner, 1992; Booth, 1994; Sayer, 2000:79). The idea of moral economy has been further developed since the 1970s, and has been applied to collectivities in Europe, Asia, Latin America, and the American South (Lichtenstein, 1995; Randal & Charlesworth, 2000; Scott, 2000; Edelman, 2005).

The "economy" of moral economy stresses subsistence and communal survival and accompanying rights and obligations. But understandings of rights and obligations are differently understood given people's experience and social position.

The British colonial regime promoted a conception of values, rights, and justice grounded in Western civil and political theory. Its conception, even for those Whites who prized fairness and the "rights of man," accommodated slavery and the inhumane treatment of Black Jamaicans. The evolution of moral economies of Blackness reflected the alternative imaginaries and interpretations of values and rights by Black Jamaicans. For example, Jamaica's slave codes required planters to provide basic necessities to slaves, such as provision grounds, housing, medical treatment, and at least a weekend day off, but planters subverted or ignored these codes. Slaves, on the other hand, knew that White (or English) rules were supposed to protect these rights. Slaves and their Black successors translated European and Christian languages of rights and salvation into their own idioms, values, and principles, cultural artifacts that contrasted with those of Europeans and the emerging capitalist market economy.

Black Jamaicans such as Paul Bogle, the Maroons, and Sam Sharpe (see below) gave voice to ideas about freedom that involved more than basic civil and political rights. They called for freedom from domination and oppression and the right to pursue a livelihood and community well-being. They joined religious expression with pursuit of their comprehensive ideas of freedom—a radical liberation perspective steeped in race (Bogues, 1997:70). Although it is incontestable that Africans, Europeans, and others mutually influenced each other in the creation of the new society (as theories of creolization contend), in some instances Blackness was the key trope around which cultural mixture revolved.

The role of "morality" in moral economy must not be underplayed if we are to make sense of symbolism and actions related to beliefs about rights, obligations, and identity that otherwise seem irrational. For example, we could read the use of race to mobilize the Morant Bay rebels as an act of desperation by a hopeless people rather than calculated action motivated by deeply held feelings and beliefs. Therefore, it is not a matter of which should have logical precedence, "the moral" or "the economy"; they are inseparable. Insurrections, small and large, have proved a felicitous source of information and symbols used in the construction of Black identity in Jamaica. Rebellions and protests disclose what oppressed people define as rights (Thompson 1971:98) and generate the conditions conducive to heightened solidarity, shared experience, and shared beliefs. The many rebellions that occurred between the mid-1700s and the present in Jamaica are a chain of expressions of dissatisfaction with established authorities and institutions and an effort to defend and assert a racialized moral economy.

The Emergence of Blackness in Jamaica: Deracination and Cultural Procreativity

Blackness as a basis of identification in Jamaica gelled within a regime of slavery. What was the ancestry and lineage of the morally configured Black identities that had emerged by the 1860s?

When Spaniards landed on the coast of Jamaica in early May 1494, perhaps 50,000–60,000 Tainos lived there (Sherlock & Bennett, 1998:48). By 1655, when the British invaded Spanish Jamaica, the Tainos were nearly extinct, and the few survivors lived in the vastness of the Blue Mountains. The Spaniards had imported a few thousand African slaves to Jamaica (Alleyne, 1988:31), and when Britain invaded, some slaves of the Spaniards escaped into the dense brush of the Blue Mountains and the limestone-pitted region called the Cockpit.

In all of British America, Jamaica was the single largest importer of slaves (Klein, 1978:141). Between 1601 and 1700, 8,500 slaves were imported into Jamaica, and another 662,000 were imported between 1701 and 1810 (Curtin, 1969:268). Despite the ending of the British slave trade in 1807, the large number of slaves imported between 1801 and 1807 meant a significant proportion of Africans remembered Africa well into the 1800s (Curtin, 1955:24).

Most of the slaves imported into Jamaica originated in territories now known as Nigeria, the Gold Coast, the Niger Delta, Senegambia, Sierra Leone, Bight of Benin, Bight of Biafra, the Congo, and Angola. Generally, the slaves were of Yoruba, Ibo, and Ashanti ethnicity. The Twi-speaking Akan peoples were the culturally dominant group, but a pan-Black identity and culture emerged out of the melding of culturally, linguistically, religiously, and regionally diverse Africans and their offspring (Alleyne, 2002:200–202). Slavers stereotyped the Ashantis or "Coromantines" as hardy and resourceful but prone to rebellion.[6] The Ashanti (originally a coalition of chiefdoms, not an ethnicity) greatly influenced the development of non-mainstream Black Jamaican religions.

Slavery facilitated the erosion of distinct African ethnic, religious, and territorial identifications, and prompted the growth of new identifications in which race figured prominently (e.g., Curtin, 1955:26; Robotham, 1994:28; Frey & Wood, 1998; Gomez, 1998). Slavery exposed Africans to leveling experiences that diminished their cultural and social differences and also provided opportunities for developing shared affinities around new identifications such as race. Among the first leveling experiences Africans had was the trauma of the Middle Passage. They adjusted to their new home under the pressure of seasoning, functional segregation (such as field and domestic work); whipping; the condition of being property; and the insecurity, injustice, and humiliation associated with the experience of imported Africans slaves (cf. Brathwaite, 1971:205, 298; Craton, 1978:166).

The effects of deracination varied according to the practices of the slavers. Slavers not only separated Africans from their communities, networks, and relationships, they began to prohibit or make difficult Africans' maintenance of their language, religion, and rituals. In Jamaica, slave owners were reluctant to allow slaves free access to European cultural resources such as Christianity and the King James Bible. One result was that Africans continued their cultural practices as circumstances allowed, and incorporated European cultural resources into their own repertoires. Gradually, specific African groups such as Ibo, Fanti, or Ashanti, and their descendants, came to call and consider themselves African and Black (see Robotham, 1994:34–36; Drake, 1991).[7] For example, as early as 1748, a slave petitioning the Jamaican House of Assembly for the right to trial by a jury of his peers identified himself and other slaves as "Sons of Chus," "unjustly and inhumanly detained in thralldom and bondage" (see Chevannes, 1994:36). This statement hints at a moral conception of Blackness preceding the Morant Bay rebellion by more than 100 years. By "Chus" the slave meant Kush, referring to the Old Testament story of the curse of Blackness placed on Noah's son Ham.[8]

The Maroon Wars:
Early Formulations of a Moral Economy of Blackness

The Maroons played an important role in the earliest phases of the development of morally configured conceptions of Blackness. Indeed, Alleyne argues there developed a "symbiotic relationship between ethnicity and freedom" among the Maroons (2002:218). The most famous Maroons were a family of Ashantis, Cudjoe, Johnny, Accompong, Kofi, and Quaco.[9] In the eastern part of the island, the stouthearted warrior Nanny (named a national heroine in 1975) led another group of Maroons. Their origins in the same region of Africa assisted in their communication, and thus their capacity to organize.

Many of the West Africans who became Maroons, especially the Akan peoples, were skilled in warfare. They displayed military prowess against the British, even though the military resources of the British far outstripped theirs. The Maroons gained their freedom more than 50 years before Haiti's Black Jacobins carried out the first successful slave revolution in the Americas.

Slaves took note of the Maroons' defense of land, their freedom, and their example of self-reliance. They also recognized that the Maroons were able to maintain their freedom by helping the British deny them theirs. The British, after decades of failing to subdue the Maroons militarily, capitulated and offered the Maroons a peace treaty. The 1738 Peace Treaty guaranteed the Maroons their freedom and ownership of a small amount of poor land in exchange for their consent to return and hunt down runaway slaves. Over time, the Maroons moved from a "deadly hatred" of Whites to a more accommodative attitude (Dallas, 1968). Thus, the anthropologist Martha Beckwith could wryly note how "Maroons became the natural friends of the whites and the enemies of their own race, a distinction which they jealously guard today. They look upon the alliance as a distinct pledge of superiority over the other negroes" (Beckwith, 1969:184).

Dynamics of Deracination and Cultural Procreativity

British policies concerning the role of Christianity in slaves' lives shifted from ambivalence to hostility. The Consolidated Slave Act of Jamaica of

1793 mandated that slave owners teach the slaves Christianity and baptize them, but slavers ignored the law. It was not long before their disobedience was codified as law. The Consolidated Slave Act of 1816 forbade slaves attendance at places of worship, as well as the practice of religion in their own homes (without a Magistrate's permit; see Phillippo, 1971:161).

White hostility toward the open practice of Christianity abetted the development of African-influenced folk religions. Enslaved Africans brought with them their own intellectual and religious traditions, and leaders in these areas helped create indigenous Black religions such as Obeah, Myalism, and Kumina. Black Jamaicans combined what they remembered of their African traditions and whatever they could glean from Christian teachings.

Myalism, of Akan-Ashanti origin, was probably the earliest form of pan-ethnic religious association among slaves in Jamaica. Myal involved religious practices centered on spirits and the use of spirits and herbs for healing purposes. Myalists believed that misfortune was the result of evil spirits and that their religion provided a means of combating them. They, like many African slaves, considered Jamaica to be the land of the dead because in their cosmology the land of the dead lay across a great watery expanse, and they believed Whites were sorcerers since they ruled the land of the dead (Schuler, 1980:93–96). Myalism elevated the well-being of the group over individual self-interests (Schuler, 1980:33), and as Robotham (1994:35) has pointed out, it contributed to "creating an ideology around which organization and broader ties could be built." Myalism morally justified resistance because Myalists interpreted slavery and slavers as evil because it destabilized community well-being. Resistance could in part be interpreted as an effort to heal a wounded people because healing was so important to Myalism.

Rebellion and Morally Configured Black Identities

Slave rebellions and religious practices mutually reinforced each other. The case of the Tacky Rebellion of 1760 is an instructive example. Tacky, a slave from what would be present-day Ghana, supported by Ashanti slaves, was one of several "Myal-men" (i.e., shaman-sorcerers) who led an uprising in St. Mary's parish that spread to other parishes (Alleyne, 1988:83; cf. Beckwith, 1969:143). Hundreds of slaves joined the uprising. The rebellion was soon put down by the colonial militia with the assistance of Maroons, but not before 60 Whites had died. Militias, Maroons, and vigilantes senselessly killed many of the captured slaves for revenge and to intimidate other slaves (authorities deported around 600 of the captives to Central America).

Subsequent uprisings displayed the recurrent patterns that involved religion and moral sensibility as a part of spontaneous and planned collective action. Slaves drew the courage to confront their oppressors from religious complexes like Myal, and used them to organize collective action.

Fusions of Religion, Blackness, and Rebellion

By the late 1700s, a Black version of Christianity was in dialogue with African-inspired Myalism, and from the interaction two different religious practices emerged: Kumina and Convince (I focus on Kumina because of its connection to Myal). One of the rituals of Myal involved a dance called Kumina. The name of the Myal dance itself eventually came to be associated with the entire ritual complex. Kumina, linked with Africans of the Angola-Congo region of Africa and in its early development concentrated in eastern Jamaica, literally meant possession by ancestors.

In 1783, George Lisle (or Leile), a Christian preacher and former slave, accompanied his Tory master from America to Jamaica. Lisle had been preaching in South Carolina, in the United States, since at least 1774 when he decided to join the church, around the same time that he discovered his "love to other negroes" (Brown, 1975:58). Lisle participated in the founding of the first two Black congregations in America: during the period 1773–75 in Silver Bluff, South Carolina, and in 1788, in Savannah, Georgia (Brown, 1975:58; Henderson, 1910; Gayle, 1982; Pulis, 1999:192). He went on to found the first Black Baptist church on the island, the Ethiopian Baptist Church.

Other ex-slaves from America made significant contributions to what evolved into Native Baptist Christianity. For example, Moses Baker, from New York, had, by 1814, built a congregation of 500 in St. James and claimed more than 3,000 adherents throughout the island (Brathwaite, 1971:163). George Lewis, of Virginia, worked as a traveling preacher, sowing his brand of Baptist teaching throughout the island. Myalists became involved in the new Black churches, facilitating syncretism through the Native Baptist Church. The Native Baptist Church became an exemplar of Black radicalism.

In Jamaica, Lisle was charged with sedition (even though he tried to remain within the law) because he was heard preaching that Whites must be prayed for, if "they must be saved" [because they owned slaves] (Brown, 1975:60), and because authorities believed that he was intending to incite slaves to insurrection (Chevannes, 1971:27). Gayle (1982) was right to emphasize how Lisle and his fellow Black Americans have not received credit for their building the

Baptist foundation in Jamaica well before the formal Baptist missionary effort of the Englishman John Rowe (1814), and which drew in slave converts in numbers that the Catholics, Moravians, and Anglicans could not touch.

Recall that Bogle and Gordon were Native Baptist leaders. Their articulation of a moral economy of Blackness was not a precedent. It was, rather, a part of a general pattern of an evolving morally configured Blackness. Let us take E. P. Thompson's advice, and look a little further into the lineage of this moral Blackness.

In 1831, the slave Sam Sharpe initiated an ambitious and deadly rebellion that led Britain to end slavery in Jamaica and the Caribbean. The rebellion was variously referred to as the "Baptist War," the "Christmas Rebellion," and the "Myalist War" (Schuler, 1980:34). Rebellions like the Sharpe uprising help us situate the origins, power, and durability of the justice motifs, and they also illustrate the emergent moral economy of Blackness, in particular the confluence of Black identity and religion with ideas about social justice. By the time the Sharpe rebellion occurred, slaves and free Blacks had incorporated the King James Bible into the racial economy of Blackness. Brathwaite, for instance, noted that one of the leaders of the Sharpe rebellion was called a "Black Israelite" (1981:88), a tantalizing hint that by 1831 at least some slaves identified themselves with Hebrew bondage in Biblical Egypt. The armed contingent of insurrectionists dubbed themselves the "Black regiment" (Reckord, 1968:117).[10]

Sharpe was either a leader of or intimately connected to the Native Baptists. His charismatic oratorical skills commanded considerable respect among slaves: "The Whites," Sharpe argued, "had no more right to enslave the blacks than the blacks to enslave the Whites" (Sherlock & Bennett, 1998:4). Under the guise of holding prayer meetings in the home of his unsuspecting master, Sharpe plotted an uprising that involved slaves on several nearby plantations.

How had Sharpe been able to mobilize so many slaves? A common explanation was that they believed the Crown had already freed them and that the planters had conspired to withhold this information (Barrett, 1988:43; Brathwaite, 1981:83; Knox, 1962:40). However, Sharpe rallied the slaves to fight for their freedom because God's Bible told them about freedom and the tyranny of oppression *and* because they believed that they had been denied rights granted by the Crown.

A deliberative body of slaves agreed to go on a nonviolent strike after Christmas, on December 26, 1831. While most slaves who were aware of the plot agreed to participate in a nonviolent demonstration, some of them wanted to violently overthrow slavery. Nonetheless, someone gave away the secret to plantation and colonial authorities, and what ended up happening was a rebellion that quickly turned violent. Jamaican militias, slave soldiers, and British troop reinforcements violently quashed the rebellion in less than two weeks, and Maroons were enlisted to capture runaways. The rebel slaves killed fourteen Whites, but 312 of their number were hanged and more than 1,000 killed in other ways. Sam Sharpe was among the last to be executed, at Montego Bay on May 23, 1832. An Emancipation Bill was introduced in the British Parliament in 1833, and two years after Sharpe's death, on August 1, 1834, the Crown granted full emancipation to Jamaican slaves.

Sharpe, and all those who took up arms in December 1831, became enduring symbols of Black Jamaicans' struggle for liberation, self-determination, and justice. This historical event and others continued to be re-lived during succeeding generations. One day when Rasta Ivey and I were walking to catch a bus at the depot in downtown Kingston called "Parade," I mentioned that I was writing about the Sam Sharpe Rebellion in preparation for an Emancipation Day committee meeting of the Rastafari Federation. Before I could finish, she told me, in a completely blasé tone of voice, "I was there. I was there at that time and I did take part in it." "What do you mean?" I asked. She repeated casually what she said. Our conversation then shifted to questioning how could a person experience something that happened more than a hundred years before their birth. Rasta Ivey explained that in the past, Africans in Jamaica could live to be 200 years old or more, but today "Jamaican people don't live so long." Rasta Ivey was old, approaching 90, which we both knew. So how did she participate in the Myalist war? Vicariously, I believe. Rasta Ivey said her grandmother lived to be 116 years old, and her mother a few years past 100. If this is true, perhaps the grandmother passed on firsthand information or firsthand experience across the generations, and perhaps through such stories a person becomes a part of the past, lays claim to it, and lives it. Rasta Ivey, like some of the oldest Rastafari I met, believe that it is possible to live for hundreds of years and that adults may disappear only to return as infants. In both cases, death does not signal finality but transformation and continuity between the past and present.

Free to Be Oppressed

Legally, emancipation granted freedom to the slaves, but in practice other rules, such as minimum property requirements, prevented their participation in mainstream civic and political activities. The former slaves thought emancipation meant "full free," but soon realized White planters would not relinquish control easily. Whites created a new thralldom, apprenticeship, that required no chains. Whites had argued that when slavery ended, former slaves would need time to learn what freedom entailed (such as working for a wage). Hence, for a period of six years after slavery, apprentices were to be required to work for their former masters for 40.5 hours each week, from sunrise to sunset. Property owners began to demand rent for the same land that the former slaves worked and lived on for free. Many ex-slaves believed apprenticeship to be a new type of slavery (Knox, 1962:75). Despite positive developments, such as the rise of the free village system, which White missionaries spearheaded as a way to help Blacks escape the control of planters, Black Jamaicans continued to sense that even though they were now free, they remained oppressed. Institutions such as the previously mentioned Black courts, often connected to local churches (Sherlock & Bennett, 1998:255), gained prominence during this era because Blacks had no expectations of justice in the formal legal system. Black identity formation was multiply and continually facilitated by the country's official and informal political, economic, and religious structures.

From 1834—immediately following emancipation—to 1865, nearly 25,000 immigrant workers were brought to Jamaica (Wilmot, 1997:4). Whites intended this labor importation as a way to simultaneously lessen dependence on Black Jamaican labor and gain greater bargaining leverage over the work force. At this point, most of the immigrants were Africans (11,380), followed by Indians (9,195), Europeans (3,890), and Chinese (464) (Eisner, 1961:142–45). The planters and other White Jamaicans hoped that the White immigrants (mainly Scots, Irish, and Germans) would numerically increase White presence in the island, populate the interior, and keep the land from Blacks. African influence on Black Jamaican life was reinvigorated during the mid-1800s when African indentured laborers were imported into various parts of Jamaica. These Africans came from various places in the Continent and were of differing ethnicities, but the Yoruba and people from Central Africa predominated (Schuler, 1980).

Beginning around 1850 into the late 1800s, thousands of Jamaicans sought to escape Jamaica's declining sugar industry, low wages, and lack of opportunity by seeking and obtaining work in Central America, especially Panama. Another exodus to Panama and Costa Rica occurred at the turn of the twentieth century (Purcell, 1993) and between 1916 and 1920 to Cuba (Eisner, 1961:148). Emigration lessened domestic tension and

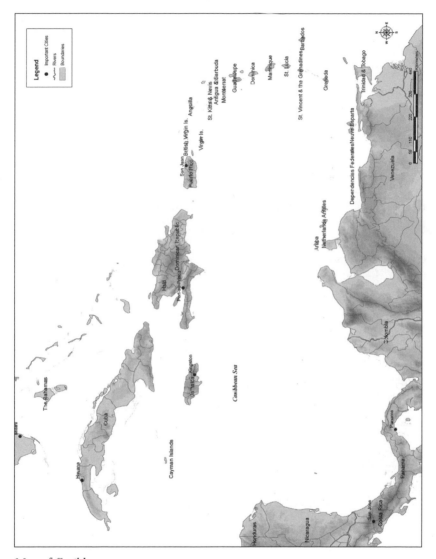

Map of Caribbean

brought Jamaicans into contact with different cultures, experiences, litera-tures, and ideologies—the latter two, as we shall see, often returning with the sojourners to Jamaica.

During 1860 and 1861, a wave of religious fervor—the Great Revival—swept across Jamaica. Thousands of Black Jamaicans became zealous spiritualists, fanatically flocking to churches. By the middle of 1862, the fervor had subsided, but the Great Revival facilitated the full-fledged emergence of African-influenced Christian churches and a religious movement called Revival Religion.[11]

Ethiopianism: A Framework for Morally Configured Black Identities

Ethiopianism provided Black Jamaicans a framework for a racial, moral, religious, and political worldview and an identity, and it was compatible with the moral economies of Blackness. Ethiopianism was likely transported to Jamaica by Lisle and other Black preachers from America, although we have much to learn about how it developed and diffused through Jamaica.[12]

Ethiopianism explained the immorality of oppression and injustice, the glorious histories of Black people, and Black suffering and exploitation at the hands of Whites. The King James Bible served as a cultural resource for Black Jamaicans who looked to it for hope, for signs of the commencement of redemption, and for answers to their questions about life's trials and tribulations. Robert Hinds, one of the founding Rastafari, was charged and tried for sedition (along with Leonard Howell), in March 1934, because of his allegiance to King Ras Tafari. When the court asked Hinds why the Rastafari held such high regard for Ethiopia, he related that they learned from the Bible that they were Ethiopians, not Englishmen (*Daily Gleaner*, 3/14/34; *DG* hereafter).

So, what did Hinds' answer to the court signify? George Shepperson has argued that in the 1611 issue of the King James Bible, the use of "Ethiopian" was synonymous with "Black people" (1968:249). In this definition "Ethiopia" included the lands and peoples of the Kingdom of Abyssinia *and* Sub-Saharan Africa. In America and England, Whites commonly used Ethiopian as a synonym for Black people into the mid-1800s (Moses, 1978:23; Scott, 1978).

Ethiopianism provided an alternative to ideas of White supremacy and Black inferiority. It was millenarian and messianic because it predicted the fall of slavery and an end to oppression and the redemption of Blacks and the continent of Africa. Brother Yendis, a well-known and widely respected Rastafari elder known among Rastafari and non-Rastafari alike for both his spiritual and political prowess, said to me in a conversation:

> Our foreparents sinned in the sight of God and they were put out to their enemies as slaves to be ruled by enemies. . . . people of a darker

complexion were discriminated upon by peoples of a lighter complexion. People of a lighter complexion presented to us a White God. And bound us as Black people to worship this White God. . . . Now, you believe those people who inflict those brutality and pain to us going get away? . . . When the day come for repatriation, people [guilty of oppression] have to be charged. Throughout the whole world. Those who are righteous and have done righteously shall be saved and those who call upon my name [Ras Tafari] also shall be saved.

Black people's fascination with Ethiopia grew out of the references to it throughout the Bible, their understanding of Israel's and Christianity's connection to ancient Ethiopia, and, later, the recognition that Ethiopia had never been conquered by Europeans (before 1935). Black Jamaicans, by connecting themselves to the venerable and documented past described in the King James Bible, and the divine promises made therein, provided a basis for creating histories and identities that contested White racism and bias. Another of my narrators, Ras Brenton, a slightly built, short, heavily bearded, and bespectacled dreadlocked man born in Kingston in 1940, echoes this sentiment:

From Menelik's time,[13] them [Ethiopians] a fight to defend that territory. Right? And [Benito] Mussolini come try at Selassie too. But him could not overcome him. Him [Mussolini] throw [launched] all bomb there. . . . them want capture Ethiopia and control the Throne Room [a spiritual space]. So we say Zion [Ethiopia] is the throne and we ain't going to leave it alone. We are like some of the throne warriors. We a defend that throne because that is Black man throne. We can't go a England to bad up and control England throne, and quarrel over it, because that is Queen Elizabeth throne and her syndicate. So, we have to have our own throne too, and when we have our throne, them get jealous and vex and spread all kinds of propaganda and bad news [about Selassie I and Rastafari]. Everybody get to . . . downgrade I and I say we no have no King. . . . them [White] king we fe bow to and worship. Rasta man come to the realization . . . and say, "No more of that. Fire for that! . . . We want Black empowerment and Black king, and everything Black for this throne." (Ras Brenton)

If Black, not White, people are understood to be primary actors in biblical narratives and living that history in the present, it follows that Whites have hidden the truth and falsified the stories they told. Thus, we have the grounds for both Black accusations of miseducation and remedies such as morally configured Black identities and a Black people's Bible.

Ethiopianism emerged in the United States, perhaps by the early 1700s. Prince Hall, a free African who fought in the American Revolution, wrote in 1797 on the injustice and barbarity of slavery and the hope of redemption offered by the 1791 slave uprising in Haiti. Hall laid his hope on a God whom he conflated with Ethiopia: "Thus doth Ethiopia stretch forth her hand from slavery, to freedom and equality" (Moses, 1978:24). This reference to Psalms 68:31 was interpreted by eighteenth-century Blacks as a divine pledge of deliverance from slavery (Scott, 1978:4), and the idea has proven to be a durable cultural resource assuring many over the centuries of the promise of divine intervention and deliverance (Fredrickson, 1995).

Ethiopianism became diasporic early in its evolution, circulating internationally and influencing religious, literary, and "trans-atlantic political movement[s]" (Moses, 1978:24; Campbell, 1987:2). Gilroy has aptly pointed to such transnational movement of Black intellectuals and the transnational dimensions of Black identity in his *Black Atlantic* (1992).

In South Africa, Ethiopianism influenced the Bantu church movements during the late 1800s and early 1900s, and later served as a rallying point for Black South Africans when Italy invaded Ethiopia in 1896. Italy's second invasion of Ethiopia in 1935 coincided with and fueled a reblossoming of Ethiopianism throughout North America, the Caribbean, Europe, and Southern Africa. And in Jamaica, movements associated with Alexander Bedward, Marcus Garvey, and the Rastafari drew deeply from the cultural well of Ethiopianism.

Two exemplars of romantic, spiritually oriented Ethiopianist racialism were Robert Alexander Young and David Walker, both of whom published notable works in 1829. Young, in his *Ethiopian Manifesto*, pointed toward the coming of a "Black Messiah" who would take up the cause of the "degraded of this earth." Walker, in his *Appeal to the Colored Citizens of the World*, took a strident stance toward fighting slavery: "kill or be killed." Walker's attitude was consistent with the attitudes and behavior we saw Paul Bogle and his followers exhibit in Morant Bay in 1865.

By the middle of the 1800s, Ethiopianism had developed a secular orientation. Black intellectuals Henry Highland Garnet, Martin Delaney, Edward Blyden, and Alexander Crummell were pivotal to this development, focusing particularly on self-reliance and repatriation to Africa.

There are commonalities in the strands of Ethiopianism that emerged in different places. For example, in South Africa, Sundkler described how the "Ethiopian mythology projects the longings of the Africans to a Christian African nation under the 'lion of Judah, King of Kings' and that its adherents sought out Mount Zion, 'City of the living God, heavenly Jerusalem' (1964:59)," which was in Ethiopia. Jamaica's Ethiopianists also emphasized the Lion of Judah, Mount Zion, and a spiritual homeland. Common to both peoples was a concern with a living God attentive to the suffering of Black people.

Some Jamaicans also revered the Biblical King David, the father of Solomon, and grandfather of Menelik the First of Ethiopia. For example, Ras Chronicle, born in 1936 in the parish of Portland, had an uncle who was a follower of Marcus Garvey (but not a Rastafari). Ras Chronicle believed that his uncle had beliefs in common with many older Garveyites:

> Ras Chronicle: My uncle him not so much a Rasta but him talk 'bout Ethiopia. That time (during the mid-1940s) them used to worship King David. . . .
> I interrupt Ras Chronicle: I never knew that!
> Ras Chronicle: Yeah, King David's Greater Son. When them a reason with you them a show you say a man will come, Great David's Greater Son to carry on David's work, who is His Majesty [i.e., Haile Selassie I].
> I interrupt again to ask whether these people had a name for themselves:
> Rasta Chronicle: Nothing different . . . when me deh [there] a country, as 12 and 13 [years old], me deh a country me hear me uncle talk 'bout the Lion of Judah and Great David Greater Son.

Rasta Chronicle's example suggests an Ethiopianist conception of divinity that could easily accommodate the divinity of King Ras Tafari/Emperor Haile Selassie I because of the expectation that something special would come from King David's Ethiopian lineage.

Ethiopianism, as an ideology and cultural resource, was malleable enough to be tailored to fit the concerns of assorted associations, organizations, political programs, and religious doctrines. The African Methodist Episcopal (AME) Church, for example, promoted Ethiopianism in various ways and maintained close ties with the independent church movement in South Africa (Sundkler, 1964; Post, 1978:161). The African American Bishop Turner stirred up Black South Africans with his Ethiopianist rhetoric:

> Why has the white man's civilization contributed so little to the advancement of Africa? . . . It is because the white man does not appreciate our

value, because he believes himself by divine right to be the dominant race and thereby privileged to maintain all the others in a state of subordination. The black is the race of the future, and one day the black man will wake up and shake off the white man's yoke. He is already rubbing his eyes and feeling his muscles. (Thwaite, 1936:37)

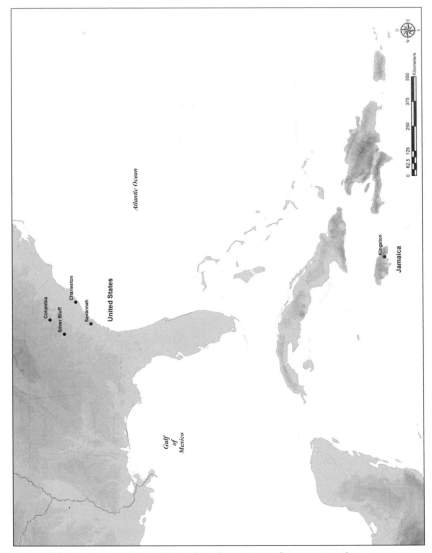

Map of the American South (Provides illustration of connection between Jamaica and U.S./South Carolina during slavery)

Rasta Ivey, born approximately 1906–1912, in Christiana, in Manchester parish. Rasta Ivey was a member of Robert Hind's camp, and knew many Bedwardites. Rasta Ivey met most of the early Rastafari evangelists, including some not based in Kingston.

Alexander Bedward and the Bedwardite Movement: The Moral Economy of Blackness and Anticolonialism

After the Morant Bay insurrection, people and identities organized through Blackness and religion became more tangibly present as collectivities. Alexander Bedward and his followers, the Bedwardites, were among the first Jamaicans to turn the cultural resources of the moral economies of Blackness, and a morally configured Black identity, into a collective identification and social movement capable of posing an organized challenge to White and colonial hegemony. Bedward used cultural resources generated in the past, such as the memories and rhetoric of Morant Bay and Paul Bogle, along with people's interest in Ethiopianism, to mobilize an army of believers willing to challenge the colonial establishment.

Some of the earliest Rastafari were once a part of Bedward's fold. Robert Hinds, for example, was a Bedwardite leader and a founding leader of the Rastafari faith. Rasta Ivey, one of my Rastafari narrators and a member of Hinds's camp, recalled listening to Bedward's talks and then discussing the issues he raised. Rasta Ivey was baptized during the early 1930s, by an "old Bedwardite," into the "Order of Melchisidec" at a place she called "Ferry." She did not recall any details about the Bedwardite, but she related that the Order of Melchisidec was "without time," and that it meant "king and priest together." The Order believed that Haile Selassie I was the Righteous One who would combine the kingly and priestly roles. The Bedwardites too had ideas about returning to Africa and the coming of a redeeming African king (McPherson, 1996:4), although we lack details about these beliefs because they remain understudied. Nonetheless, Rasta Ivey's baptism by a Bedwardite, Bedward's racialized language of "war" and healing, ideas about King David, Melchisidec, and Africa, call our attention to the connections and transitions between Myalists, Native Baptists, Kumina, Revivalists, and the emergent Rastafari. They demonstrate how cultural resources were passed on, and reformed into new identities.

Bedward's birth is placed in 1859. Like other Jamaicans of his time, he traveled to Colon, Panama, in 1883. The emigration of some Black Jamaicans had the effect of vivifying their racial identity, a result of experiences they had while traveling abroad. In 1885, Bedward had two religious visions that compelled him to return to Jamaica to be baptized and save other Jamaicans (Brooks, 1917; Pierson, 1969). Apparently these visions were experiences that set Bedward on an identity transformation path (see chapter 3 on the encounter). In April 1889, he joined the Jamaica Native Baptist Free Church (JNBFC), newly founded by the hermit H.E.S. Woods (from the United States) in August Town, a small community located on the northeastern fringe of Kingston (Brooks, 1917). In October 1891, Bedward claimed that God had called on him to become a savior of Black Jamaicans.

Bedward turned his revivalist church into a movement. He and his followers spread their beliefs widely across the island by organizing their congregations into "camps" under the tutelage of a "shepherd." Bessie Pullen-Burry, who visited Jamaica at the turn of the twentieth century, estimated that there were 6,000 Bedwardites in these camps (1971:142). People from all over the island came to be healed and baptized by Bedward in the "healing" waters of the Mona River. His following consisted primarily of small farmers, casual and household workers, higglers, craft workers, and the unemployed. They were drawn to his religious message and to the moral economy of Blackness that he "lifted up": the need for land and justice, the injustices associated with White rule, and the necessity of setting up social welfare schemes that addressed the needs of the aged, infants, sick, and illiterate. Like Bogle, Bedward advocated that Blacks establish their own institutions such as courts of law to administer justice and protect fair play.

While the language of Ethiopianism may have been familiar to some Jamaicans, it could also be unsettling to those more readily accepting of the racial status quo, especially in its Black God and anticolonial forms. Bedward's confidence in his own authority as a *Black* savior and his capacity to call God to his side in a struggle to overturn the injustice inflicted upon Black people was aggressive. In 1895, he publicly delivered one of several indictments of Whites to a large throng of listeners:

> The Pharisees and Sadducees are the white men, and we are the true people. White people are hypocrites, liars, thieves; Ministers of religion are all rogues and vagabonds. There was a white wall and a black wall. The white wall was closing around the black wall, but now the black wall was stronger than the white wall, and must crush it. The Governor is a scoundrel and robber, the Governor and Council pass laws to oppress the Black people, take their money from their pockets and deprive them of bread and do nothing for it. . . . I have a sign that black people must rise. Remember the Morant War. The fire of hell will be your portion if you do not rise and crush the white people. (Chevannes, 1971:35)

Describing the struggle in no uncertain racial and religious terms and grounding it in ancient biblical history, Bedward warned that the power of Black people was increasing to the point that it could resist and bowl over the hypocrisy and hegemony of Whites. The condemnation was deeper than it sounded on the surface; it invoked the justice motifs associated with the moral economies of Blackness. To call Whites robbers and thieves was to indict them for slavery, for exploiting Blacks as free workers by withholding pay and paying meager wages, and for heavily taxing poor Blacks without due return of benefits. To call Whites liars was to remind listeners of countless false and broken promises regarding freedom, land, and employment, and by this point in time, to condemn religious and historical miseducation resulting from White writing and interpretation of history. Bedward's preachings were but one of the racially and politically subversive religious beliefs circulating in Jamaica between the 1880s and 1920s (see Elkins, 1977; Burton, 1997).

Between the mid-1890s and 1921, Bedward's movement grew in strength, and there were frequent clashes between his followers and the colonial authorities. The British branded racial activists as mad and delusional, used vagrancy laws to arrest them, and remanded them to the asylum (see Price, 2003, for an account of how Bedward's claim that he would fly to heaven was used to discredit him). In April 1921, Bedward organized a display of strength in the form of a major march from August Town to Kingston. The government prepared for the worst while also scheming to destroy him. Bedward and nearly 700 of his followers were arrested and tried under the Vagrancy Law (Post, 1978:8). Authorities sent Bedward to an asylum, although he showed no evidence of the madness with which they charged him (Reynolds, 2000). Bedward died in the asylum on November 8, 1930. King Ras Tafari had been crowned Emperor of Ethiopia just six days earlier. Perhaps this spectacular event was unbeknownst to Bedward. Many of his followers, though, took close note of the occasion. A new but also familiar dialogue of Blackness and redemption was about to begin.

Marcus Garvey: Modernizing Ethiopianism

Another movement in which Ethiopianism played a prominent role co-existed with Bedward's. Marcus Garvey, a Jamaican, internationalized his idea of Black uplift and unification, and in doing so he held out new ideas for interpreting Blackness. While much of Garvey's organizing occurred outside of Jamaica—in the United States, the Caribbean, South and Central America, and England—his United Negro Improvement Association (UNIA) had tremendous impact upon Jamaica. Unlike Bedward, who spoke especially to rural residents and the dispossessed, Garvey's message took hold among urbanites and Jamaica's Black petit bourgeoisie.

Marcus Garvey was born in 1887, in the parish of St. Anne. He left school as a teenager to work as a printer and traveled through Central America as a young man. He became racially radicalized through his travels. He saw the common degraded situation of Blacks across the world, and he was influenced by the "New Negro" movement in the United States and the teachings of the Pan-Africanist, Robert Love (Lewis, 1987).

Garvey founded the UNIA in 1914 in Jamaica and sometime between 1916 and 1918 founded the first international chapter in New York City. When he left Jamaica for New York, Garvey was rumored to have uttered a prophecy that a Black African king would soon be crowned and this man would be the redeemer of the race. Whether Garvey actually said this is contested (Hill, 2001, claims not). Perhaps some people confused Garvey's ideas with those of Reverend James Webb, who in 1924 pronounced the coming of a redeeming Black king in a speech delivered in Liberty Hall).[14] Garvey "modernized" Ethiopianism by embedding it within an emergent modern Black nationalism that emphasized organization, empowerment, and economic development more than the purely cultural and spiritual concerns that had energized previous versions (Carnegie, 1999). He used the justice motifs just as effectively as Bedward, though toward different ends. Notice, for instance, how Garvey used biblical tropes of weariness and autonomy to speak to a Black audience: he stated that the desire of the UNIA was "not to disturb the tranquility of other men, but to lay down our burden and rest our weary backs and feet by the banks of the Niger and sing our songs and chant our hymns to the *God of Ethiopia*" (Garvey, 1989:120, emphasis added).

Garvey argued that Black people should imagine God as Black not because of some essential truth, but because it was appropriate on cultural grounds:

Whilst our God has no color, yet it is human to see everything through one's own spectacles, and since the white people have seen their God through white spectacles, we have only now started (late though it be) to see our God through our own spectacles. The God of Isaac and the God of Jacob let him exist for the race that believe in the God of Isaac and the God of Jacob. *We Negroes believe in the God of Ethiopia, the everlasting God . . . we shall worship him through the spectacles of Ethiopia.* (Garvey 1989 [1923]:34, emphasis added)

Brother Woks, a short, dark-skinned Rastafari, born in 1938, who does not wear locks and has been an ardent supporter of the Ethiopian World Federation since the late 1950s, believed Garvey had a tremendous effect on how Black Jamaicans imagined themselves. "Hearing Mr. Marcus Garvey preach, and teach," said Bother Woks, "encouraged Black people to rise up because if we are not able to see ourselves as a Black race, nobody is going to show you [your history and common experience]."

The Rastafari and Garveyites coexisted for some time, but there were conflicts, most starkly represented by Garvey himself. Garvey favored "civilized" religions over grassroots religions like Kumina, Native Baptist, and Rastafari; for him they represented racial backwardness. Garvey's disdain for the "cults," however, may also have reflected pragmatic concerns for the organizational integrity of his following. Sister Mariam, a Garveyite who converted to Rastafari during the 1940s, believed that "Garvey, him really see him people start to take up and follow the Rasta people and from that him is very vexed."

Garvey became an acerbic critic of Haile Selassie I, which put him strongly at odds with the Rastafari and Blacks who held the Emperor in favorable regard. He admired the Emperor's challenge to the invasion of the Italian fascists but lost respect for the Emperor after he turned to the colonizing nations for assistance. Selassie I delivered himself to his enemies, so Garvey believed (Garvey, 1937). Garvey lost support through his anti-Selassie stand, which suggests that Black identification with Ethiopia and Ethiopianism was ultimately about more than an attraction to charismatic leaders. Paradoxically, Garvey was a prophet in the mind of Bedward, and has remained an icon to the Rastafari in spite of his disdain for them.

The Text Augments the Word

Oratory prowess has been central to Black intellectual traditions, at least partially because of the long period of time that so many Blacks lacked text literacy and access to textual information (e.g., Banks, 1999; Bogues, 2003). Of course, some Blacks mastered reading and writing on their own or with the assistance of Whites, but the building of a Black intellectual tradition based in printed media was slow to develop in Jamaica. By the 1920s, though, the printed word had become an important means of transmitting ideas on Blackness and Ethiopianism. The spread of printed material increased the circulation of ideas and increased the possibility for more people to learn about Blackness and grapple with the implications of oppression, miseducation, and deracination.

The Holy Piby, The Royal Parchment Scroll of Black Supremacy, and *The Promise Key*, three important Ethiopianist-oriented texts, influenced the early Rastafari. Robert Athlyi Rogers, an Anguillan, settled in Perth Amboy, New Jersey, founded the Afro-Athlyican Constructive Gaathlyans (a.k.a. the Hamatic Church). It was there that he wrote *The Holy Piby* (1924), which preached the " . . . doctrine of the divinity of Ethiopia" (Scott, 1999:141).

The development of a literature that spoke to Black experiences in terms of Ethiopianism exposed White suppression and distortion of Black history and culture:

> The Bible which the Bantu now have is the wrong book. There exists, they
> say, another Bible, hidden away from the Bantu by the Whites, a book

containing the real truth, whilst the "old Bible"—as the Bible is called in such circles—was written only to cheat the Black man. One source of this propaganda seems to be the Afro-Athlican Constructive Church, of Negro origin . . . they know and possess "another" Bible, the right, Ethiopian Bible, called "The holy Piby." According to them, the "old Bible" was given to the children of the house of Israel, whereas the Holy Piby has been given to children of the house of Ethiopia. (Sundkler, 1964:278)

It is no coincidence that the "King of Kings," the "Lion of Judah," and "Zion," construed in terms of Blackness, existed in the United States, Bantu South Africa, and Jamaica. The contributions of Blacks based in America were instrumental. For example, Rogers (who revered Garvey) founded a branch of his Ethiopianist-inspired church, the Afro-Athlyican Constructive Church in Kimberly, South Africa. Around 1924–25, Rogers met two Jamaicans in Colón, Panama—Charlie Goodrich and Mother Grace Garrison—who resettled in Jamaica and formed a branch of the Afro-Athlyican Church there. The church, however, was not well-received by Jamaican Garveyites, and they forced it to move from Kingston (Scott, 1999:142).

The Holy Piby turned up in St. Thomas, where key founding Rastafari evangelist Leonard Howell would later preach his vision of Rastafari (Scott, 1999:142). Hill believes that Howell found *The Holy Piby* in Port Morant (142,143). Reverend Fitz Pettersburgh's *The Royal Parchment Scroll* (ca. 1926) refers repeatedly to King Alpha and Queen Omega, and emphasizes the "resurrection" of Ethiopia. It is likely that Reverend Pettersburgh, an African American preacher, visited Jamaica. Leonard Howell, himself, authored *The Promise Key* (ca.1934), a document that was circulated in the meetings of the early Rastafari. Hill (2001) suggests that Howell plagiarized *The Royal Parchment Scroll*, which, from an academic perspective, might be true. However, the contemporary term "open source literature" perhaps better describes the attitude of Howell and his followers toward ideas.

Other media contributed to the well of cultural resources drawn on by the Rastafari. These include news stories on Ethiopia and Emperor Selassie I published in the *Daily Gleaner, Pittsburgh Courier,* and information and images collected by seafarers and brought to Jamaica, such as pictures of the Emperor, and the June 1931 issue of *National Geographic,* which carried photographs of life in Ethiopia. These texts had a deep impact upon some:

> But the thing what convince me now [about the divinity Selassie I], a man come from Cuba and give me a book. And the book is a underwater book, Geographic book [*National Geographic*] . . . Well in the middle of the Geographic book, it have the entire crowning of His Majesty. And when me read all them things, me get powerful you know. . . . Because the book say "We are now ready for the crowning of the first Ras Tafari," you know. A that the book say, you know. [he repeats to emphasize the significance for him]. We are now ready for the crowning of the first Rastafari. . . . Me about twenty-something at the time. . . . no bwoy can't get them book fe buy you know. (Brother Yendis)

Brother Yendis was born in 1935. So even in the 1950s, texts such as the issues of *National Geographic* were important pathways to learning about and identifying as Rastafari, but also precious because such material was so difficult to acquire.

The Rastafari: A New Configuration of Moral Blackness

Many Black Jamaicans believed in 1930 that the second coming of Christ would be signaled by war, rumors of war, famine, pestilence, and hard times. They were looking to their Bibles for answers to the turmoil and instability engulfing the world. They sought ways to recognize the Messiah when He returned, which required piecing together experience and cultural resources.

> Mortimer Planner [also spelled "Planno"] say him and Skipper (from down a Dungle, as we woulda call down Spanish Town Road) and Skeewi, and some more man, did sit down . . . [one] morning when it come out in a de *Gleaner* say Emperor Haile Selassie crown King of Kings in Ethiopia. . . . Morti Planner was around to bring the paper come show Skipper . . . Him say "See it ya Skeewi, Haile Selassie crown at Ethiopia, King of Kings and Lord of Lords," and we have the whole of the picture . . . . we see we King sit down 'pon him throne as King of Kings and Lord of Lords. . . . You no see it? Isaiah [the Prophet] tell we say him a go come and Revelations bring him come. You no see it? And all a them, Daniel and all a them prophets there. So a something what we a read and overstand. (Ras Brenton)

Some elder Rastafari credit Garvey with pointing them toward King Rastafari:

Now, when Mr. Marcus Garvey talked about [how] a King shall be crowned in Africa, and when that time comes, Black people deliverance draweth nigh. These informal groups that usually protest against injustice and against the colonial masters . . . check with the Bible. . . . the brothers said, "This must be the man that Mr. Marcus Garvey is talking about, the King of Kings, The Lord of Lords, The Conquering Lion of the Tribe of Judah, Elect of God and the Light of this world." That is the basis from which we all come to the acknowledgement that His Majesty is the returned Christ seated on the throne of David. . . . We read ourselves the Bible. (Brother Woks)

While the Emperor adopted some of the highly symbolic titles of the Book of Revelations, it was the durable, racialized cultural resources that allowed Jamaicans to attribute even greater significance to his crowning. For example, some older permutations of Ethiopianism, such as that of Robert Young, explicitly identified a redeeming Messiah consonant with what Black Jamaicans were thinking in the 1930s:

As came John the Baptist . . . to spread abroad the forthcoming of his master, so alike are intended these our words, to denote to the black African or Ethiopian people, that God has prepared for them a leader, who awaits but for his season to proclaim to them his birthright. How shall you know this man? By indubitable signs which cannot be controverted by the power of mortal, his marks being stamped in open visage. (Moses, 1996:65)

A White-led organization, the Salvation Army in Jamaica, voiced similar rhetoric. According to Bryan (2000:35), thousands of Jamaicans were members of the Salvation Army in 1895, and its presence in Kingston carried into the 1920s. When I first met Ma Lion, she introduced herself as the "woman with the growling lion," and then literally made a noise that flowed from her throat and chest that sounded a mixed growl and purr. I asked her how she "got" the lion. She sang an answer while rhythmically clapping her hands: "The Lion of Judah, will break every chain . . . " and at the end of this phrase she sounded her purr growl. Her lion offered courage and liberation; it broke chains of oppression. Ma Lion was born in 1922 and identifies 1950 as the year she "vision" and became Rastafari. I was unable to formally interview Ma Lion, but what she pointed me to was a still vague part of the early Rastafari years: the role of the Salvation

Army. Rasta Ivey talked of how, during the late 1920s, "Salvation Army come say . . . 'the Lion of Judah will break every chain.' [But] Nobody listen to them . . . them only a sing and clap hand. . . . Them also say 'blood and fire' . . . " would arrive hand-in-hand with redemption and the return of the Messiah. What Rasta Ivey is pointing to is that inquisitive people were connecting and integrating the various discourses of race, religion, and justice that had been circulating before the time of Selassie I's coronation.

During our first in-depth conversation, Rasta Ivey repeated, like a mantra, that "The five become one . . . the five become one." I was puzzled. Rasta Ivey spoke in undulating fits, breaking up her narrative with excited but abrupt inhalations of air—as if she needed a deep breath—and pregnant pauses. It seemed she had moments when she really could not articulate what she wanted to say so badly. I felt I had to hang on every word or else I might be unable to make sense of what she was saying. Some people considered her a mad woman, perhaps because of her idiosyncrasies. I found her brilliant, but quirky. She was a masterful observer of people; she had a good memory; and she was judicious in how she shared her analysis. I never witnessed Rasta Ivey doing what we might call speculating about people. She talked of what she personally knew or what someone had told her:

> Price: You think Mr. [Leonard] Howell knew Bedward?
> Rasta Ivey: I do not know of that. I do not know. But the two of them were at chord and it was the same thing they were talking about. I put [together] four or five of them who work in chord.
> Price: Which five?
> Rasta Ivey: Mr. Bedward, Mr. Brown, Brother John, Mass Howell and Garvey. Howell came last. . . . After Mr. Garvey disappeared [to England?], Howell came. Four of them put together and then five of them and everything complete. Then the King came [Ras Tafari was crowned as Emperor]. The Kings of Kings. When Salvation Army was preaching, they said the "Lion of Judah." "Who is the Lion of Judah? Isn't it Ras Tafari? Ras Tafari is the Lion of Judah." . . . That time he was in Ethiopia kicking hell in Ethiopia, but we did not have the understanding to know" [she and others were only beginning to learn of Selassie I].

What Rasta Ivey was explaining to me was that there were several different groups speaking to a common theme of Blackness and redemption.

They were not saying the same things, but there was overlap. They were "at chord," emphasizing the coming of a Black Messiah; the "upliftment of Black people"; an end to White oppression of Blacks; and Black redemption, repatriation, and liberation. What Rasta Ivey and some of her contemporaries during the late 1920s and early 1930s "pieced together" were the messages of the various carriers:

> I see the end of Mr. Bedward, and I see several man come after Mr. Bedward. In the midst of that and after that coming right down until I see Salvation Army and Marcus Garvey . . . and I hold on to that. I hold on to that because the Salvation Army said . . . "The Lion of Judah shall break the chain." Everybody else tells you of King of Kings, but the Salvation Army says, "the Lion of Judah come."

Rasta Ivey felt she was on to something important. People such as Bishop Brown, a seafarer who preached of a coming Black king and redeemer, gave credence to her conclusions: "I did have the understanding you know . . . the people them a listen . . . but the people . . . didn't all come [to seriously consider Ras Tafari as divine] 'til Bishop Brown come preach we have a [Black] king . . . where him go I don't know [Rasta Ivey does not know what happened to Brown]." Brother Dee, like Rasta Ivey, had much to learn about Ethiopia. However, he was not immediately taken by the crowning of Rastafari. Brother Dee was in his late eighties when I met him. He was among the trailblazing Rastafari who was during the 1950s among the militant Rastafari who had the courage and conviction to express defiantly the identity that elite Jamaicans wanted to stamp out. However, Brother Dee, like his peers, had to *become* Rastafari, which entailed embarking on a journey of discovery and learning as a part of internalizing the new identity Rastafari: "When Ras Tafari did come me didn't accept it you know . . . Bishop Brown come tell us we have a Black King . . . [but] we never know anything 'bout Ethiopia . . . 'til Selassie crown."

There is widespread consensus that four men, Leonard Howell, Joseph Hibbert, Archibald Dunkley, and Robert Hinds, were pivotal founders of Rastafari. Howell, who dominates most accounts of the early days of Rastafari, lived for a while in America. Hibbert had resided in Costa Rica and was a president of a UNIA chapter there (McPherson, 1996:7). Dunkley was a seaman who worked for the Atlantic Fruit Company who later was among the first members of the Ethiopian World Federation:

coming to '31 [1931] . . . anytime the ship come it take a certain amount of Jamaican boy carry them away, to go work . . . and bring them back. [Archibald] Dunkley, the Red man, one Red man, him go get magazine book and bring them [to us]. Him used to preach 'pon street. . . . him dead now. (Rasta Ivey)

We don't know much about Robert Hinds either, but Rasta Ivey mentioned that he worked on the docks of Kingston and that he too "went on ships." He may or may not have been a seafarer, but he was certainly in contact with international seafarers. Rasta Ivey credited another man, Bishop Brown, as a founding Rastafari. However, we know almost nothing about him and his contributions to the fledgling people and identity. All of these men were preaching the doctrine of Ras Tafari by 1933. Brown, according to Rasta Ivey, was preaching about a Black king before Bedward died. What role women played in these initial moments of Rastafari is a question waiting to be addressed. While Rasta Ivey does not say much about other women in her stories about the early days of Rastafari, they were present, just as she was, though perhaps not as active as she was.

Now that a new people and identity—one configured around a moral conception of Blackness—is on the scene, we must wonder what will happen to both. Brother Bongo, an elder who received an official medal of commendation from Emperor Selassie I during his visit to Jamaica in 1966, explained:

[A]ll who came after Howell in Jamaica go on to spread the word Rastafari as the doctrine of the Black King. . . . [Queen] Elizabeth was demoted because the Black subjects started to turn to His Majesty. Not paying no attention to Elizabeth's sovereignty. Her troops and agents started to harass the doctrine because it created a diversion just like when Christ used to preach in his days against the Elders, Sadducees, and the Philistines, and they rose up against him saying that this man seeks to take away the people from Caesar. So, they said that this Man [Selassie I] was taking the worship away from the Queen.

Both the Bedwardites and Garveyites were short-lived, perhaps because so much of their identity and direction depended on their leader. How will the Rastafari evolve, and what drew people to associate and identify with this new, morally configured Black identity?

2

Ethnogenesis, Surprise, and Collective Identity Formation

The Rastafarian movement stands for *freedom* in the fullest sense
and for the recovery of the dignity, self-respect and Sovereignty of
the Black people of Jamaica. Many deplore and accuse the black
people of raising the colour question in this island. But White supremacy was the official policy of this Island for hundreds of years
and white supremacists never regarded black men as good as the
dogs in their yards.

> (Ras Sam Brown, the "Foundation of the Rastafarian
> Movement," [1966]; emphasis added)

One June morning in 1998, I picked up Rasta Ivey from her
one-room dwelling behind the Ethiopian Orthodox Church, and together we drove to a vast sea of hovels, a community called Waterview,
adjacent to the bustling Spanish Town highway. I parked at the top of the
entrance road, and the two of us made our way through a maze of dirt
paths separating rows of tiny residences constructed of tin, wood, and assorted scraps. We were visiting Brother Dee, an octogenarian like Rasta
Ivey. Brother Dee had become an invalid, confined to a decrepit wheel-
chair. His locks and beard were snow white, and his eyes a cloudy, gray-
ish blue. He lived with his daughter and several of her children in a one-
room home of ill-fitted board. A curtain hung on a string served as a wall,
turning one room into two. I was reluctant to invite Rasta Ivey with me
because I knew how cantankerous she could be. I had already interviewed
Brother Dee and spent time with him, so I knew that he too was argu-
mentative. I was prepared for the visit to be short. However, I was very
wrong. The elders warmed up to each other and began talking. I asked

some questions about Rastafari and the past, and they each answered, often at the same time, at first disagreeing and hurling snippy remarks at one another. When Brother Dee made wild statements, such as the *Titanic* being one mile long, Rasta Ivey would get agitated and say, "No, no, no, no." Brother Dee would retort huffily with phrases like "What you a say, man?" As the discussion warmed up, though, Rasta Ivey's voice took control of the conversation, and Brother Dee began to affirm her recollections and thoughts, intermittently adding his own contributions. Their conversation ranged between World War I and the late 1990s and focused especially on people and events in and around Kingston such as seafaring and wharf-working Jamaicans and early Rastafari people. The result of getting these two elders together and listening to them proved felicitous. Their conversation provided additional information to compare against other Rastafari life stories and news stories, and it helped me construct a narrative of Rastafari ethnogenesis. We will now turn our attention to collective or social identity formation among the Rastafari, between 1931 and the mid-1970s.

Early Rastafari organizers attracted crowds in the eastern parts of the island with their justice-laced message of racial redemption. Some listeners must simply have been curious or nosy onlookers. Law authorities, however, heard speeches stirring up racial hatred and contempt for the government and Jamaican elites. Some clergy saw Rastafari evangelists as a threat that drew members from their congregations, diminished their authority, and encouraged racial interpretations of scripture. Members of the elite feared that Rastafari evangelists were influencing the consciousness of people, pushing them to contest the established racial, political, and economic order. Such concerns led a group of elites to ask the Inspector of Police in Seaforth district to investigate Leonard Howell (*DG*, 3/14/34:21). Thus, elites opposed the Rastafari almost from the start. I stress the efforts of elites because of their power to mold the portrayal of the Rastafari and their capacity to ascribe Rastafari identity through mediums such as news stories. The tension between elites, ordinary citizens, and the Rastafari increased as the Rastafari contested how elites and other citizens depicted and treated them. These were struggles over Black identity, historical interpretation, moral authority, and a racially configured religiosity, and not merely that the Rastafari were bucking Jamaican sensibilities of decorum and acceptable beliefs.

Ethnogenesis, Complexity, and Collective Identity Formation

How did Rastafari evolve from pariahs to celebrated exemplars of Black culture and identity? Why did they view themselves collectively as a persecuted and chosen people? I focus on watershed moments in the evolution of the Rastafari in order to provide sociohistorical context,[1] and to illustrate instances of disruption in their ethnogenesis. I also want to be able to situate personal identity formation within the context of ethnogenesis. Ethnogenesis is the study of how groups form and evolve. It is not a theory per se, but a framework for theoretical development. William Sturtevant, a pioneer in the approach, revealed, for example, how in the United States some of the Creek Indians transformed into a new ethnicity, the Seminole Indians (e.g., 1971; Sattler, 1996). Studies of ethnogenesis have helped us come to terms with why and how identities shift over time, especially in the context of oppression, dislocation, and colonization. Ethnogenesis focuses on the history, collective identity, and other factors involved in the emergence and development of a people (e.g., Taylor, 1979; Bilby, 1996; Hill, 1996; Whitten Jr., 1996; Galloway, 1998; Greenbaum, 2002:8).

Ethnogenesis is conceived as taking two major forms (Bilby, 1996). One is the birth of an entirely new group, such as the Maroons of Jamaica. The other involves redefinition of ethnicity over time, especially where social, economic, and political contexts change. In the shifting situation, ethnicity and identity can be mobilized by various actors for different purposes. The distinction is useful, but questionable empirically because of the too neat a division between the two types. The Rastafari are a "new people" whose identity and ethnicity have shifted in relation to changing circumstances. The ethnogenesitic approach remains valuable, though, because it helps us keep in view what is happening at different levels of action, reminds us of the agency of the people involved, the influence of institutions and power, and how these mutually influence each other.

The story of Rastafari ethnogenesis is one of complexity. Surprise, disruption, and perturbation are metaphors for an empirical reality: the consequences of particular acts or actions by different actors often had unintended and unforeseen consequences that proved vital to the durability and persistence of the Rastafari. For example, the efforts by elites to discredit and liquidate Rastafari sometimes had the effect of drawing

additional attention to them, stirring interest in and diffusing their beliefs, and fortifying personal and collective identity. Signal events or perturbations—sometimes traumatic, typically surprising—have mutually
influenced the evolution of the Rastafari and how they were depicted.
Students of complexity draw attention to how change and instability
characterize the workings of our life worlds, despite that these processes
may be imperceptible to us much of the time (De Greene, 1997).

Complexity is about "agents" that "interact" and "adapt" within a social system (Hornstein, 2005:120). There is growing awareness that the
ideas of complexity offer new ways to think about how sociocultural
systems work (e.g., Escobar, 2004; Chesters & Welsh, 2006; Hornstein,
2005; Lansing, 2003; Mosko & Damon, 2005). The fundamental ideas
of complexity urge us to view sociocultural phenomena as dynamic,
open systems with shifting boundaries. We identify "initial conditions"
to situate these systems and the semblances of order and trajectories
of development that we perceive. However, we can only approximately
pinpoint initial conditions, because determining a single originating
point in the social world is tremendously complicated. We can begin
with emergence, though. For instance, we can identify several individuals as Rastafari founders, but each had his own history that he brought
to the new effort, and previous movements such as the Bedward and
Garvey movements influenced the emergence and initial trajectories of
the Rastafari. Open systems are influenced by feedback from various
sources, and as such, order is unstable and ephemeral, always vulnerable to disruptions that shift existing arrangements or patterns within
the system and perhaps even influence wider systems. Thus, we have
limited capacity to predict the consequences of actions, events, or the
direction change will take: surprises are a part of the process. Inde-
terminate systems also display self-organizing capacities, that is, such
systems can become more complex over time, the result of adjust-
ment to relatively simple or small interactions, as well as pronounced
perturbations.

We saw in chapter 1 the emergence of several charismatic Rastafari
evangelists within a vibrant and diverse field of groups focused on religion, justice, and Blackness. However, two of these evangelists, Leonard Howell and Robert Hinds, were accidently thrust into the national
spotlight. Government's attempt to quash the Rastafari had unintended
consequences.

Unintended Consequences:
Spying and Reporting on the Rastafari, 1934–1938

Officer Isaac Brooks and Constable Gayle went to Seaforth District in St. Thomas Parish, around seven o'clock in the evening of December 10, 1933. They found Leonard Howell, standing on a plank supported by two barrels, addressing a crowd of 300 or so people (*DG*, 3/14/34:21; 3/15/34:20). The two men, with the aid of an oil lamp, recorded in longhand the parts of Howell's speech they believed to be seditious. Brooks noted that the audience periodically cheered for parts of Howell's speech, and that Howell was selling pictures of King Rastafari (Haile Selasie I) for one shilling each. Robert Hinds was also there.

Howell and Hinds were working together, preaching a similar message, but not in the same way. Hinds, the former Bedwardite leader, was an illiterate but talented orator and battle-seasoned militant evangelist. Hinds had, on his own, paid close attention to the pictures he saw of King Rastafari and his coronation, and he was connecting it with an interest he already held. Both men completely concurred, though, with the idea that King Ras Tafari was the Messiah and redeemer of Black people (*DG*, 3/17/34:6). They recognized that a combination of religion, race, politics, and social justice would appeal to the gathered throng. Howell was also a skilled orator, and his speech artfully combined racial critique with hope. He knew that Black Jamaicans were suffering from economic duress, lack of cultivable land, high taxes, many of the same problems that had led to the Morant Bay rebellion. He knew how to mobilize these sentiments. He claimed, for example, that Whites financially benefitted from Black privation: "The Governor of this country lend out £20,000,000 at interest as belonging to the people. . . . He lend it to the white man to settle on their estates" (*DG*, 3/17/34:6). "Do you want to see better times?" Howell asked the Seaforth crowd (*DG*, 3/15/34:20). Finally, he persuaded his Seaforth audience to consider themselves Abyssinian instead of British subjects.

Police arrested Howell and Hinds based on the report filed by officers Gayle and Brooks and charged them with sedition. Their trial began March 13, 1934, in Morant Bay, and was presided over by Chief Justice Sir Robert William Lyall. The courtroom could not accommodate all the people who wanted to observe the proceedings. Some attended the trial for its luridness, and the press emphasized moments when the audience erupted into laughter. Such was the case when Howell, with a straight face, explained that the King of Abyssinia was the same Messiah that appeared in the King James Bible, and he would redeem Black people (*DG*, 3/15/34:20; 3/16/34:16).

While on trial, Howell and Hinds had the opportunity to expound upon their practice. Both men spoke biblically in Ethiopianist language. Hinds argued that Christ would not return in spirit but in flesh. The Christ in his view had returned as King Ras Tafari. Hinds read from Revelations 19. He said, "I told them . . . that we got it from a magazine that he was crowned in 1930—November 2." Hinds believed that Blacks were Israelites, "otherwise Ethiopians" (*DG*, 3/17/34:6). Howell read from Thessalonians and Revelations to support his claims. The *Daily Gleaner* (*DG*) reported that such statements drew bursts of laughter from the court audience who were, in effect, laughing at Howell and Hinds and the idea that Black people could have their own history and God. Both men were undaunted by the ridicule, firm in their belief in a "God of righteousness" that had returned to earth to redeem Black people and lead humankind (*DG*, 3/15/34:20). Howell and his witnesses claimed his speech was religious, while the government insisted it was political (*DG*, 3/16/34:16). Several of Howell's witnesses were women, suggesting the visible presence of women from the earliest days of the Rastafari.

The jury found Hinds guilty of talking against the government to "make people rebel against it," and the judge sentenced him to a year in jail. The judge believed that Howell had duped Hinds into promoting Rastafari and gave him a lighter sentence. He found Howell guilty of "uttering seditious language," and sentenced him to a term of two years (*DG*, 3/17/34:6). The judge, Sir Lyall, had spent time in a region of East Africa near Ethiopia and made reference to his firsthand experience with anti-White, anti-government movements and how they led to "serious rioting" (*DG*, 3/17/34:6). Given Lyall's African experience, he might have sentenced them to longer terms. Perhaps he had not yet reason to believe them a serious threat.

Elites unwittingly provided Rastafari with an audience—antagonistic, sympathetic, and curious—which they could never have reached on their own. *The Gleaner*, Jamaica's primary news organ from the 1930s to 1960s, was the voice of its elites. By reporting on Howell and the Rastafari and by reprimanding Howell, the authorities' effort to disrupt the emergent Rastafari had the unanticipated consequence of amplifying their beliefs. Imprisonment did not dampen the faith of Howell or my narrators in the rightness of their beliefs and identity. Soon after his release from jail, Howell returned to preaching Rastafari, in Kingston and St. Thomas, to any who would listen. Rasta Ivey remembers it this way: "Him tell them [the court] 'bout Rasta and them send him asylum, and when him go asylum and come out [he] come preach every night . . . them time me live a town you see."

Following the sentencing of Howell and Hinds, the denunciations did not let up. In a letter to the editor, a man wrote: the Rastafari "live the lowest lives, while they keep the ganja trade, not only alive, but flourishing. They paint the white man with colours of hate and teach that God and Christ are black. Decent coloured people who won't stoop with them are dubbed 'black-white'" (*DG*, 8/20/34:12). The writer had reason to worry: people in St. Thomas were refusing to pay taxes. When a Crown Lands agent asked residents why, they responded they need not pay taxes because they would be delivered to Africa, August 1, 1934, and would "trample upon the stomachs of the white men" when they walked to Kingston to board awaiting ships to Africa (*DG*, 8/20/34:12). News columnists and editorial commentators assumed that by showing the Rastafari to be fools—a tactic the elites would vainly repeat for the next 40 years—people would reject them. Relying on attributions of simple-mindedness and escapism proved an inadequate political response to or an explanation for the expanding ranks of Rastafari. What the critics failed to recognize was the potential of Rastafari identity to build a Black community and address concerns of oppression, miseducation, and deracination.

Although we can call the parish of St. Thomas the "birthing ground" of the Rastafari because of the base built there during the earliest phases of the Rastafari's evolution, Portland parish was also an important early site of activity. Portland's southern boundary adjoins St. Thomas and has the Caribbean Sea as its northern boundary. The two parishes make up the far eastern tip of Jamaica. During 1935, two "young" devotees of Ras Tafari attracted attention by organizing in Mt. Moriah, Port Antonio, and Bog Bridge, in Portland. One reporter called the young evangelists "extremely aggressive and belligerent," criticizing the "wholesale robbing of the rights and privileges of the black race by the whites" (*DG*, 7/30/35:4). The discourse of these Rastafari evangelists was of such interest that in a case in Port Antonio, their audience prevented four police officers from breaking up the meeting. They hurled stones at the policemen, forcing them to retreat. The police reported that what caught their attention was not only the crowd but also the speech: a "vitriolic diatribe" against the police.

The trajectories of the emergent Rastafari connected with events happening outside of and within Jamaica. Newspapers, including the *Gleaner*, reported on Mussolini's 1935 invasion of Abyssinia and the subsequent war. Tens of thousands of Black people in America and the Caribbean mobilized in solidarity as a reaction to the 1935 invasion of Ethiopia (e.g., Weisbord, 1970; Robinson, 1985; Scott, 1993; Yelvington, 1999). Race-conscious Jamaicans were connecting their current plight with past and then-current struggles in Africa. For the Rastafari, they saw their opposition paralleling that of the African Nyabingi. The Nyabingi were a politico-religious, anti-European movement of Africans native to present-day Uganda and Rwanda, led by a charismatic African woman, Muhumuza. The Nyabingi were finally suppressed in 1928, after more than two decades of challenging the colonial policies of Germany, Britain, and Belgium (Hopkins, 1971).

Frederico Philos (a pseudonym, perhaps an Italian aware of the African Nyabingi) published an ominous article on the "Nya-Binghi" in the *Jamaica Times*, in 1935. Philos's propagandist piece claimed that "Nya-Binghi" meant "death to Whites" and that they had developed into a worldwide movement under the aegis of Haile Selassie I. Philos's claims had some substance—the Nyabingi were a real movement antagonistic to Whites—but he used that kernel of truth to spin a frenzied fable. He turned historical events into propaganda aimed at instilling fear in Whites and status quo Blacks. His propaganda may have been additional inspiration for the name of one of the oldest Rastafari sects, the Nyabinghi Order. The Order emphasizes liberation, truth, love, and righteousness—racialized motifs of justice—and designates Haile Selassie I as the "head" or leader of the Order.[2] The Rastafari defined Nyabinghi to mean, among other things, *Death to White and Black oppressors*, reminiscent of Paul Bogle's racialized call to arms, "Death to the Whites and their Black allies," during the Morant Bay rebellion. For Rastafari, the death threat, though, is symbolic, not a literal threat.

By mid-1935, systematic suppression of the Rastafari had begun, and, in St. Thomas, officials banned them from holding public meetings; talking about Rastafari could not be conducted in public (*DG*, 8/19/35:19). In August 1935, a *Gleaner* reporter noted that the Rastafari had been "brought to a standstill," that they had "ceased to exist" (*DG*, 8/19/35:19; *DG*, 3/18/37:4). Whether from wishful thinking or ignorance, he was wrong. Authorities had driven Rastafari evangelists and their adherents underground, some moving into Kingston to carry on their activities. Despite the loss of charismatic evangelical organizers like Howell and Hinds, the Rastafari had become a reticulated network of cells that could not be completely stamped out through repressive means.

In 1937, at the instruction of Haile Selassie I, Dr. Malaku Bayen, an Ethiopian who had studied at Howard University in the United States, founded the Ethiopian World Federation (EWF) in New York City to raise money and build support for Ethiopia's war against the Italian fascists. The EWF, in the Preamble to their Constitution, emphasized racial solidarity between the Black Diaspora and Ethiopia. The Rastafari did not miss that the EWF Constitution defined Ethiopians as Black, encouraged Black solidarity, and emphasized justice motifs compatible with those of Jamaica's moral economy of Blackness: "We the Black people of the world, in order to effect Unity, Solidarity, Liberty, Freedom, and self-determination, to secure Justice and maintain the Integrity of Ethiopia . . . " A group, organized by Paul Erlington, Leonard Howell, and other seasoned organizers, all Rastafari, founded Local Chapter 17 in Kingston in 1937.[3] The Rastafari formed other EWF locals and other groups and, as a result, developed a visible but often frail organizational infrastructure that provided means for "abeyance," structures and networks that would sustain the Rastafari in periods of repression and political inactivity.[4]

Dynamic Equilibrium and Disruption: Pinnacle and Rastafari, 1940–1941

Between the mid-1930s and 1940, the number of Rastafari slowly increased. Howell left EWF Local 17 in 1939 to form his own organization, the Ethiopian Salvation Society (ESS), a race-focused mutual aid society. That same year, he convened a "Jubilee" at the Liberty Hall Club on King Street in Kingston (formerly Garvey's headquarters), that attracted hundreds, including travelers from St. Thomas, Portland, and other parishes (*DG*, 4/3/39:24; 4/4/39:6). Howell, who saw himself as the successor to Marcus Garvey, was reputed to have said during the weekend Jubilee, "Marcus Garvey gone down, Howell gone up."

Having successfully brought together like-minded Jamaicans, Howell moved his Ethiopian Salvation Society (ESS) from Kingston to a remote location in rural St. Catherine's parish, sometime between 1939 and 1940. Howell described himself as "socialistic," and a *DG* writer described the ESS as both a business organization and a "true communistic lifestyle" (Carradine, 11/23/40:26). Howell installed himself as the highest, divinely anointed, authority of the ESS compound, known widely as "Pinnacle," for its elevation and commanding views of Kingston, the sea, and the surrounding countryside, from its perch in St. Catherine (*DG*, 7/15/41:1).

The estimated 700 men, women, and children of Pinnacle lived on a relatively self-supporting commune of 485 acres that had its own cobblers, carpenters, and coal makers. A common fund provided the means to feed everyone, and living arrangements were gender-segregated. Many of the practices associated with the Rastafari such as communalism, gender segregation, small-scale production, and ganja cultivation were core features of life at Pinnacle, and these practices would eventually be associated with a generic Rastafari identity.

During 1941, the authorities disrupted the rhythm of daily activities that Howell and his flock had developed, and again they forced the Rastafari into the public spotlight. Several members of the surrounding community reported being robbed and beaten by Pinnacle residents, claiming that Howell ordered the punishment (*DG*, 7/29/41:14). The plaintiff's claims, along with similar reports, lead to a police raid of Pinnacle and Howell's arrest and subsequent imprisonment.

On July 13, 1941, more than 150 constables in "high powered cars and wagons, and two motor buses," armed with rifles, sped to Pinnacle to arrest the Rastafari. The police apparently received poor intelligence; when they arrived at Pinnacle there were few Rastafari on the commune. Apparently, they were out collecting water and wood. Howell was nowhere to be found. Over the next few days, constables detained 70 Pinnacleites, mostly men. The police confiscated quantities of cannabis plants, pictures of which they displayed prominently in the *Gleaner* (7/29/41:14).

Several days later, police apprehended Howell in his home at Pinnacle. Authorities charged him with "occasioning actual bodily harm" and violation of the Dangerous Drugs Act. The trial of Howell and his flock began July 28, 1941, in the Spanish Town Courthouse. Again, there was tremendous interest in his trial: "It was impossible to keep away the large crowd of loudly talking, jeering, cheery people who flocked the passages leading to the courtroom" (*DG*, 7/26/41:1; 7/23/41:9). Howell received a sentence of three months for each of four charges, to be served consecutively. The Court sentenced 28 of the roughly 70 detained Rastafari to six months of hard labor (*DG*, 8/25/41:16; 7/31/41:16).

The *Gleaner* covered the Pinnacle raid and trials of the Pinnacleites and reported stories of torture, gaunt and tattered men, women, and children, suffering under the hardened "dictator" Leonard Howell. Pinnacleites contested the plaintiffs' and reporters' claims. One of Howell's "deputies," a widow named Louise Anderson, pointed out in a call to the *Gleaner* that the people of Pinnacle were cruelly treated by many who lived in areas surrounding the commune (7/16/41:16). Her account accorded with themes of hostile citizens and police in the 1940s through 1960s I heard from elder Rastafari. "You had to [be] careful where you walk in those days," said Brother Dee, "A man might fling one stone and lick you inna the head, draw blood [from your head], and all you hear is dutty [dirty] Rasta, go weh [away]."

The elites saw in the raid on Pinnacle another opportunity to cripple if not destroy the Rastafari. Though the elites most wanted to eliminate people such as Howell, Brother Yendis recognized that they also wanted to rid all traces of this morally configured racial identity from Jamaica: "[It] is something plan [by the powerful] since 1937 . . . everything [was done] fe get rid of Howell. And is not [only] Howell them want fe get rid of either. It is the doctrine [of Rastafari]." The Pinnacle raid, though, spread the Rastafari and their beliefs into rural areas and back into Kingston and Spanish Town.

Signs of Rastafari Identity

Since at least 1934, Rastafari men were known by their beards. Other identifying symbols of the Rastafari were the red, gold, and green "pom-pom" (a tassel-like object), a tri-colored badge, or some similarly colored token. A woman might wear a tri-colored sash, ribbon, pom-pom, scarf, or some similar distinguishing emblem. Although it is difficult to exactly place when the Dreadlocks faction of the Rastafari emerged, they do not appear in the stories of my narrators before the late 1940s. The Dreadlocks gained their name from the uncombed and uncut tresses that adorned their head. The wearing of uncombed Black hair in a society that greatly valued hair management disgusted most Jamaicans, increasing the scorn directed at the Rastafari. Brother Woks remembers seeing his first Dreadlocks in the late 1940s, which is consistent with other accounts.[5] Brother Woks recalled how, "During those times [before the mid-1960s], those who combed their hair were more in the predominant number than those who did not, for most of us the trim and comb business was a general thing until after some time when the Rasses [the Dreadlocks] emerged, then that kind of thing really stopped." Rastafari men like Brother Woks came to be called "Combsomes"—they combed their hair some—in distinction to the Dreadlocks who "dash 'way the scissor and comb." There are many accounts of how the early Dreadlocks explain the significance of their locks, and Ras Sam Brown offers us one version. In a very loud and affected voice, he said:

Ras Sam Brown was born in 1925 in the parish of Trelawney. Ras Sam became an ardent Rastafari activist who was involved in the founding of several
Rastafari organizations, participated in the planning of the Mission to Africa,
ran for political office in 1962, and traveled on several international Rastafari
missions during the 1980s and 1990s. Ras Sam was a prolific author, poet, and
painter.

"We are warriors . . . we take on the vow of the Nazarites. . . . When the
people them look on I n I, them see I n I art dreadful and awesome, and
them tremble in them boots!" The divergence between the Combsomes
and the Dreadlocks is also relevant to evolving gender dynamics between
the Rastafari. A larger number of women were actively and visibly involved
in the affairs of the Combsome Rastafari than in those of the Dreadlocks
(for example, one-third of Chevannes's [1994] Rastafari interviewees were
women). Since the 1970s, the Dreadlocks have been cast as the normative
representation of the Rastafari, and gender is situated within this frame.
We have neglected the active and public participation of women Rastafari

through the 1950s. From an ethnogenesitic perspective, the reduced public participation of women in Rastafari activities between the 1960s and 1980s is an interruption in a pattern, rather than the pattern itself (today, Rastafari women are again publicly active and visible).

The Rastafari grew more radical from the late 1940s onward, with several factions of the Dreadlocks developing an anti-establishment orientation. Some Dreadlocks, endeavoring to live in a state of nature—like modern-day John the Baptists—strove for an ascetic lifestyle and followed a code adapted from the Old Testament. Some dressed in sackcloth. Others refused to wear shoes or eat processed food. Some stopped eating "flesh." They frequently fasted. Ras Jayze says that he is a "prehistoric" Rastafari. He is one of the dwindling number of ascetic, monk-like Rastafari. Ras Jayze's dwelling is a small stack of unmortared blocks covered with a couple of sheets of zinc, on the edge of a tiny glade in Spanish Town. "Rasta has to go all the way into the past, past all the [biblical] ancients, all the way to prehistoric people, before Rasta can move forward." Ras Jayze believes that progress for the Rastafari must entail first a return to nature, premodern living. He argues to me that a return to nature is what is needed to "save the human race." He is struggling, though, to align his self-concept with the urban, material world around him. "I am at war with I-self these days," he said. I must leave this shitty [city]. Look. Me eat outta iron pot, and cook food 'pon fire. I-man supposed to eat what nature give. I must go away from the cooked food. I must go away from all these dutty people in this dutty shitstem [system]." Rastafari asceticism was not new to Jamaica. During the latter half of the 1800s, religious devotees engaged in similar "wandering prophet" practices (Elkins, 1977). However, the most militant Rastafari rejected Jamaican society in a way that exceeded their forerunners. For them, Jamaica was fully equivalent to a modern-day Babylon, and they distinguished themselves from "Babylon" through language, diet, dress, and lifestyle. These practices and rhetorics gradually diffused among the Rastafari to the point that they became defining themes.

Surprises, Perturbations, Unintended Consequences: 1954–1966

The front page of the *Daily Gleaner*, April 17, 1954, carried a story of the arrest of 29 Rastafari, including eight women, for marching without a permit (4/17/54:1). An adjacent news column told the story of Kenya's Mau Mau movement, the purportedly "secret anti-White society" that had threatened Queen Elizabeth's royal tour. The stories related information about Black people in Jamaica and Kenya, respectively, who were barometers of the local, national, and international racial climates. National liberation and anticolonialism were in the air, and the Rastafari and Mau Mau were two examples of how race, oppression, and colonialism could manifest in Black identity and race-centered resistance. Such peoples and movements made identity a part of overturning the hegemony of Whites and the indigenous comprador groups that benefitted from White hegemony and Black subjugation.

The arrested Rastafari had embarked on what they called a religious march, but which authorities deemed a political march. Among the 29 Rastafari detained was one C. A. Jackson, known to his colleagues and the public at large as Constable Jackson. When he appeared at the bar, the Magistrate queried if he was C. Jackson, a policeman? Jackson replied: "My name is Ras Jackson. C. Jackson was my name when I was in Babylon, but now my name is changed." Ras, derived from Ethiopian vocabulary, conveyed nobility and dignified lineage. By the early 1950s, it signaled a man's identity as Rastafari (it seems that the honorific "Queen" for Rastafari women was not widely used before 1968). It was a bold act to renounce a high status role of policeman and to identify as a Rastafari, especially because the Rastafari had come to stand against everything that the police represented (*DG*, 4/17/54:1). Changing one's name is often an aspect of Black identity transformation, signaling a change in a person's identity. Surely, Ras Jackson had lost his mind, his colleagues concluded. The authorities demanded that Jackson submit himself to medical examination. What Ras Jackson shows us, though, is the growing appeal of Rastafari identity and the sacrifice that people of that time were willing to make to identify as such.

Octogenarians Rasta Ivey and Brother Dee related similar stories of police repression and Rastafari resistance between the 1940s and 1970s. Standing before a judge along with several of his brethren during the mid-1950s, Brother Dee reminisced, "I ask the judge, 'Who give you power to be a judge over Israel' [Rastafari people]? Him say him a prosecutor. I say, 'You is raas clot,⁶ you know!' [a serious insult] . . . [the Judge told me] 'take one year.' This was in Spanish Town." Framing his vignette in terms of race, Rasta Ivey questioned Brother Dee: "Is [it] a White man try you?" Brother Dee retorted in his deep, gravelly voice, "One Brown man." Rasta Ivey replied: "I say White man wouldn't give you a year. If it was a White man [he], wouldn't give you a year. It is just because it is [a] Brown man [that] him give you two years."

Brother Dee, born approximately 1910–12. Brother Dee worked on Kingston's wharves during the early 1930s, and met most of the earliest Rastafari evangelists in the Kingston area.

What Rasta Ivey was getting at was the gross conspiracy of the colonial order that put Brown and Black people in the position of disciplining each other under British rules. Rasta Ivey and Brother Dee interpreted the racialized colonial order from the standpoint that some Blacks willingly assumed the oppressor's role, maintaining the very system that stifled them. Rastafari interpreted Blacks punishing Blacks as a 'tribal war' that pit Ethiopians against each other. There is reason to believe that the British knew what they were doing by using Blacks to discipline each other. In 1902, for example, a Black regiment of the Constabulary, under White leadership, violently put down the Montego Bay riots (the melee proper began with attacks on perceived symbols of injustice: a police station and courthouse in Montego Bay). Bryan sees such examples as a "victory for white hegemony" and evidence of the limitation of ethnicity as a binding tie between Blacks (2000:xii). My narrators, however, believe that ethnicity and race *should* be the basis for binding ties.

In 1954, in a final effort of law enforcement authorities to close down the commune, the police destroyed Pinnacle. Its destruction had the unintended consequence of dispersing the Rastafari once again. Those leaving Pinnacle, many of whom were more militant than during 1940–41, further spread Rastafari beliefs and practices, especially communal living, elder leadership, and the idealization of "natural" living and self-reliance as an alternative lifestyle.

The Tension Rises: The Visit of Mamie Richardson

As early as 1934, the Rastafari had imagined themselves leaving Jamaica for Africa. It was an important idea and a desired goal. The idea had different lineages, and the Rastafari gave it their own spin. Indentured African laborers who settled in St. Thomas parish during the mid-1800s, for example, imagined returning to their homes in Africa, and these longings informed durable myths such as avoidance of salt because it prohibited a person from flying across the sea to Africa (see Schuler, 1980:93–96). By the early 1920s, Marcus Garvey was promoting ideas of African colonization, African redemption, and Black emancipation, and within these frameworks, he talked about an idea of repatriation. There was no singular definition of repatriation, but by the early 1950s many Rastafari had set their sights on the nation-state of Ethiopia.

Brother Woks, whose godfather was one of the founding Rastafari evangelists, Joseph Hibbert, noted that when Mamie Richardson, a deputy of the New York City EWF, visited Jamaica in 1955, she "blessed the informal groups of BSUE [Brothers Solidarity of United Ethiopia, a.k.a., the African Cultural League] . . . with a charter and named it His Imperial Majesty Emperor Haile Selassie I Local 37 of the Ethiopian World Federation." The BSUE, a self-proclaimed "organized race group," promoted its "Immigration and Repatriation Plan," which it delivered directly to Winston Churchill in 1954 during his visit to Jamaica. What the BSUE sought was to get the British government to formally recognize "Ethiopian" as the designation for all Black people in the Empire who so desired (Spence, 1959:n.p.) Thus, for all of the so-called otherworldly beliefs of the Rastafari, such as Africa as Zion and ships to ferry them there, there were Rastafari working politically and strategically through organizations such as BSUE to assert their African identities and beliefs.

Mamie Richardson, an international organizer for the EWF, visited Jamaica in September 1955, on a goodwill tour of the Caribbean. She came to celebrate the reunification of Eritrea and Ethiopia and bring a message from Haile Selassie I. It was a message that would capture the imagination of the Rastafari. Haile Selassie I wanted Black people in the Caribbean to learn their "ancient" history, their native language, more about their own religion, and learn about Christ (*DG*, 9/30/55:n.p.) What Sister Mariam and other Rastafari also heard Richardson discuss was the Shashemene land grant, a gift from Ethiopia to Black people who wanted to repatriate. Sister Mariam said, in reflecting on hearing Richardson's message, "Me already have Selassie in me heart, so it is the land that really catch me [attention]." With a grant of land and direct access to Ethiopia for Blacks of the Diaspora, Haile Selassie I was fulfilling Rastafari beliefs in his role as redeemer. Brother Bongo and some of his clique began studying and learning Amharic for what they imagined to be impending repatriation. According to Richardson, Haile Selassie I was building a merchant navy that would venture to American ports with the possibility of Jamaica as a port of call (*DG*, 9/30/55:n.p.). Recall that as early as 1934, Howell and Hinds promoted stories of ships arriving in Jamaica from Abyssinia or Africa to rescue its stranded Black wayfarers. Thus, as supernatural claims were manifesting, prophecy materialized.

Richardson's visit inspired the Rastafari and affirmed a common identity for their various groups. Regardless of the EWF's goal, Richardson had substantiated Rastafari belief in Haile Selassie I's redemptive role. The Rastafari ratcheted up their pursuit of repatriation. The experiences and beliefs that led individual Rastafari to identify as a "peculiar" people, a persecuted people, and a chosen people, were validated by events such as the Richardson visit, reinforcing a sense of "we" or "I n I." Their purpose and identity, as they variously imagined and described it, was acquiring empirical credence.

Misapprehending the Rastafari: Identity, Ideology, Language

By the mid-1950s the Rastafari, especially the Dreadlocks, were enacting a symbolic repertoire that included instilling fear and dread in the non-Rastafari. The Rastafari saw their cause advancing while the colonial and racial order, at home and abroad, was crumbling. Africa was stirring politically; Black Americans were mobilizing against segregation; and Jamaican independence was on the table.

The Rastafari used harsh language as part of an elaborate linguistic system based on a Rastafari theory of "word, sound, and power." Subscribers to the theory believe that words and their sounds hold power, that it can be directly harnessed and used. For example, when a Rastafari shouts,

"White heart!" "Brimstone!" or "Fire bu'n!" at someone it could have been an effort to intimidate, insult, condemn, suggest control of the natural elements, or all of these. They understood that their words when associated with a Rastafari identity could make people recoil. Word, sound, and power celebrated stigmatization, which Rastafari used against their stigmatizers. It is in this context that we can grasp the meaning of violent-sounding slogans such as "Death to all White and Black Downpressors" or, as the *Sunday Guardian* reported a Rastafari railing, "This is black man's time. We are not going to stop 'til we get what we want. Any man, black or white, who tries to stop us, will be killed. Blood is going to flow into this country" (*Sunday Guardian* 5/1/1960:n.p.). There are also the divinely mystical uses of word, sound, and power. Brother Yendis explained:

> Jah is the word, Ras give it sound, and Tafari power. Jah-Ras-Tafari! Anytime one say "Jah," and other ones add "Ras Tafari," that sound go like lightning into the Throne Room . . . Jah can work but [now tilting back his head and calling in a loud, deep voice] "Jah Ras Tafari!" is the most powerful sound . . . doan take that sound lightly . . . It call forth the strength of His Imperial Majesty.

This symbolic swagger offered Rastafari a method to confront the people and institutions they held culpable in perpetuating oppression and miseducation. We could, using contemporary parlance, say that the Rastafari grasped the utility of "shock value." However, many more literally interpreted Rastafari symbolism as violent threats. Millenarian and messianic groups, confident in their power and immanent millennium, may literally and violently contest the evil they perceive in their midst (Taylor, 1990:192). Whether or not millenarian accurately describes the Rastafari, a consequence of this largely symbolic and ritualized violence of words was misapprehension on the part of the public: it encouraged elites' depictions of them as pathological. Despite elite fears, the Rastafari preferred to live their slogan, "peace and love." It was a greeting and parting phrase used by Rastafari from the 1950s into the 1970s, which prefigured Black harmony, an idea and behavior integral to the identity many Rastafari were trying to instill in the midst of a social order that cultivated Black discord. Rasta Ivey and Brother Dee, for example, often talked nostalgically about "peace and love" as something lost to the present: "See what happen to them Black people now?" Rasta Ivey rhetorically said to Brother Dee and me while the three us sat and talked about Rasta history in Brother Dee's one-room abode. "Them don't have no love [today, for each other]." After pausing for a moment, she qualified her statement: "But some of them still have love." To which Brother Dee wryly added, "Some of them." These elder Rastafari affectionately recalled the sense of racial and religious fellowship the phrase evoked and lamented how unimportant Black harmony had become in the post-1970s era.

Symbolic Invasions and Conquests

The Rastafari, emboldened by Richardson's message, flexed their newfound muscle. In addition to their linguistic activism, they engaged in a range of disruptive activities that emphasized their growing influence.

In March 1958, the first Rastafari "universal convention" drew participants from across the island to the Coptic Theocratic Temple in Kingston (*The Star*, 3/6/58:n.p.). This event, which came to be called "Groundation" or "Nyabinghi," was most likely the first grand convening Rastafari ceremony. The month-long event attracted Rastafari of both sexes, including children. It was also reflective of a cohesive moment in Rastafari ethnogenesis. Both Gad (Vernon Carrington) and Prince Emmanuel (Charles Edwards), who would later become leaders, respectively, of the Twelve Tribes and Bobo Ashanti sects of the Rastafari, participated as members of the Nyabinghi Order. Citizens complained about the all-night, all-day ritual, the copious ganja-smoking, and confrontational name-calling. *The Star* framed the event with the title "Rastafari convention a nuisance" (3/3/58:n.p.).

A collection of Rastafari symbolically "captured" Victoria Square, an important landmark in downtown Kingston. More than 300 Rastafari men, women, and children converged on the park in the early morning hours, raising their black, green, and red flags and banners, and planting them on the Victoria statue. They had "conquered" a symbol of the colonial and racial order, the park named for Queen Victoria of England (*The Star*, 3/24/58). Later, nine Rastafari families, each headed by a "bearded, shaggy-headed cultist," carried out an even more symbolically significant invasion when they "captured" Kings House, the former home of Jamaican governors and an entertainment haven for royalty (Tribune, 6/30/58: n.p.). As in other invasions, they raised their flags and proceeded to make themselves at home, setting up iron cooking pots upon blazing fires.

Claudius Henry: Disruption, in Two Acts

The Reverend Claudius Henry, self-proclaimed "Repairer of the Breach," recognized leader in repatriation efforts, which by the mid-1950s were called the "Back-to-Africa" movement, became the lightning rod in a two-part debacle that further marked the Rastafari as dangerous and added to their identification as persecuted and chosen.

During the last week of September and the first week of October 1959, hundreds of Rastafari flocked to the African Reform Church (ARC) headquarters in Kingston. A rumor was circulating that a ship would arrive on October 5, to pick up passengers who wanted to leave for Africa. People (not only Rastafari) from across the island walked, hitched rides, and took taxis to the Church headquarters. Among the hopeful were many women, some with infants. The newspapers reported that some had sold or given away their possessions and mocked their zeal by noting that they had neither passports nor tickets for their journey to Africa (*DG*, 10/6/59:1). When the ships failed to arrive, many disappointed Rastafari and non-Rastafari desirous of leaving Jamaica for Africa were stranded (*DG* 10/7/59:1). Henry's debacle was used to portray the Rastafari as hopelessly and perhaps hazardously out of step with reality.

Like many of my interlocutors, Reverend Henry had several visions that had set him upon the path toward Rastafari. Early in his life, he became dissatisfied with the teachings of the established churches. He lived in the United States for 13 years until a vision told him to return immediately to Jamaica (Chevannes, 1976). When he returned in 1957, he embodied a morally configured conception of Blackness and set immediately to build a congregation that worshipped Haile Selassie I.

Henry again found himself in the public eye in 1960, precipitating further disruption. Before sunrise on April 6, 1960, police raided his African Reform Church. Both Henry and Edna Fisher (who helped Henry develop his church) were present while the police searched the rooms and discovered ganja, dynamite, a shotgun, revolver, numerous machetes sharpened on both sides, cartridges, conch shells, and more than 4,000 detonators (*DG*, 4/7/60:n.p.). The police arrested Reverend Henry and 11 others. His arrest put the Rastafari onto a different trajectory. Elites now conflated their threatening symbolic performances with the weapons seizure and constructed the Rastafari as an imminent danger to the citizenry and state. That Henry's many sympathizers from across the island took to the streets to protest his arrest only contributed to negative assessments of the Rastafari (*DG*, 5/11/60:n.p.). While it can be argued that Henry was involved in his son Reynold's plot to "liberate" Jamaica and recruit Rastafari as rebels serving his bigger plan to liberate Africa, the effort involved a small number of people, few of them Rastafari (see Meeks, 2000:29–34).

During the trial, Deputy Superintendent Wilfred McIntosh produced a letter to "Dr. Fidel Castro, Prime Minister of Cuba," signed by Henry and 11 of his co-defendants. The letter used the tropes of the moral economy of Blackness and the morally configured Black identity of Rastafari to make a political statement:

> [We are] . . . poor, underprivileged people which were brought here from Africa by the British Slave traders over 400 years ago to serve as slaves. We now desire to return home in peace, to live under our own vine and fig tree, otherwise a government like yours that give justice to the poor. All our efforts to have a peaceful repatriation has proven a total failure . . . we must fight a war for what is ours by right. . . . Jamaica and the rest of the British West Indies will be turned over to you and your government, after this war which we are preparing to start for Africa's freedom. (Chevannes, 1976:277)

The court charged the accused with feloniously seeking to "incite insurrection against the Government of this island in order to intimidate and overawe the Governor, Legislative Counsel, and House of Representatives" (*DG*, 5/6/60:n.p.).

The Rastafari were hardly in agreement about Henry's reputation or his role in furthering their goals (van Dijk, 1995:81). Several of my activist Rastafari interlocutors remembered the Henry trials and resented him and his followers for several reasons. They were critical of Rastafari who proclaimed themselves powerful and those who followed "self-styled leaders" and "idiots": "Him [Henry] make we look like fool," said Brother Yendis. Some Rastafari held Henry responsible for the increase in the flagrant violence directed toward them. Elites used the fear they whipped up around Henry's trial to gain further support for repressing the Rastafari. Clinton Parchment, writing in the *Gleaner* a few weeks after the arrest of Henry and his followers, argued that

> perhaps the Jamaican authorities will at last move against the lawless and dangerous sect of Rastafarians, most of whom might better be called rascals. . . . There may be a few sincere and decent Rastafarians . . . but it is self-evident that the majority are lazy, dirty, violent, and lawless

scoundrels mouthing religious phrases to cover up their aversion to work and their ill habits. . . . they are mostly useless and quite unpicturesque. (Parchment, 4/30/60:n.p.)

Death in the Red Hills

Another perturbation connected to Henry followed his two disruptive acts. In May 1960, three Rastafari men were found shot dead in the Red Hills, a suburban area northwest of Kingston. Two British soldiers were killed in an ensuing manhunt. One of the suspects in both killings was Reynold Henry, the son of Claudius, and several others hailed from the United States. The weapons cache discovered at the ARC, the letter to Castro, and the spate of murders generated fear and anxiety that caused the Rastafari to suffer more strain. Minister of Home Affairs, William Seivright, made the situation graver by implying that the Rastafari had become "pawns" in a greater political conspiracy that several reporters implied might involve communists.

The police captured four Black Americans in Sligoville on June 27, 1960, and the next day, Premier Norman Manley assured the public that security matters were under control, even though a few suspects remained at large. Manley gave the security forces the green light to "investigate" Rastafari settlements and individuals, investigations that in many cases were nothing more than cruel and senseless intrusions. The manhunt came to a close on July 11, 1960, when police took Albert Gabidon and Eldred Morgan, so-called "members of the Rastafarian cult," into custody in Annotto Bay, in St. Mary's parish. They were not self-identified Rastafari, though. Already in custody were five Black Americans who were charged with the deaths of the three Rastafari and two soldiers. Four Jamaicans were charged with the murders of the three Rastafari. Why the men killed the Rastafari remains unclear (*DG*, 7/12/60:n.p.).

Four of the convicted men were sentenced to death. Reynold Henry, Claudius's son (and Albert Gabbidon) were hanged, March 28, 1961, at 8:30 a.m. The last words of Reynold were, "I die for Marcus Garvey." Why would a man die for Marcus Garvey? Perhaps out of an intense concern with race and liberation? According to Reverend Carter Henry, who met with Reynold while he was on death row, Reynold meant no harm to Jamaicans. He had come to Jamaica to "gather an army to liberate Africa." He, like many Ethiopianists, believed that Whites stole Africa and, in exchange, Black people received the Bible (*DG*, 12/23/60; 3/29/61:1).

Even though the repression of the Rastafari grew more severe in 1960, it did not lead Rastafari like Herben Walters, Brother Bongo, Brother Yendis, Sister Mariam, and Rasta Ivey to apostasy. The reasons that led them to become Rastafari were more important than the tribulations associated with the identity. Persecution reinforced conviction and conviction reinforced personal and collective identity.

Results of Self-Organization: Desires Materialize

Theories of complexity propose that emergent and patterned properties resulting from the interactions of countless individuals can, without planning or coordination, result in substantial transformations that lead to greater complexity. This is called self-organization (e.g., Goerner, 1995:11; McClure, 2005:43–44, 51). By July 1960, the Rastafari, the government, and the citizenry recognized they all were in a complex, combustible situation, and that something had to be done. The tribulation and turmoil, though, offered promising reward for the Rastafari. Ras Brenton, during a conversation, told me:

> The Elders had to face police and battles and soldiers, and all that just to talk about Rasta business in the streets. Rasta man had to hide from Babylon to wear his locks on the road or walk freely on the road. Police would want to chase you or find some way to embarrass you to get you out the way. You see me? Because why! They know within themselves that we are fighting for our continent [Africa], but because Babylon bribe them to beat us off the streets, and beat us up and do us all manner of evils . . . we have to stand up for our rights. Like I was telling a brother last night. . . . Mr. [Mortimer] Planno get some contacts through a man named Dr. Arthur Lewis [a celebrated economist] who was a Black professor at the University of the West Indies. Because Mr. Planno found him to be a lenient Black man who was on Black people's side, like the Rasta man's side, Planno used to go and look for him and reason with him sometimes. . . . It would happen that Planno and Dr. Arthur Lewis were friends some sort of way.

Three University College of the West Indies (UCWI) scholars, M. G. Smith, Rex Nettleford, and Roy Augier, at the urging of Lewis and prominent Rastafari, conducted and published in approximately two weeks a study of the Rastafari. The authors ran off nearly 10,000 copies of the research report and published the entire document (the *Report*) in the *Gleaner* in 12 install-ments, beginning August 3, 1960. The *Report* identified several chief desires of the Rastafari, such as their desire to be recognized as a legitimate people and that there be an immediate end to their persecution by the police and government. Perhaps most important, though, was the research team's rec-ommendation that government immediately convene a meeting of Rastafari representatives[7] to "discuss matters of mutual interest" (*DG*, 8/2/60:n.p.).

"Rasta, Africa Does Not Want You": The Mission to Africa

In 1934, repatriation to Africa appeared an unrealistic dream, and elites harped on how the Rastafari were hopelessly out of touch with Africa. Until Mamie Richardson visited Jamaica and announced the plans of the EWF, repatriation was a strongly held idea, but it existed foremost as a matter of faith. Suddenly, the Rastafari, having witnessed the tragic results of Henry's debacles and having suffered government crackdowns, were facing the real possibility of migrating to Africa. And, their benefactor would be the government, not Haile Selassie I!

On August 3, 1960, the *Gleaner* reported that Premier Norman Manley agreed to meet with prominent representatives of the Rastafari and ac-cepted in principle the idea of sending a mission to Africa (n.p.). Why Manley decided to support repatriation remains a mystery. Did he have sympathy for the racial and religious sentiments of the Rastafari? Did he see the Rastafari and repatriation as a political opportunity to build a Black grassroots constituency and cement ties with newly independent African nations? Was he seeking to defuse or co-opt the growing militancy of the Rastafari? Or, did his personal connections to prominent Rastafari such as the early evangelist, Altamont Reid (who in 1940 became his body guard), influence his thinking (*DG*, 8/3/60)? Then, there were charges that Norman Manley made commitments to Claudius Henry in exchange for his political support. All of these factors probably influenced his support for repatriation, although we can only speculate on the importance of each.

Rasta J, born in 1940, grew up in a race-conscious household. Both of his parents were Garveyites interested in Jamaica's politics, and his mother was a Rastafari active in Rastafari affairs. Rasta J believed, like many Ras-tafari of the 1950s, in their power to effect change through their cultural practices and identity. Their conviction and their word, sound, and power helped put Premier Manley in his position of authority:

Bustamante now start [repression] again . . . Rasta get pressure 'pon them until now Michael Manley come now and say well, "Ease up off a Rasta. . . ." Father [Norman] Manley, him was the man who make Marcus Garvey come home from Spanish Town prison, you know . . . but through Bustamante turn rigid in a Rastafari back, we have to wake him up, rise him up . . . we have to get rid of the wicked man . . . we rise him . . . Rastaman chant him, chanting Norman, chanting Norman, Norman win in '54. . . . Norman send the first delegation a Ethiopia.

Manley stressed that migration to Africa would be open to Jamaicans, irrespective of race or creed. Others were interested in repatriation, and Manley constructed the issue as if he had always supported it: "This Government has always been in favor of migration and had never put any obstacles in the way of any person or group wishing to leave Jamaica" (*DG*, 8/19/60:n.p.).

Jamaica's elite critiqued the Mission plan, and by implication the Rastafari, noting that Africa wanted people with skills, not the poverty-stricken, unpracticed, and itinerant. Their prejudice was that the Rastafari lacked any reasonable idea about Africa and that Norman Manley was taking an irrational risk. This, to some extent, rang true. Other than news stories and a few hard-to-get books, the Rastafari had little opportunity to learn about Africa.

My interlocutors believed that the time had come for them to push forward their identity and beliefs, and not slink away from the violence, discrimination, and vilification directed against them. They were seeing their beliefs materialize, feeling and expressing a sense of self-righteousness, and the government was concurring with their desire to repatriate. This reciprocal influence of Rastafari, Jamaica's institutions, elites, and non-Rastafari was integral to the evolution and growth of the Rastafari in ways similar to a positive feedback loop. Disturbances were fueling the upsurge of the Rastafari rather than retarding their evolution and influence.

The delegation departed Jamaica for Africa via New York on April 4, 1961. The Mission boarded their B.O.A.C. plane at the airport at the edge of the Palisadoes in Kingston, buoyed by the hearty and joyful singing, cheering, and drumming by the throng of Rastafari and other Jamaicans who had gathered to see them off (Douglas, 1961).

The official adviser for the Mission was Dr. L. C. Leslie. He spoke on behalf of Manley when the Premier was absent. The Antiguan Minister for Social Service accompanied the Mission. Douglas Mack and Philmore

Alvaranga represented the Rastafari of eastern and central Kingston, and Mortimer Planno represented the Rastafari "movement" (Ras Sam Brown ended up being dropped from the Mission). The UNIA was represented by W. Blackwood, the EWF by Cecil Gordon, the Afro-Caribbean League by Dr. M. B. Douglas, and the Afro-West Indian Welfare League (AWIWL) by Z. Monroe-Scarlett. The Rastafari delegates disagreed with the Mission adviser over the procedure for publishing a public report on the Mission's experience. As a result, two reports were published. The *Majority Report* was the official report, and the *Minority Report* provided the account of the Rastafari delegates.

ETHIOPIA

The Mission arrived in Addis Ababa on April 21, 1961. Premier Manley noted that Haile Selassie I greeted them as "brothers of one blood and race." The "Emperor said that Ethiopia would always be open to people of African origin who lived in the West and who desired to return," wrote Manley (*DG*, 7/31/61a:1). All delegates noted the magnanimity of the Emperor in his willingness to accept Black repatriates in Ethiopia and in his acknowledgment of their shared blood and race. For the Rastafari this confirmed what they had been claiming for three decades.

While Rastafari representatives found support for their identity in Haile Selassie I's words, authors of the *Majority Report* emphasized the messages that *they* heard. Dr. Leslie denied Rastafari insistence on the Ethiopian leader's divinity. He reported to the *Gleaner* that the Ethiopian Minister of Foreign Affairs told him that "His Imperial Majesty Haile Selassie I is a devout Christian, and as such, he could not encourage any attempt to make him a deity, as it would be entirely against his Christian principles" (*DG*, 7/31/61b:n.p.). The Emperor, however, did not shun the Rastafari delegates. Dr. Douglas noted a quiet exchange between the Rastafari delegates and the Emperor:

> At the conclusion of our "official" interview [with the Emperor], Messrs. Planner, Mack, and Alvaranga, in the act of presenting gifts to His Majesty had a "private talk" with him. Mr. Scarlett and I who were standing a few feet away were pleasantly surprised to hear the "private" audience being conducted in English. . . . it must be emphasized that this audience was "private." So impressed was the Emperor that he immediately

ordered that all our expenses while in Ethiopia be borne by His Government. (Douglas, 1961:n.p.)

Douglas's account suggests that the Rastafari delegates made a very favorable impression upon Haile Selassie I and corroborated the story the Rastafari delegates tell in their *Minority Report*. Dr. Leslie denied that there
was any "private interview" with the Emperor, but granted that the Rastafari delegates "lingered behind and spoke to Haile Selassie I."

The Rastafari delegates used their *Minority Report* to frame their ex-
perience and analyses of the Mission in idioms familiar to the ordinary
Jamaican. They likened their meeting Haile Selassie I to that of the three
Wise Men who traveled from the West to the East to deliver gifts to the
Baby Jesus:

> When we presented our gifts to the Emperor, before we could tell him
> who it was from, he said "Is it from the Rastafari Brethren?" We told
> him "Yes." That show that H.I.M. knows of Rastafari Brethren. H.I.M.
> also gave each member of the Mission a gold medal for our work, ful-
> filling biblically, equality cometh for all. Only the Rases presented gifts
> to H.I.M. and the rest of the Mission left us in the palace, fulfilling the
> parable of the ten virgins—five had oil in their lamps and five had none.
> (DG, 7/31/61c:n.p.)

NIGERIA

The Mission left Ethiopia for Lagos, where Nigeria's Governor General reported his government was "fully in favor" of repatriation of West Indians to Africa. The then-current King of Lagos informed the Mission that
"West Indians migrating to Nigeria would be welcomed as people 'returning to the land of their fathers.'" The Nigerians enthusiastically received
the idea of repatriation. The Minister of State for External Affairs equated
repatriation with the "Jewish restoration to Israel" (*DG*, 7/31/61a:n.p.). The
King's main concern was that repatriates be sensitive to the disparities in
economic development between Jamaicans and Nigerians (he imagined
Nigeria was vastly poorer than Jamaica).

Premier Manley confessed during a speech in Nigeria that one of his
ancestors had been a "principal slave raider" and that he felt a duty to
help repair the damage done to those descendants of Africans wrested

from their land and kin and enslaved. The premier's self-incrimination probably played well with the Rastafari and deflected criticism of his status as an elite Brown man.

GHANA

On May 8, the Mission arrived in Ghana, and two days later, Dr. Kwame Nkrumah received them in his home. Manley and Leslie had attended Ghana's independence ceremony in 1957, and Nkrumah repaid that courtesy by hosting the mission twice, once officially and once unofficially at his home, even though Indonesian President Sukarno was visiting Ghana at the same time. Nkrumah told the Mission, "Our meeting is historic. It has historic significance not only because we are blood relations but also because so many attempts [to repatriate] were previously made and failed. Marcus Garvey tried but was prevented." Nkrumah expressed his pleasure that the Mission was energizing the Back-to-Africa movement. "Look upon yourselves as Africans and land is here for the asking" (*DG*, 7/31/61c:n.p.). He set up a special committee which resolved that the Mission should produce a comprehensive memorandum and declaration that described who and how many would migrate.

Ghanaian officials, like the Ethiopians, were interested in the kinds of skills Jamaicans could bring to their nation. Nkrumah said Ghana could employ all Jamaica's skilled seamen because they were building a merchant fleet, the *Black Star Line*, and he speculated that the fleet would travel to the West Indies in a year or so.

LIBERIA

Liberian President William Tubman told the Mission that his nation would accept all people of African descent. Tubman's primary stipulation was that migrants not have a police record. Liberia was interested in attracting farmers and prior to the visit of the Mission, had offered people of the Black Diaspora free land and three months of free housing to relocate. Premier Manley noted that Jamaicans had been "trickling" into Liberia since the 1940s and several had attained prestigious positions within the nation. Liberia, the Rastafari delegates pointed out, had since its founding an open-door policy for people of African descent. President Tubman spoke highly of Marcus Garvey, and thoughtfully engaged the Rastafari delegates on their spiritual beliefs. Douglas lightly, but with a trace of seriousness, claimed that Planno almost persuaded President Tubman of the divinity of Emperor Haile Selassie I (Douglas, 1961:n.p.).

SIERRA LEONE

The final stop was Sierra Leone, where Prime Minister, Sir Milton Margai, informed the Mission that his nation had been founded to repatriate emancipated slaves from Britain, the West Indies, and the United States. As early as 1776, some 200 Black people of the Diaspora were sent there to build that nation, and Sierra Leone had a direct link with Jamaica. In 1796, Britain sent more than 500 unruly Jamaican Maroons from Trelawney parish to Halifax, Nova Scotia, as punishment. Nova Scotians aided the Maroons, who had not adapted well, in relocating to Sierra Leone in 1800. President Margai accepted the Mission's idea of repatriation and offered to receive "West Indians whose ancestors had been forcibly removed from Africa," but he displayed little of the enthusiasm of the other African governments (*DG*, 7/31/61a:n.p.).

The Mission's Accomplishments and Politics

On Saturday, June 3, 1961, the Mission arrived at the Palisadoes Airport, at 2:45 in the afternoon. The Rastafari delegates estimated that 5,000 people waving banners, singing, and shouting were there to greet them. The Mission participants were decked out in the garments given them by the African dignitaries (*DG*, 7/31/61c). The three Rastafari delegates had become heroes of the Rastafari movements.

Premier Manley noted that the Mission's goal of exploring the "'repatriation of Africans living abroad' to the 'ancestral land'" was achieved and the idea was well-received by the African host nations who appreciated the first serious repatriation effort undertaken in a hundred years (*DG*, 7/31/61a:n.p.). The Mission, however, was not empowered to negotiate any agreements. The people of Ethiopia especially impressed the delegates, and they stressed how Ethiopians saw Blacks of the Diaspora as their brothers and sisters. This account contradicted those who argued that Ethiopians, and especially Haile Selassie I's lineage, denied their Blackness or connection to the Black Diaspora.

The Mission's international public relations work gave Jamaica a chance to connect with Africa during a period when the tide of nonaligned nations was rising. It was no coincidence that the African nations the

Mission visited were interested in the anticolonialism and decolonization fervor of the time. The Mission was a smart political move on the part of Manley, even if it alienated some of his home constituency.

While the Mission's achievement further strengthened the confidence of the Rastafari and validated their identity and beliefs, it little changed how elites perceived them. Rastafari remained subject to sensationalism and abuse. For example, one writer penned the scandalous title "Some Rastas are cavemen," and described how "The less fortunate ones . . . live in shallow caves like animals" (*The Star*, 4/9/62:n.p.).

By 1960, however, a tiny but growing number of contributions to the newspapers were grappling with the world from the vantage point of the Rastafari. For example, an author writing in the *Jamaica Times* argued that the "gravest injustice to minority groups in any society is either a failure, or a refusal, on the part of the majority group of that society to try and understand fully the aims and goals and thinking of such minority group" (4/24/62:10). The writer asked his audience to try to "observe the tremendous hardships the Rastas endure in order to be themselves, to live their own lives, and to avoid—and to even escape—the hostility of the majority group of the Jamaican society, to realise these men and women have at least the courage of their convictions."

In 1962, Ras Sam Brown ran for a seat in Parliament in the general election on an independent ticket, the *Black Man's Party*. Brown was not the only Ethiopianist testing the waters of formal politics. Brother Bongo noted:

> There were groups in addition to those I already named. There were others such as Millard Johnson who came about in 1959 to 1960 with Mr. Garvey's philosophy, "Africa for the Africans. Those at home and those abroad." He emerged to continue the works of Mr. Marcus Garvey and competed in the 1962 elections, but that organization eventually faded after a while. It was unable to compete against the two major political powers. Sam Brown contested in that election, too, and he only got 82 votes. So, I try to tell the brothers that if they try to field candidates saying that they are looking for seats in Gordon House [Parliament so to speak], as far as I am concerned, because of the Jamaica political psyches we will not obtain it.

Ras Sam Brown himself had a slightly different opinion in 1998:

> The brethren was not wise in those days, and still many of them not wise right now towards politics. You see, them [Rastafari] claim them wasn't

supporting politics because politics is graft and those sorts of things. We know that. We know a lot of graft in politics, but at the same time, we know say that . . . [it] is the only way you can express yourself if you have people in a desperate situation.

While Brown and Johnson sought to set examples that Black people should not shun the political system, and not support the two primary parties, they received little support. My view is that their lack of votes had more to do with their cantankerous temperaments and lack of a political organizing machine than a lack of interest in their platforms. Both men had no sustainable capacity to reach beyond a few Kingston neighborhoods, and Brown, for example, represented a faction of the Rastafari—the Rastafari Movement Association—and thus could not count on the support of those Rastafari, such as those attached to the EWF locals, who might vote. Brown's move led Mortimer Planno to leave the RMA for the EWF and the "spiritualist" Rastafari Shadrach, Meschach, and Abednego to leave the RMA and form their own orga-nization. Rex Nettleford (1972:77) interpreted Brown's move as betray-ing a "willingness and desire to participate in the normal power process of the country despite the doctrine of Exile." Sam Brown explained to me that he ran not because he wanted to be a part of the "system" but so that he could advocate for "the poor, the infants, the shelterless, the starving, and the sick" and so that he could "shake up Duke Street." He was among the few Rastafari interested in state power as a means of em-powering poor Black Jamaicans. Brown's view caused him and similar Rastafari perspectives to be branded "communist" and thus a threat to the already sensitive status quo. Nonetheless, these racialized forays into politics were on the forefront of an emergent large-scale shift in percep-tions of Blackness.

The Coral Gardens Incident

The Coral Gardens Incident was another watershed in the evolution of the Rastafari, confirming their interpretation of themselves as persecuted. On April 11, 1963, responding to a report of a fire at a gas station in the Coral Gardens area, near Montego Bay, the police arrived to discover that a guest at a nearby motel had been hacked to death. They were told that a band of bearded men—Rastafari—committed the homicide, and they were also responsible for setting the gas station afire (*DG*, 4/13/63:1).

Authorities called in the Jamaican Defense Force, and Prime Minister Alexander Bustamante flew to the scene with Roy McNeill, Minister of Home Affairs, and other government officials. Alexander Bustamante was elected Prime Minster in 1962, and he had no interest in the Rastafari, other than seeking to eliminate them. In less than two years, the attitude of the government toward them had completely changed. Even though they suffered abuse under Premier Manley's regime, it was worse under Bustamante's. For one, Bustamante was unwilling to support anything related to Black Nationalism, even though he fancied himself a champion of Jamaica's grass roots.

The government treated the Coral Gardens incident as an attempt at insurrection rather than a crime of arson and murder. Many ordinary citizens quickly became dangerously hostile toward the Rastafari after the "Holy Thursday massacre": "[A] roundup of beards had begun. As each set of captives was brought to the police station the crowds that gathered outside far into night rushed forward, jeering." Police and military forces arrested more than 150 Rastafari in the parishes of St. James, Trelawny, Hanover, and Westmoreland in two nights. They charged them with vagrancy, unlawful possession of property, and violation of the Dangerous Drugs Act (*DG*, 4/13/63). Senator Hugh Shearer reportedly said to bring in the Rastafari "dead or alive."

Despite the intensified suppression, the Rastafari continued agitating and organizing for repatriation. They were encouraged by the signals they were getting from different quarters, especially messages that allegedly came from the Emperor himself. Brother Bongo noted how

> Our father is looking for us to come together, to unite because it is His Imperial Majesty who told a [second] delegation of Rastafari brethren . . . "You are here long enough to see the condition of Ethiopia and what is needed. So I would advise that you return to Jamaica and tell the Rastafari brethren to organize and centralize themselves because their redemption is near."

Brother Bongo and other Rastafari continued to work actively on repatriation and identity issues in the midst of suppression.

> Brother Bongo: We decided to organize a united front that brings all brethren together. Well, we started having meetings at Back-O-Wall. Meetings go on sometimes from 6:00 pm until 3:00 o'clock next morning. The

centre was at Back-O-Wall, West Kingston. There were brethren like said Sam Brown, Shedrack, Meschach and Abednego, the said Chinese brother there from the Unemployed Rights Workers Council. . . . we kept meetings at Spanish Town Road by the Coronation Market, and at one stage, our program was *Ethiopian Nationality Claim for Resettlement to Ethiopia.* . . . we endorsed the resolution at a meeting, a street meeting, public meeting, which was very well attended, at Coronation Market, over some 3 to 5,000 people.

Price: When was that Iyah [Rasta]?

Brother Bongo: That was 1964, somewhere about that time, and that resolution was declaring that we state our claim to our [Ethiopian] nationality. In it, we asked for audience with the Minister of Home Affairs of the Jamaica Government. It was the Honorable Roy NcNeil at the time. So, audience was granted to a three-man delegation from the Rastafari community to meet with the Minister to discuss the possibility of renouncing the Jamaican identity and claiming our Ethiopian nationality and the findings around that. Well, when the day came, we had a march of about some 200 followers with placards claiming our Ethiopian nationality, and we are Ethiopians, originated in Ethiopia, but was born in Jamaica.

The Rastafari continued working in international arenas. Rastafari Philmore Alvaranga and Sam Clayton visited the United States in 1964, seeking to raise funds to support a second African mission, this time to Kenya, Nigeria, Ghana, and Ethiopia. The Rastafari "executives" (the designation activist Rastafari gave to them) noted the strong interest in repatriation expressed by Kenya's Jomo Kenyatta, who said that that their "great-grandparents were once sons of Africa" (Evans, 1964:n.p.). The United Churches of Kenya promised free land for up to 10,000 people of "African descent." According to the executives, Haile Selassie I remained "enthusiastic" about the idea of repatriation and "assisting the Rastafari Brethren to settle in his country" (Alvaranga, Clayton, & Mack, 1965:2).

Slowly, Jamaican popular consciousness was shifting to acknowledge the Rastafari as a legitimate people and cultural expression. In 1964, Rex Nettleford and Jamaica's National Dance Theater Company put on a play called "Two Drums for Babylon," a story that revolved around a middle-class woman's involvement with Rastafari. For a middle-class person to involve oneself with Rastafari meant scandal and shame for his or her family. A seismic perturbation that shifted the social position of the Rastafari was impending, though no one could have predicted what actually would happen nor the consequences: Emperor Haile Selassie I would visit Jamaica, the land where he was recognized as God.

God Lands in Jamaica

"Poor Haile Selassie," sigh. This highly civilized Christian gentleman would throw a fit if he ever saw the people who use his name in vain. (Wright, 1960:n.p.)

After nearly four decades of ridicule and marginalization, the Rastafari had witnessed a rapid succession of events that confirmed their convictions. Now Emperor Haile Selassie had confirmed his plan to visit Jamaica. The Rastafari, though, had already raised the question of preparation for meeting their God, as this chant attests:

Will you be ready when Rastafari trod?
Will you be ready when Rastafari trod?
It must be morning noon or night
Let your heart be pure and right
Will you be ready when Rastafari trod?
I n I ready when Rastafari trod (reprise)

On April 21, 1966, the most significant event in Rastafari experience occurred. The God of the Rastafari came to Jamaica. It was an event deeply etched in the memories of my narrators. It confirmed their identity, their ideology, and rendered more meaningful the tribulations they had experienced.

In 1966 there remained hope among elite Jamaicans that Haile Selassie I would tell the Rastafari that he was not God. This obsession on the part of the elites in proving the Rastafari to be fools had become pressing, as the mood among the Rastafari had reached a feverish pitch in anticipation of the Emperor's visit: "Their enthusiasm has never been this high. The greatest harm that Haile Selassie I could do to the Rastafarians, his followers, is to personally and publicly tell them that they should stop worshiping him. . . . Haile Selassie fervently desires that all Rastafarians should discard the belief that he is God" (*The Star*, 1966, n.p.). Whether the Emperor said these words is an unresolved question. However, elite contentions did not deter the Rastafari.

In droves the Rastafari struck out to the Palisadoes airport in Kingston to greet the Emperor. It was cloudy and raining lightly on April 21, 1966.

For several days, Rastafari had been converging on Kingston. Some had walked from as far away as Montego Bay, a four-hour drive today by car. Some carried crocus bags stuffed with ganja. Both Ras Sam Brown and Brother Bongo related that in their excitement they shouted to police and dignitaries that it was "Rasta time!"

The plane floated down from the clouds to the ground. Brother Alex, a self-described "peace and love brother" in his mid- to late sixties, recalled when we talked that

> It was raining, a mist-like rain you know. But nothing could hold we back from we God, you know. So, man no really pay no attention to the rain. . . . none of we did know from which direction His Majesty would come. Rasta say him God no live in no sky, but God did come from sky that day. When the plane break the clouds the rain stop. Immediately. And a wind blow, and all man dry again, just like a miracle. Then we see seven white doves. And the crowd of people go crazy. When plane touch ground them couldn't hold the people no more and them burst forward and dash out 'pon the runway. . . . It was a serious situation. You see man all light him chillum [ganja] pipe under the plane . . . them man don't know say them coulda explode the plane. Chaos did run the place. And the authority them, well them didn't do anything because them didn't know what to do. . . . too many people, too much disorder. One Brethren [Mortimer Planno] did calm the crowd and greet His Majesty. Him [Planno] said when the plane door open and him did see His Majesty, the King, was weeping.

Brother Bongo offered a slightly different account:

> His Majesty came out [the airplane] and the crowd was in jubilation. He put his hand up [lifting his fully opened right hand into the air, he performs the story for me] and the third time the Man did like that, if a pin was dropped, you could hear it. If you drop a pin in the audience, you could hear it. Silence. Silence [he himself is silent for a moment]. When Morti Planner said that His Majesty would like to leave the plane, and asked the crowd to make a way for His Majesty, the crowd obeyed. Planner came on and bowed to His Majesty. . . . Before His Majesty's plane landed, there was a shower of rain that just passed over. Like a squall come over. . . . everyone was soaking wet out at the airport and immediately everyone realized that they were wet and as they were thinking that,

"Imagine I am wet, how am I going to get dried?" We heard a hum of a plane engine coming and immediately the hum was heard, the sunlight could be seen while the hum was getting louder. The sun came brightly, and within the sun, the plane could be seen as if it were coming out of the sun. As the sun came up, those who were wet became immediately dry as if it were a miracle. It is something to think about because I was there. Immediately dry again and the plane came, and circled and landed. I tell you it was a jubilation. I was at the foot of the plane. I saluted as His Majesty passed. I did not make any effort to touch [Him] nor anything. I knew I would meet His Majesty later because I already had an invitation in my possession to meet His Majesty up in Kings House.

Many elders told me the story of the Emperor's landing at Palisadoes. The details and focus vary slightly, but the rain, the clouds, the drying breeze, the seven white birds, the intervention of Planno, and the weeping Emperor, are consistent leitmotifs. These recollections, crafted into stylized stories utilizing widely shared and accessible cultural resources and constituting social memory, will probably become as durable as Rastafari claims that the slaves never received any of £20 million the British paid to Jamaicans as compensation for ending slavery.

The Emperor's actions contradicted claims that the outpouring of emotions Jamaicans showered upon him disturbed him. He invited a group of Rastafari to lunch with him in Kings House. This must have caused the greatest stir among the elites who shared the Emperor's company with the so-called unwashed heathens. Brother Bongo provided details of the meeting of the Rastafari and Haile Selassie I:

Thirty-two brethren at that meeting . . . were presented to His Majesty at Kings House on the 22nd of April, 1966. Each of the thirty-two received a medal of goodwill. I did not hear at that time, but afterward His Majesty said continue on the good works that we are on. We were invited to three separate occasions with His Majesty. One at Kings House, one at the stadium when His Majesty was at the National Stadium, and one at Sheraton Hotel where he met all the people. At Sheraton, His Majesty sat on a dais . . . and people went and made their obeisance, saluted and greeted him. When I went up, I saluted, paid obeisance, prostrated; I had an attaché case with the documents surrounding the whole issue and whole works [of repatriation, Ethiopian identity], and I bowed to His Majesty and turned to His Majesty's Minister of Foreign Affairs who was Dr. Abebe. He was standing beside His Majesty, and I said, "We have some documents for you, Your Majesty" and Dr. Abebe, his Minister of Foreign Affairs, just beckoned to us and we just turned to him, knelt down, opened the attaché case and took out the documents. The [Jamaican] government gave us a letter that stated to the delegation that our case needs documentary evidence from Ethiopia. I took that letter out especially and handed it especially to the Minister of Foreign Affairs.

Though the authorities strove and struggled to keep people at a distance, everywhere the Emperor went huge crowds gathered to see him.

Haile Selassie I sent a powerful message. The Emperor, by inviting the Rastafari to eat with him, and by giving them gifts of gold medals, used his authority and presence as a monarch and world diplomat to empower them. Moreover, the Emperor acted in a Christ-like fashion. He sat and broke bread with pariahs. He did it openly, in the view of the world, at the risk of inflaming the "Romans." The Emperor's actions, if construed though the biblical lens that Jamaicans drew upon, confirmed a divine, or at least special, status toward the Rastafari.

The authorities who spurned the Rastafari now had to sit with them. Ras Trevor Campbell wrote in the Rastafari weekly, *Ethiopia Calls*:

> For the first time in the history of Jamaica, Ras Tafari Brethren and persons of Back-to-African movements were officially invited to Kings House, Glory be to the visit of the Emperor Haile Selassie I. Although we were born here, the privilege was never granted to us until April 21, 1966. . . . It was a mixed assemblage at Kings House. The Ras [Rastafarians] were there, the aristocrats were there, the peasants and the outcasts. It was a real occasion of the mixing of the haves and have nots. It took Ras Tafari in person to occasion the reality that "all men were created equal." The King of Kings and Lord of Lords did not think himself too high to leave his High Throne in Ethiopia to sit on a chair in King's House among the servants of the earth.

Haile Selassie I spoke his native Amharic during his public engagements, and used an interpreter, even though he had a thorough command of English. Of note, though, are the few occasions when the Emperor spoke English. For example, the Emperor thanked the representatives of the 20-odd "African groups" in English, and he thanked Rastafari Douglas Mack in English and remembered him from his two visits to Ethiopia in

1961 and 1964. The Emperor said, "I am glad to know, and thank you for continuing your work with your people here. You have done purposeful work" (*DG*, 4/23/66:24). Acts and messages such as these bolstered the Rastafari's conception of their beliefs and the divinity of the Emperor while undermining the efforts of the elites to discredit the Rastafari.

The perturbation unleashed by the visit of Haile Selassie I contributed to shifting the social position of the Rastafari, a transition under way before his visit. The Emperor's visit and subtle but positive attitude toward the Rastafari account for much in the transition of the Rastafari to exemplars of Black culture and identity. This transition, though, was in process; no one could predict what would come next even though the Rastafari themselves were buoyed by turned events. There were more surprises in store, and it would be the mid-1970s before the Rastafari became widely recognized, nationally and internationally, as cultural exemplars. Nonetheless, as Brother Yendis noted, "Yes. 1966. When His Majesty come a Jamaica, and the whole a Jamaica come look upon him [Haile Selassie, I] and see say, yeah, a this [is the] man them a talk bout. The thing change . . . Rasta get respect. Things have to happen to fulfill certain things. Like showing the world say this is Rasta country."

The Rodney Riots: 1968

By the late 1960s, a Jamaican Black Power movement had emerged; the nation was recovering and constructing its African roots and taking pride in its Black culture. Rastafari, of course, had been doing this from the 1930s, and Ethiopianists even longer. Jamaica's Black Power movement was not an imitation of the movement in the United States, although it shared some commonalities, such as an appreciation of Black phenotypes, culture, and history. As in the United States, it was social movements in Jamaica— Bedwardites, Garveyites, Rastafari, Black Power—that played a central role in valorizing Blackness and contesting how it was used to oppress.

In January 1968, the University College of the West Indies hired Walter Rodney, a historian from Guyana, to its faculty. He uniquely combined Black Power philosophy, history, Marxism, and Freirian-like pedagogy. Rodney gave lectures in notorious ghetto sections of Kingston, and many Rastafari were his students: "I have spoken in what people call 'dungle,' rubbish dumps, for that is where people live in Jamaica. . . . I have sat on a little oil drum, rusty and in the midst of garbage, and some black brothers and I have grounded together" (Rodney, 1996:64).

Rodney was one of the figures who introduced Rastafari to theories of imperialism and Marxism. His ideology and politics meshed with the sentiments of the time and resonated with the sentiments of a morally configured Blackness. He illustrated this in his definition of Black Power as: "(i) the break with imperialism which is historically white racist; (ii) the assumption of power by the black masses in the island; (iii) the cultural reconstruction of the society in the image of blacks" (Rodney, 1996:28).

Rodney's critique of the Jamaican Labor Party (JLP), his pursuit of cross-class and cross-race alliances, and his rhetoric about the need for revolution to break imperialism, caused him to become the government's number one enemy. Here was a man speaking the language of Sharpe, Bogle, Bedward, and Garvey in the radical vernacular of the 1960s. The government's reaction to such champions of Black Power had always been liquidation. Rodney was no exception. Roy McNeill, Minister of Home Affairs, believed that Rodney was the gravest current threat to Jamaica (Payne, 1994:22). Elites sought to contain the growing racial awareness through policies such as the Forbidden Publications Act, which banned importing books by Malcolm X, Stokely Carmichael, Eldridge Cleaver, and even Jamaican sociologist Orlando Patterson's *The Children of Sisyphus*.

Brother Yendis shared his perspective on Rodney, and in doing so offered a critique of the political system that Rastafari found oppressive and offensive. He reserved special opprobrium for Prime Minister Shearer, who sought to crush Rodney and the movement he had tapped into:

Rodney see injustice in a system, him speak out. . . . That causes the up-stirs. . . . It was the status quo of the day feel like Rodney was a threat. And Brother [Prime Minister] Shearer, again, he was sitting down on a limb what him wasn't to be on [he shouldn't have been Prime Minister]. . . . Him never know nothing about government, he never know nothing about care for people, and as a Black man, he never even finish his education, and Bustamante take him up, and help him parents with him, and so on and so forth, and him come up with this glorious benefit that him get. Tell you better than that. When Independence [came], them did a blow up [honor] Sangster and Sangster dead . . . you must independent [liberate] yourself from British Colonial system, for that is why we get Independence . . . to take weself from British Colonialism and Imperialism. . . . [The Brown and Black] leaders were so backward that they go right back into the same thing [dependence] what them come out of. Them never know say we a come we come out of it.

Brother Yendis evoked the irony of the times. Rodney and many of the Rastafari were aware of the ethos of liberation pulsing through the metropoles and satellites of the world, while Jamaican politicians were simultaneously pursuing independence and neglecting what Bob Marley called "mental slavery." Political independence was on the table, while cultural dependence on British culture and Whiteness continued to be exalted in a predominantly Black nation.

Rodney sought to "ground" various left-of-center dissenting groups such as the Unemployed Workers, the Young Socialists, the New World Group, and some of the race-focused groups (Payne, 1994). Government leadership must have concluded that if they could eliminate Rodney's influence, then they would have defanged the opposition. The government decided unilaterally to prevent Rodney from returning to work and live in Jamaica. Rodney's attendance at a conference in Canada provided the opportunity for government to keep him from disembarking from his plane upon his return to Jamaica on the afternoon of October 15, 1968, forcing him to return to Canada. Once the UCWI student dissenters discovered the "ban on Rodney," they planned a protest march to the offices of the top government leadership. The march was disrupted by Jamaica's police and army. The faltering march turned violent as JLP supporters stoned marchers, and Jamaica's inner city residents joined the fray. The disturbance turned riotous as the police and army battered whoever got in their way, and looting and arson spiraled into a conflagration. The violence subsided within a couple of days, and the damage was limited largely to Kingston's commercial district (Gray, 1991). But the impact of the disturbance had far-reaching consequences.

The unintended consequences of the Rodney riot gave prominence to discussions of Black identity in Jamaica's history, culture, and future. And, it momentarily created a space in which Rastafari and other civil society groups such as labor, leftist, and student organizations could build coalitions.

Joshua, Democratic Socialism, and the Black Exemplar Status of Rastafari: 1970–1975

In 1969, Michael Manley indirectly condemned the race-based injustices of Jamaica's past, and made plain the relationship between Black identity and miseducation, deracination, and oppression:

An epoch of brainwashing in a white-oriented society has left scars, which, however unconscious, mar the inner assurance with which Black people accept their own norms of beauty and excellence. . . . The acceptance, with joy and pride, of the fact of Blackness, of black dignity and black beauty . . . [and to] use political Black Power to make the black man free in his own country to live a decent civilised and happy life. (Waters, 1989:120, 121)

In the 1972 national election, the charismatic politician and intellectual Michael Manley, son of the founder of the PNP, Norman Manley, used Rastafarian lexicon and symbolism to appeal to the majority black and poor population who were re-imagining themselves through the positive messages found in Rastafarian and Black Power ideologies. Manley garnered massive support among the majority Black population who dreamed aloud that "better must come." The infusion of Rasta influence into the national election came not only from Manley but also his coterie of campaign personnel working at the grassroots level. D. K. Duncan, for example, sometimes wore a tam (headwear associated with Rastafari) and used Rasta phrases at PNP rallies (Waters, 1989).

Michael Manley was the embodiment of the shepherd leader, as was the opposition JLP leader, Edward Seaga. Both knew how to tap into the moral economy of Blackness to mobilize support. Manley considered himself a socialist, a leader in the Third World movement. Policy-wise Manley pursued development of a mixed economy grounded in an ideology of Christian love and "equality of man." He brilliantly displayed his capacity to grasp and utilize the justice motifs that pervaded the discourse of so many Black Jamaicans. The phrase "socialism is love" and socialism is the "philosophy that best gives expression to the Christian ideal of equality of all God's children" aimed directly to appeal to the ideologies of two influential groups, Rastafarians and Christians (see Keith & Keith, 1992:18).

Manley adopted the name Joshua, allegedly given to him by Claudius Henry, the scandalous leader of the two debacles detailed above. Joshua was a prophet and leader who succeeded Moses. God counseled his servant Joshua that: "There shall not any man be able to stand before thee all the days of thy life: As I was with Moses, so I will be with thee. . . . for unto this people shalt thou divide for an inheritance the land, which I sware unto their fathers to give them" (Joshua 1:5).

The Rastafari adopted elements of Manley's vision and reworked them into their own idiom, "social living," rather than socialism. The Rastafari were attracted to the promises of socialism, especially free education and school uniforms, land reform, cooperative farms, food subsidies, work, youth and relief programs, expanded health care, and access to housing. Manley's appeal to brotherly love, equality, and eradicating exploitation resonated with the Rastafari's concern with the justice motifs. Ras Brenton, for example, argued that "We (Rastas) must be socialists. We support socialism because we want to be able to have a house too, to have some land, to be able to make a living without so much sufferation. . . . Capitalism is not fe we. It is fe them who already have."

Manley linked himself and the PNP to the Rastafari in several ways. He allowed a Rastafari group, the Mystic Revelations, to represent Jamaica abroad; he rallied crowds by lifting aloft and shaking a stick he called the "rod of correction," which he claimed Haile Selassie I gave to him; and he publicly used Rasta language (such as "I man"). The rod invoked Haile Selassie I, overturning injustice, and the biblical imagery associated with Moses.

Manley's co-optation of Rastafari culture and symbols helped him and the PNP win the 1972 and 1976 elections. The symbolic association of the Rastafari with new sociopolitical possibilities, and the concomitant rise to national and international prominence of Rastafari musicians such as Bob Marley and the Wailers, further contributed to the validation of the Rastafari as exemplars of Black culture and identity, in Jamaica and internationally. Such an outcome would have seemed as outrageous in 1954 as the arrival of a fleet of ships to repatriate the Rastafari to Africa. However, in the nonlinear social world, a particular outcome can be maintained only for a while. Manley and the PNP were able to make only minor changes, not the seismic transformation they promised, and whatever optimism they may have stirred in some Rastafari was replaced with cynicism. "They [politicians] tried to make us their lapdogs," Ras Sam Brown told me in the late 1990s, referring to the heady days of democratic socialism. "But we are survivors like the mongrel you see on the street. We don't allow no master, you see. We free." The demise of the socialist vision and the PNP's reign was an important watershed, giving way to the emergent sociopolitical configuration called neoliberalism, the antithesis of Michael Manley's rhetoric of equality and justice. The Rastafari, however, were unsettled by another humongous perturbation around the same time. On August 27, 1975, Haile Selassie I was supposedly killed during a political coup. So, the Rastafari were confronted with the question, "How can your God die?" This question really got at Rastafari identity and commitment to it. We shall return to this scenario in chapter 6.

The chaotic and complex nature of the evolution of new peoples and social movements involves surprises—events that change substantially the evolutionary trajectory of a group. We can never know when their experience, their story, will shift radically to another script, perhaps overlaying, conjoining, the narratives that already exist. The Rastafari survived the ridicule and suppression of the 1930s and 1940s, greatly increased their numbership and influence between 1955 and the mid-1970s, moved beyond the devastating impact of Henry's twin debacles and the Coral Gardens incident and the crackdowns that followed these. The *Report* and the Mission to Africa lent credibility to the Rastafari that did not immediately lead to changes in their status, but set in motion a concatenation of factors that would validate the Rastafari as a legitimate people and identity. The meaningful symbols, collective identity, and ideological cultural variation generated by the Rastafari, along with the interventions of non-Rastafari and the motivations of individuals to explore the emergent community identity, help explain the growth and durability of the Rastafari.[8] Therefore, let us examine closely the personal dynamics of a morally configured Black identity.

3

The Positive Power of Stigma and Black Identity

I myself was one of those [underprivileged ghetto] youths [of the late 1950s] who accepted the Rasta Faith, as in it I saw something to identify with; it gave me a feeling of belonging and a brighter perception of the future because it helped me to understand the past in a way impossible before.

(Jah Bones, 1986:41)

I am one of those who believe that to find a new order of things with Europe means putting new order in oneself.

(Memmi, 1965:147).

Early in my research, a close Jamaican friend who was knowledgeable about Jamaican culture, history, and politics urged me to seek out Brother Yendis. He said that Brother Yendis was a well-known and respected Rastafari who presently headed the Rastafari Federation. I took my friend's advice. Finding and meeting Brother Yendis was not difficult. At that time, the Rastafari Federation was prominently located in lower Kingston, and a visit there led to an invitation to one of their upcoming conferences. Brother Yendis, then in his early sixties, exhibited a physical frame and musculature that conveyed strength and a bodily presence that fit his reputation as a determined and charismatic man. His very dark skin, imposing hands and forearms, dangling locked grey beard, and huge, single lock that led from his head almost to the ground, made him imposing and unmistakable. His dark eyes could cast a glance that seemed on more than one occasion to have the power to look deeply inside of a person. At the same time, Brother Yendis laughed frequently, a sort of "hee-hee" chuckle almost incongruent with his commanding features. Over the ensuing months, I learned that Brother Yendis was an experienced organizer, a world traveler, and intelligently informed on left politics and Jamaican history and religion.

Conversations preceding our formal interviews offered tantalizing tidbits about Brother Yendis's identity and experience. He was born to poor parents who practiced Catholicism. At an early age he became aware of the Rastafari and how they were mistreated and portrayed as a menace. Brother Yendis's racial awareness and sense of injustice were detonated during a visit to Florida on a farm work visa during 1961. He was asked to move to the rear of one of the buses that carried him to the fields where he worked. He remembered how he did not understand the bus driver's "accent" (Southern American), and why he was urged to sit in the back. In the back of the bus he saw only African Americans. They were laughing and joking. He then noticed that in the front of the bus there were only Whites. Brother Yendis could not comprehend why the African Americans were jovial in what struck him as an incomprehensible arrangement: racial segregation. He would soon learn about Jim Crow and the Civil Rights movement. He reflected how that experience and others made him feel he "had to do something" about the condition of Black people in Jamaica and the Diaspora, that he had to fight against injustice, and that he had to begin in Jamaica.

Brother Yendis gradually came to encourage my research efforts, after many conversations. He made few but important suggestions. He said, "Don't focus on the politics [only] . . . you must tell the different ways I n I (Rastafari) sight up his Majesty and develop [Rastafari identity]. . . . some come to a realization through the Bible . . . and some say His Imperial Majesty speak directly to them. Capture this, man." Brother Yendis also told me that I should talk to older Rastafari women.

Unbeknownst to me, I had been steered by a Rastafari interlocutor in directions that would profoundly shape my thinking. Talking to Brother Yendis and other Rastafari helped me arrive at the idea of morally configured Blackness, and thus contribute to expanding Black identity theory. After several interviews, I began to notice similarities in narratives. One striking pattern involved the careful identification of a specific experience or set of experiences that moved the narrator onto the path of becoming Rastafari. These experiences involved particular racial and religious encounters in the real world and "interior" dialogues about Black history and culture, miseducation, deracination, oppression, justice, and biblical history. Both types of experience were part and parcel of a social process of discovery and learning about Rastafari. "Encounter," "active resistance," and "turning point" are social science concepts that describe the kind of experiences involved in my narrators becoming Rastafari. Brother Bongo encapsulates the complexity and effect these descriptions entail:

> I renounce Trevor Campbell, which is my slave name. That is my slave master's name. I come of age and to the consciousness to my ancestral rights, my original rights, my original identity as an Ethiopian. So as an Ethiopian, I cannot be identified as Trevor Campbell. There is no such Ethiopian name as Trevor Campbell. It must be a slave that is named Trevor Campbell. So, now that I am redeemed from mental slavery, I am now Gabi Selassie.

Before Ras Brenton came to identify as a Rastafari, he was intrigued by the language he heard them use to talk about themselves. He recalled how he would "take in" the information delivered by Rastafari orators lecturing or preaching on the streets to whomever would listen. Ras Brenton was smitten by the messages of Black pride and history and meditated on these positive framings of Black identity, history, and religion. He reflected on how these orators exhorted people to absorb and live the ideas and to work collectively in preparation for their redemption.

Thus, we want to know how people like the Rastafari come to place Blackness and religion at the center of their self-concept, how they turn stigma into an asset, and how these acts relate to fashioning a collective identification called Rastafari people. An account of Rastafari identity, especially its personal formulations, must address both identity and acts of conversion—the transformation of a person's self and conception of reference group—which are both religious and racial in content. Indeed, Blackness and religiosity are not separate domains for many Black peoples of the Western hemisphere (Hall, 1995) and to slight this interrelatedness would ignore people's self-knowledge.

I use nigrescence theory, a discrete formulation of Black identity theory, to explain the processes involved in becoming and being Rastafari. The nigrescence model explains why and how people elevate Blackness to a primary identification imbued with satisfying meaning (Cross Jr., 1995). In order to attend to the moral and religious dimensions of Rastafari identity, I incorporate into my conception of nigrescence some ideas from religious conversion theory. For example, "seeking" may be a part of Black identity transformation, while the moral ideas associated with religion, such as suffering, justice, and redemption, can operate as master frameworks within which people seek to situate themselves racially. For my Rastafari narrators, the durable discourse of Ethiopianism is a cultural resource that serves as a framework for uniting race, religion, identity, and culture in a manner that critiques White hegemony and Black people's complicity in their own oppression. Both nigrescence and religious conversion ultimately grapple with how individuals attach themselves to a collectivity. Before explaining nigrescence and religious conversion theory in detail, however, I will lay out some general ideas upon which my conception of a morally configured Black identity rest.

Identity Purposes

Identities are storehouses of information that persons draw on to navigate their lives, elements of the human capacity to reflect and be self-and-other aware. Identity helps us deal with two perennial and perhaps universal concerns: "What do I make of you?" and "What do I make of myself?" Our identities, both the ones we assume and the ones imposed on us, are continually open to and undergoing modification as we draw on what we learn and experience. Identities are especially influenced by those aspects of ourselves that others pay attention to and "reflect back to us" (Tatum, 1997:21). While we cannot say that every culture has some language for identity and self-concept in the peculiar sense used by Western academics (e.g., self-actualizing), every culture recognizes what the "West" acknowledges as an identifiable and durable person with some degree of "unity" (Strauss & Quinn, 1997:31). Psychologists and, to a degree, some psychological anthropologists, discuss these durable and recognizable patterns in terms of a "self-concept."

We can imagine the complex self-concept as having two major dimensions: personal identity and reference group orientation (Cross Jr., 1991). A person's self-concept changes during his or her life course, although some features, such as what psychologists and lay people call personality, may remain stable. But, even these personal patterns can change, for example, when a person moves from being shy to outgoing. In this use, "personal identity" is the configuration of biographical experiences that influence how someone imagines and evaluates himself. Personal identity is unavoidably shaped by a constellation of roles and relationships (to people, nature, time), especially one's reference groups. The term "self-concept" may imply an analytic primacy given to an overarching notion of Rastafari as an identification, but it matches how nearly all of my interlocutors talked biographically about their selves. This is perhaps because Rastafari serves for some people as a master identity that informs other identifications. At the same time, though, my interlocutors and I were aware of other salient identifications such as those involving work.

The Rastafari evolved both through a combination of the effort of individuals to define themselves and profess a particular understanding of the world and through the reactions and labeling of other actors such as Christians, law enforcement officials, and journalists. In these and other interactions, the Rastafari demarcated themselves from other Black Jamaicans through conspicuous "us-them" boundaries signified through cultural, linguistic, ritualistic, symbolic, ideological, and phenotypic expressions. Through my interlocutors we can learn how racialization and identity transformation manifest in individuals. In 1953, then 33-year-old Herben Walters described his encounter and identity transformation: "'I was living in Kingston Pen, near the Queens Theatre, and I saw how they [the Rastafari] lived loving together. And one day I suddenly changed in body and spirit and knew *the truth*. So I became a Rastafari and will die a Ras Tafari'" (Wright, 1960:n.p., emphasis added). Although Walters's conversion was probably preceded by much reflection and questioning rather than occurring instantly as he implied, people like Walters noticed a disconnect between negative depictions of Rastafari and their actual messages and behavior.

Black Jamaicans could use Blackness to oppose White hegemony and provide an alternative to it. Although stamped with many stigmas (including those created by Blacks themselves), Blackness was never totally devalued. As I wrote in the Preface, subversion could entail "deficient" people weaving a different story about themselves in which their status exceeds that of their oppressors, if not everyone else. Ras Chronicle, like many older Rastafari I met, shared exalted definitions of themselves and their comrades: "So, why me become a Rasta is because Rasta is a specific development in the Black people business. Rasta is the cream of the Black people, of the African race." Undoubtedly, many Black and African people might contest such an assertion. Nevertheless, self-exalting is a common human practice. The Rastafari, however, have no capacity to impose and enforce their beliefs on others as is the case with Whiteness.

Wishful thinking cannot alone make a new identity. A person literally needs culture, history, and the involvement of other people. Identity transformation involves a person's desire to reconfigure their own identity, and their drawing upon relevant cultural resources. It also involves internalizing the new identity through introspection and practice. And at some point there will arise concern with commitment to and maintenance of the new identity.

Each of the Rastafari I interviewed had, in varying degrees, reworked their self-concept, developing a positively heightened racial and religious conviction and a sensibility of relationship to Black people past and present. Many of my Rastafari interlocutors had experiences where they made "connections" or experienced epiphanies that urged them to embark upon a journey in search of information and answers:

> From I was a young girl visit [Pentecostal] church with me mother, I wonder how Jesus never look like we. Him have beard, and him hair hang so [touching her shoulders]. But him White. And I look at all a we [in the Church]. We Black. So I come say that God must White. And so if God White and we Black, then White must better than Black. I hold that [belief] for a long time. . . . So, now, I learn why the Rasta get such fight. Him say God not White. And him do things different because him say this. This is not easy to accept if you hold onto the White Jesus. (Sister Pear)

Sister Pear's puzzlement about the racial identity of God and Jesus provided the context for her to entertain some of the claims of the Rastafari. Her curiosity, however, involved a lengthy interior dialogue. A person may engage in such an interior dialogue for months or even years before actively pursuing identity transformation.

Becoming Rastafari involved making connections between many dimensions of one's experience. These connections involved linking an acute awareness of oppression, a recognition of being a member of a maligned group, a realization that there exists a long-standing tradition of positive understandings of Blackness, an awareness that one's cultural heritage has been hidden, and an insight into how White cultural hegemony had distorted one's earlier understandings. These are but a few of the connections my interlocutors made and internalized through the interior and interpersonal dialogues that identity transformation requires to produce a different primary identification. Through particular experiences, often interpreted with the help of living exemplars of Rastafari, each convert had become sensitive to, in various ways, their own miseducation, deracination, and oppression, and how these were implicated in a greater chain of social, historical, and existential predicaments. The converts used identity—Rastafari identity—to address the quandaries raised by what became for them a nagging awareness of injustice, racial pride, White hegemony, and the promise of Black redemption. Identity transformation proved a route to an attractive possibility: liberation through identification with a living collectivity that endows itself with the attributes of divine connection, soul, intellect, and a special gift for the capacity to "see" and know what others do not.

Theories of Black identity formation explain Blackness as a primary identification, but Black identity theory is rarely used outside of a small corner of social and counseling psychology. My reading of their narratives suggested that the experiences of my narrators had much in common with what researchers have to say about the formation of Black identity. There was not a total convergence between the patterns in the data and the theories of Blackness, though. For example, theories of Black identity do not explicitly incorporate religiosity (though Cross Jr. claims that nigrescence conversion has a spiritual dimension[1]) or address in detail contextual factors such as cultural understandings of Blackness.

My perspective on Black identity transformation draws substantially on nigrescence theory's idea of the "encounter" (e.g., Cross Jr., 1991, 1995, 2001). The encounter explains why and how a person's racial understanding and worldview can be shaken to the point that they no longer want to be who they were. The concept helped me grasp why my narrators were motivated to embark on a mission of soul searching and developing a critical racialized perspective on the world around them. Unlike theories of race and race relations, which are legion, Black identity theory delineates and explains the specificities of Blackness as a particular categorization and experience of race in relation to the self.

Black Identity and Internalized Oppression

Franz Fanon, in *Black Skins, White Masks* (1967), and *Wretched of the Earth* (1963), convincingly demonstrated the negative impact of colonization and colonialism on the psyche and identity of colonized and subjugated people, as well as on the oppressors. Fanon demonstrated how the colonized and oppressed internalize their colonization and oppression and turn it upon themselves. He argued that the abnegation and displacement of colonized people's culture, identity, and history, overwritten if not replaced by the culture, identity, and history of the colonizer, creates a dynamic that has to be negated by the colonized themselves. From his perspective, a colonized or marginalized people must liberate themselves.

Liberation cannot be granted or bestowed upon them, especially by the colonizers. Paulo Freire (1970) amplified this point by showing how oppressed people can internalize the negative opinions of their oppressors. Liberation was one of the antidotes to internalized oppression that Fanon (and Freire) identified. He saw violence as the most effective and cathartic route to liberation, reasoning that the acts of overturning domination and exorcising the hegemony of Whiteness restored the self-confidence of the oppressed and inspired respect, if not awe, in the oppressor. My research suggests that the kind of liberation Fanon desired is regularly achieved without violence—though not necessarily removed from it—through identity transformation. The Rastafari, if you will recall, *symbolically* enacted violence, especially through language.

Many scholars of Black identity explain its primary operations as being a cultural and psychological defense medium, a source of meaning, and a social anchor (Allen, 2004; Cross Jr., 1991, 1995, 2001; Helms, 1990; Harrison, 1998:156). Blackness is learned, and it is learned through reflection, socialization, and interaction; it is not heritable, as unfortunately many people continue to believe (including many Rastafari). People use the various social constructions of Blackness in making sense of the world, especially in locating themselves and others in history and place. Yet, because Blackness is learned and transmitted across generations, and likewise because much misinformation about it is also transmitted, we should expect people's understanding of it often to be incomplete and unevenly distributed. Even among people who have been socialized into positive conceptions of Blackness, such as some of the children of Garveyites, we should expect to find an array of understandings, which also lend themselves to the potential for racial contention within Blackness.

Racial misunderstanding, in the form of miseducation, has great significance for identity. For Black people in the West, miseducation created a great dilemma, but a dilemma that also has a solution:

> If you teach the Negro that he has accomplished as much good as any other race he will aspire to equality and justice without regard to race. Such an effort would upset the program of the oppressor in Africa and America. Play up before the Negro, then, his crimes and shortcomings. Let him learn to admire the Hebrew, the Greek, the Latin and the Teuton. Lead the Negro to detest the man of African blood—to hate himself. . . . With the *truth* hidden there will be little expression of thought to the contrary. (Woodson, 1933:192–193, emphasis added)

One solution to the dilemma miseducation posed for Black self-knowledge involved countering it with a positive and accomplished Black history to which one was an heir.

Many of my Rastafari interlocutors talked about their identity in terms of an interest in, and pursuit of, "truth." Truth, similar to Woodson's usage, concerned knowledge involving race, religion, history, and culture. This interest in and pursuit of truth resembled a quest:

> Leonard Howell, the patriarch of Rastafari, say we have a new [Black] God and King . . . I want to know more about this . . . I search out the Bible . . . I reason with other Brothers . . . you see we find weself in a situation where we do not know anything about weself . . . [but] we know 'bout England. (Brother Dee)

It is within such contexts that we can see "nigrescence," or "becoming Black," as a part of the cultural production of race. Racial identity transformation can aid in changing how a person understands, projects, and positions herself in relation to others. The transformation of which I speak involves resocialization and reeducation to positively define and evaluate Blackness, Black history, and Black culture.

Being "Peculiar" Can Be a Good Thing: Rastafari, Blackness, and Managing Stigma

Blackness is multiply stigmatized, but not entirely defined by it (Cross Jr., & Strauss, 1998). Students of Black identity have in the past promulgated misleading pronouncements about oppression and stigma causing self-hate. Stigmatization can influence a person's primary identification in ways that do not lead to self-hate or identification with the dominant group. The Rastafari were, for several decades, a multiply stigmatized group, and in some ways remain so despite the post-1960 events that lifted their identity and beliefs to an exalted position in Jamaica. Their belief in a Black and embodied God was heretical; their positive evaluation of Blackness was befuddling to many; their use of cannabis cast them as deviants; and Black people themselves often denigrated Blackness. In these ways and others, the stigma of the Rastafari was so powerful that it could contaminate friends, family, and even strangers who did not inoculate themselves through distancing or ridicule.

So, why would someone become a Rastafari given its many stigmas? My interviews suggest that emergent Rastafari recognized their capacity to manage the stigma, the power of Rastafari identity in the Jamaican context, and the capacity of the identity to address problems attendant to miseducation, deracination, and injustice: "When me hear a man a call me Rastafari or a Rasta man, me feel strong, me feel good because me know say is not me go out there to tell a man, say, 'See me, me is Rastafari,' you know. No. Man say: 'See the Rasta man deh'" (Brother Yendis). Recognition by others, without his prompting, affirms what Brother Yendis is feeling inside.

Stigmatized people may see themselves as normal, even while others see only the stigma (Goffman, 1963). It may draw the attention of an audience and excite their imagination without the awareness, or intent, of the bearer of stigma. Ras Chronicle, like many of the elder Rastafari, had many stories that illustrate the powerful stigma attached to being Rastafari. Even minor actions by non-Rastafari could convey stigma: "Them time there [early 1960s], when you [a Rastafari man] sit down in a bus, near a girl, she want go through the bus other side . . . it's just a little beard me have [no dreadlocks], you know . . . me a tell you man, you see it, society teach them how Rasta a Blackheart and Rasta a thief." I asked Ras Chronicle what "Blackheart" meant to him. He replied, while grimacing as if in pain: "'Blackheart man?' Them teach people say Blackheart man will eat out ya heart."

Rastafari see themselves as normal, but a "peculiar" kind of normal. They juxtapose their self-understood normality against what they pose as the abnormality of the non-Rastafari. The abnormality of the non-Rastafari involves their complicity or promotion in deracination, injustice, and miseducation. The Rastafari reconfigure the estrangement that can result from stigmatization into normality. The reconfiguration has an insulating effect that buffers the pain that comes with stigmatization. Their self-created special status as the elect of Emperor Selassie I plays an important part in managing the power of stigma.

"Self-elevation" by members of stigmatized collectivities is mastered as a part of a person's identity work, which is another way that they create a sense of parity in relation to other people (Goffman, 1963:38–39). It involves a stigmatized group creating a rationale for their normality or even transcendence. The stigma Rastafari see others stamping upon them they interpret within the framework of their justice motifs, as another illustration of non-Rastafari iniquity. It is not necessarily taken person-ally but still recognized, reinforcing the conviction of individuals in their identity beliefs, providing further evidence of their being a "peculiar" and "special" people. Like the early Christians, the Rastafari believe that they must bear the burden of the cross—the travails of stigma and elect status—in order to obtain the crown (redemption). Self-elevation is en-acted in mundane settings, woven into various kinds of discourse: casual conversations, meetings, gatherings, and their own publications. For ex-ample, the opening vignette described in chapter 1 was a scene in which the Rastafari were engaged in self-elevation. In the language of the Rasta-fari, self-elevation includes being the elect of God, a chosen and peculiar people different from normal people. Bongo J offers us a perspective on self-elevation:

> Me is a king, a priest, a prophet. . . . me no come in with no frauding [falseness], no bowing, no begging. My word is a lamp unto my feet and light unto my body. . . . it is merciful and true to the man who can keep this convenant and TESTAMANT [of Rastafari]! To do good, to do the right (I capitalized "testamant" because Bongo J shouted it).

Self-elevation helps explain how my interlocutors called up the fortitude to embrace a stigmatized identity. Rastafari like Brother Yendis, Herben Walters, Sister Pear, and others came to realize the Rastafari were not the dangerous and abnormal people they were made out to be. In cases such as theirs, stigma was not only overshadowed by self-elevation, but it was also a powerful attraction because it was construed as marking their nor-mality (as a special or chosen people) in the midst of a society of abnor-mal people.

Rastafari both neutralized internalization of the stigmas used to mark them as deviant and continued to do things that reinforced the stigma-tization. For example, tending one's hair had special meaning for Blacks who believed that they had "bad hair" and that "good hair" was equiva-lent to the silky, soft, or straight hair of Whites and mixed-race people. In Jamaica, many Black men were obsessed with hair management, see-ing regular trimming as a sign of respectability; for Black women the hot comb and lye were remedies for bad hair. Dreadlocks Rastafari ve-hemently objected to these and other body-crafting practices that were construed to denigrate Black physiognomy and mimic Whiteness. In-deed, between the 1950s and late 1970s, the Dreadlocks Rastafari were the aesthetic vanguard, leading with new definitions of beauty within the context of Blackness. Not combing and not cutting "bad" hair, letting it grow into unruly tresses became a positive sign, defined by the Rastafari for themselves. What "madness," so many Jamaicans wondered aloud. "Them is like wild animal!" Acts such as these increased the visibility of Rastafari by further marking them as outside of the realm of a normalized racialization. While they were constructing themselves as peculiarly normal, they were also marking themselves off from the "normals." The dreadlocked Rastafari engaged in "voluntary disclosure," a kind of stigma management (Goffman, 1963:48). They told Jamaica, and the world, "I am who I am," eschewing any need to "pass" because they respected themselves and their identity; they had nothing to hide (we saw this aspect become prominent, if not flaunted, by the late 1950s). Anyway, concealing their identity was not an option for the Dreadlocks. They could not pass. The Combsome Rastafari, however, had the option of passing. All they had to do was to code switch and remove identifying signs such as buttons and sashes that indicated "I am Rastafari" and it would be difficult for anyone but the "wise" or someone who already knew them to penetrate their cover.

Theorizing Blackness

There are few empirically oriented models that speak specifically to Black experience. Typically, it has been White researchers, using White experience or their interpretation of Black experience as the baseline, who have developed models that they have applied to the experience of non-Whites. W.E.B. Du Bois was among the influential Black scholars, though not the first, who addressed the particularities of Black identity formation around the same time as William James, Charles Cooley, and George Herbert Mead were developing dialectical, social, and dialogical understandings of identity formation. They left their accounts generic and universal. On the other hand, Allen argues that Western conceptions of identity with their emphases on independence and autonomy are insufficient for understanding Black identity (2004:127–128). Du Bois applied the idea of mutual interaction between a person's primary identification and society to race. His conception of double consciousness revealed how the "Negro" was constantly reminded of his restricted, inferior, and marginal position—of who he is—through interaction with others, especially as the subject of the gaze of Whites (1969). Yet, Du Bois understood that Negroes knew themselves to be fully human and deserving of rights and respect. While there is a lineage of researchers, primarily Black, who have addressed the complexities of Black identity, including the positive dimensions, there are Black and White researchers who have stereotyped Black identity as a cluster of pathologies that are the result of internalized debased conceptions of Blackness and the acceptance of Whites as the primary reference group. It is only in the past 30 years that research has substantially undermined this thesis by showing how other Blacks are the primary reference for Black people (Allen, 2004; Cross Jr., 1991). That Black people affirmed themselves and made positive achievements under oppression was infrequently investigated by scholars before the 1970s.

Black identity theory is based primarily on the experience of Black Americans. There is scant empirical research that compares Black identity theory against Black experience outside of the United States or the experience of Black immigrants to the United States (some exceptions include Semaj, 1980; Cha-Jua, 1998; Charles, 2003; Akbar, Chambers, & Thompson, 2001; Henry, 1982). Historically, however, Black American experience has much in common with the experience of people of the Black Diaspora in other parts of the Americas, even with their particular histories of development. Several Black identity theory assumptions, concepts, and explanations are useful to explaining Black identity transformation among the Rastafari in Jamaica.

Theorists of Black identity assume that Blackness consists of distinct matrices of experience and meaning, which call for analyses attuned to these considerations. For example, theorists single out the enslavement of Black people, the equating of slaves to property, the legal denial of equality and opportunity to Blacks, the pernicious denigration of Blackness as a degraded cultural expression, stigmatization, and other forms of discrimination and racism (e.g., Cross Jr., 1971, 1981; Sellers, Smith, Shelton, Rowley, & Chavous, 1998; Adams, 2001). The remembrance of slavery (and other forms of oppression) was vital to the identity of my interlocutors, as exemplified in the view of Ras Sam Brown: "Our ancestors came here as slaves . . . slavery has enriched the European and impoverished the African . . . we will never let that be forgotten. It is the history of Black people in this land [Jamaica]." Such understandings of the real influences of history and oppression must be accounted for as factors that influence Black understandings of their self-concept and collective identity. Stuart Hall argues that any search for identity involves a search for "origins," and that the Rastafari have used identity to create a language for "suffering" and for re-appropriating and re-telling history (1995:5, 13).

Many Black identity theorists recognize that it is problematic to presume that "traditional African American [or Black in general] culture has had to be grafted onto the cultural practices of the European/American society to form an original cultural expression" (Sellers et al., 1998:18). This old problem of whether cultural practices can survive across generations or whether it is possible to completely erase them (e.g., *Melville Herskovits v. E. Franklin Frazier*), is irresolvable and misleading. Black people in the Americas have developed recognizable cultural formations deeply influenced by their African heritage and connections, but they have also incorporated beliefs and practices from Europeans, Native Americans, Indians (of the subcontinent), and other cultural formations. Some theories of Black identity incorrectly suggest a "tendency" of Black (or African) people toward collective identification (e.g., Allen, 2004). This attributes too much determinative power to Blackness and distracts our attention away from the real cultural production of collective identification. Nonetheless, it is reasonable to center the experience—historical and current—of Black people of the West in theories of Black selfhood and collectivities. More than three centuries of similar trials and tribulations experienced by Blacks in different settings constitute an enduring well of imaginaries, memories, and cultural resources from which to draw and develop understandings of commonality and difference. Sister Amme, a slender ebony-skinned woman who rarely smiled, was perhaps the "youngest" of my Rastafari narrators. She began her Rastafari identity odyssey in 1966 after Emperor Selassie I visited Jamaica. She says she did not put on her "covenant" (dreadlocks) until 1977. She related how her transformation to Rastafari involved her growing awareness of Blackness in the context of world history: "I went to the Institute [of Jamaica] regular, for several months . . . I read all about pan-Africanism and slavery and Black Nationalism. . . . I see Black people everywhere get a beating [suppressed]. . . . I realize I am a part of this too." Her testimony speaks to one of the products of the racialization process itself: enduring sources of achieved and imposed identities.

Black Identity Analyses: From Pathology to Positivity

The earliest empirical studies of Black identity date to the mid-1930s, carried out in the United States. Children were frequently the source of data for this early research into racial attitudes. Conclusions drawn from analysis of children were extended to Black adults, and findings based on racial attitudes were discussed as if personality had been studied (Cross Jr., 1991:10). By the 1940s, a view of Blackness as a stigma had taken hold, promoted by intellectual luminaries such as Kenneth and Mamie Clark, Kurt Lewin, Gordon Allport, Gunnar Myrdal, Abram Kardiner, and E. Franklin Frazier. The idea that Black identity was stigmatized and tarnished by self-loathing was informed by a psychological perspective that myopically assumed that a positive self-concept required a positively valued reference group, which, ergo, Black people could not have been because of their inferior status, the deracination of slavery, and their unachievable desire for Whiteness. The Black self-hatred thesis remained dominant for three decades, overshadowing works that favorably or positively interpreted Blackness, such as those of W.E.B. Du Bois, J. A. Rogers, Marcus (and Amy Jacques) Garvey, Carter G. Woodson, St. Clair Drake, and Zora Hurston. Indeed, the liberal Gunnar Myrdal saw the effort to positively portray Black life, culture, and history as a futile effort because he believed the energies of Black people would be better directed to assimilation rather than to displays of distinctive achievement (Cross Jr., 1991:30; Baker, 1998:181).

During the 1960s, studies of Black identity began to engage with changes in Black personal and collective conceptions. In retrospect, the era of the Civil Rights movements was a watershed in American history, where not only discriminatory policies were overturned, but also Black consciousness and identity shifted among Black people of all kinds. Indeed, the social-movement dimensions of racial identity emerged as an important concern in the early study of Black identity. Theorists of Black identity like William Cross Jr. and Bailey Jackson III recognized that the Black social movements in America and the growing positive views of Blackness were related. The movements raised issues that encouraged Black people to question their own indifference or naiveté toward political issues, acts of injustice, oppressors, and oppressive systems. Indeed, Cross Jr. has argued that Black social movements provide context and stimulus for individual Black identity transformations (e.g., 1991). You did not have to listen to Macolm X, Elijah Muhammed, or Stokely Carmichael to recognize conditions were changing. James Brown, for example, released "Say it Loud ('I'm Black and I'm Proud')" in 1969. Around the same time in Jamaica, Prince Buster released "Pharaoh House Crash," Pharaoh being a vernacular name Rastafari gave Jamaica's Black Prime Minister Hugh Shearer to identify him as a part of an oppressive system (Waters, 1989:97). The 1968 Rodney Riot in Jamaica was additional proof that Black consciousness had moved to the front stage in Jamaica.

By the 1980s, theorists of Black identity were wrestling with incorporating the heterogeneity of Blackness and its many quotidian functions into their explanations (e.g., Tatum, 1997; Sellers et al., 1998; Parham, 1989; Cross Jr., & Phagen-Smith, 2001; Jackson III, 2001; Cross Jr., Smith, & Payne, 2002). Contemporary models of Black identity with their focus on Blackness, its salience, centrality, regard, buffering, and ideology, or some combination of these, take a long view of Black identity development, recognizing that key socialization experiences occur during childhood and adolescence (e.g., Parham, 1989; Tatum, 1997; Cross Jr., & Phagen-Smith, 1999; Jackson III, 2001). These frameworks help us appraise where Blackness sits in relation to other identifications, how individuals perceive Blackness, how they think others perceive it, and what they accept as appropriate acts of Blackness, e.g., how a Black person ought to act. Sellers and his coauthors (1998) promote the collection and use of self-evaluations of Black identity as a key source of data but, at the same time, urge researchers not to neglect the capacity of institutions and people to ascribe categorical identifications. Their approach to Black identity stresses meaning, which they see as preferable to an emphasis on stages (Sellers et al., 1998:23–24).[2]

Most contemporary Black identity theories treat Blackness as a nominal identity but do not assume that everyone accepts or recognizes the imposition or ascription of Blackness. Nor do those theories characterize those who do not accept Blackness as pathological. Thus, Blackness is understood as highly varied, supple, and more or less salient in a given person. Empirically and personally, Blackness as a highly significant and positive identification is something to be discovered and revealed. This makes it all the more important that our understanding of Black identity draws on experience-near data such as life narratives.

Identity Transformation and Becoming Black

Cross Jr.'s nigrescence model is a distinctive formulation of Black identity theory. There is some consensus in Black identity theory that a positive Black identity provides individual defense mechanisms for anticipating and responding to racism by focusing blame on a system or institutions (e.g., Tatum, 1997; Cross Jr., 1995; Helms, 1995; Adams, 2001; Jackson III, 2001). Cross sees the nigrescence model as applicable to Black identity

(Cross Jr., 1995:95) across history, culture, and other social positions—an important claim which we will interrogate. He argues that nigrescence can explain identity-related transformations from that of Nat Turner, the Virginia slave who led a major slave revolt, to those of the Black intellectuals W.E.B. Du Bois and Malcolm X (Cross Jr., Parham, & Helms, 1991; Cross Jr., 1995:95). All developed a strong racial consciousness as a result of particular experiences. Nat Turner changed from a humble slave into a racially conscious and rebellious one; W.E.B. Du Bois' pre-Fisk University outlook did not entail a strong racial consciousness; and Malcolm X's transformation involved moving from disinterest in Black history and culture to becoming one of the leading promoters of it. Marcus Garvey offers another example illustrative of what nigrescence theory attempts to explain. When Garvey's travels led him to notice the common plight of Black people of the West, he became discontented with his stance, leading to a change in his outlook and mission:

> I saw the injustice done to my race because it was black, and I became dissatisfied on that account. I went traveling to South and Central America and parts of the West Indies to find out if it was so elsewhere, and I found the same situation. I set sail to Europe to find out if it was different there, and again I found the same stumbling block–"You are black." I read "Up From Slavery," by Booker T. Washington, and then my doom—if I may so call it—of being a race leader dawned upon me in London. . . . I asked, "Where is the black man's government? Where is his King and his kingdom?" . . . I could not find them, and then I declared, "I will help to make them."[3]

Black identity, in nigrescence theory, investigates the self-concept from the vantage points of personal identity and reference group orientation (see Cross Jr., 1991:39–42). Personal identity describes behavior involving how we interact with each other and how we assess ourselves and others. Personal identity, generally speaking, involves what it means to be a person and unique being. The other key aspect of a person's self-concept in the nigrescence formulation is the reference group orientation. The reference group orientation (RGO) focuses on the specifics of experience that relate to values, culture, group identification, symbols, and so on. It represents the interaction between the social world and one's personal identity and can reveal the whys and hows of meaning that are attributed to understanding, preferences, and worldview. In this way, RGO is a particular

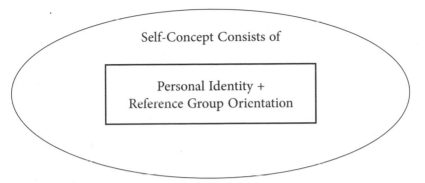

Diagram of the Self Concept. Source: Adapted from Cross Jr., 1991.

portal for situating the specifics of culture, class, race, gender, ethnicity, ideology, and worldview, offering us the "ethnographic dimension of the self-concept" (Cross Jr., 1991:45). Indeed, as far as Blackness is concerned, we are dealing with worldview, ideology, history, and cultural and political propensities more than with psychology per se (Cross Jr., 1991:187). Nonetheless, I am not advancing any grand claims about identity based on the nigrescence model. Cross-cultural studies of identity in displaying the variability of conceptions of "the person" challenge rigid conceptions of what (or even whether) personal behaviors or traits are universal. Nigrescence theory, however, offers an exciting strategy for explaining Black identity.

Nigrescence locates identity transformation primarily in the realm of RGO, not personal identity. Personality characteristics such as shyness or extroversion do not change much, if at all, because of a shift in emphasis on Black identity (e.g., Cross Jr., 1991; c.f. Glazier, 2006). Intuitively, it seems that self-esteem would be enhanced as a result of the move toward positive affirmations of Blackness. Research, however, including work done for this book, suggests self-esteem does not have to change because of nigrescence. A person does not become more "unified" or "whole" because of the nigrescence experience, although values such as Black pride may become salient.

The nigrescence model represents Black identity transformation in terms of five "stages" (Cross Jr., 1995): pre-encounter; encounter; immersion-emersion; internalization; and internalization-commitment. I describe recognizable states in Black identity transformation as "processes" (rather than stages) in order to underscore the tension between change and stability, to suggest the experience of multiple states simultaneously, and to deflect equation of "stage" with static-ness or a progressive teleology of development.[4] There are recognizable patterns, orientations, and moments that manifest during Black identity transformation, and to identify them is neither reductionist nor insensitive to nuance. There are no neat or once-and-for-all transitions between states of identity transformation. A person can "spiral" back and forth between states as new identity-related challenges or crises arise[5] (e.g., Cross Jr., 1995:95; Parham, 1989; Rambo, 1993:16). Said differently, people and their identities are always in a state of becoming, always contingent on something else (Hall, 1996; Holland, Lachicotte, Skinner, & Cain, 1998). What can be deceiving, though, is that any particular "becoming" may look almost exactly like what has been common for a long time; the idea of identity as open-ended does not necessarily mean that people are authoring totally novel selves.

The *pre-encounter* state is a person's pre-transformation identity, the identity and awareness that will be redefined. The *encounter* focuses on the revealing experience or experiences that make someone feel unsettled and in need of change. The transition from a person's pre-encounter identity to a reconfigured and emerging one is called *immersion-emersion* and signals the beginning of active identity transformation work. The social process through which a person seeks to forge the new identity and integrate it into his or her self-concept and social networks is called *internalization*. The state where a person feels comfortable with his or her new identity is deemed *internalization-commitment*. Cross's definition of commitment stipulates that a person must also be comfortable reaching beyond or outside of "Black only" concerns. This stipulation can be taken as a critique, intended or not by Cross, of rigid and delimited Black identifications that demand Black-only loyalties, which is different from Black-first loyalties which permit bridging across racial and ethnic difference. The gist of the idea is whether one is first and foremost pro-Black rather than anti-White.

The pre-encounter Black identity is defined in terms of three general attitudes or orientations: low salience of race; social stigma; and anti-Black. Low salience describes people who do not accentuate their Blackness, but neither do they deny some relation to it. Indifference to Blackness is another way to portray this orientation. Such people's sense of self, well-being, and purpose in life are not tied to Blackness but other things, such as career, religion, political affiliation, lifestyle, or status. As long as these other identifications are meaningful, attraction to Afrocentricity is unlikely (Cross Jr., 1995:98). A second pre-encounter orientation is that of Blackness as a stigma or problem. For these people Blackness is defined as a burden. Such people may be defensive about Blackness, reacting to its stigmatizing dimensions and the possibility that these will negatively bear upon their aspirations and life chances. Thus, there is an acknowledgment of Blackness, and perhaps some appreciation of its significance, but no abiding concern with learning about Black history or culture, or becoming politically involved in issues related to Blackness. The burden, and not Black history or culture, is the focus. Note that stigma is not managed in the way I suggest that Rastafari handle the challenge. For other pre-encounter people, Blackness can function as a negative referent. It captures everything they find problematic with Black people. This orientation is called anti-Black. If there is a line between the rhetoric of the anti-Black Black and White racism, it is a very thin one. The anti-Black-Black is likely to be estranged from Black people who do not share his or her view and is likely to evaluate positively Whiteness and Eurocentrism.

The pre-encounter Black identity is that sense of self that has evolved through childhood socialization and is grounded in a person's understanding and experience related to kin, education, communities, and prior social interaction. It is during the socialization and education attendant to the formation of the "pre-encounter" Black identity that people inadequately come to terms with the implications of deracination, miseducation, and racialized oppression for themselves and their reference group. Deracination stresses the implications of uprooting, extirpation, and cultural alienation for identity (e.g., the issues that Fanon and Césaire raised). Enslavement, life as chattel, Black codes, Jim Crow laws, denial of formal education, the promotion of Eurocentric perspectives, and persistent poverty are only a few of the obvious ways in which deracination has shaped the contours of Blackness in the Americas. Miseducation feeds deracination because African descendants may go through life without an awareness of how deracination relates to them, of how much of their understanding is informed by stereotypes and half-truths about Black people, or how an appreciation of Black culture and history might change how they relate to the world. Coming to terms with such realities might be comparable to the shock of inadvertently finding out that one is an adopted child or that a parent has committed a heinous crime. As long as one does not know, the game continues to be played as usual. But when what was once "hidden" comes to light, or when the "half that has never been told" is revealed, a person's understandings may turn topsy-turvy, prompting anger and questioning: Many of my narrators made precisely this point. Bongo J, for example, became visibly enraged when he talked about information and education hidden from him:

> Them hide those things, man [positive achievements by Black people] and preach colonialism system at all times . . . the White man want to be hanged by his tongue. . . . talk[ing] a wrong doctrine [Eurocentrism]. We [Black people] are wrong doctrinized. And [it] is Rastaman [that] know about it and give him [Black people] back a concept of reality. And them still don't want accept us. You na see?

The encounter describes a compelling racialized experience. Something happens that makes a person enter into engagement with Blackness as a social category and lived experience. As an analytic category, such an encounter points to the emotion and shock that may result from a jarring experience (or experiences) and lead to repercussions for a person's self-concept. It can be a personal perturbation. For example, W.E.B. Du Bois, on reflection, attributed a hurtful slight by a White female acquaintance as one of his earliest recognitions of his racial different-ness:

> I remember well when the shadow [of race] swept across me. . . . In a wee wooden schoolhouse, something put it into the boys' and girls' heads to buy gorgeous visiting-cards. The exchange was merry, till one girl, a tall [White] newcomer, refused my card—refused it peremptorily. . . . Then it dawned on me with a certain suddenness that I was different from the others. . . . shut out from their world with a vast veil. I had no desire thereafter to tear down that veil. . . . I held all beyond it in common contempt. (1969:44)

Black people commonly experience such jarring racialized encounters, as Du Bois discovered. The encounter, though, does not always have to be a painful experience. For instance, through a book, story, dreams, or reflection on accumulated experience, a person might learn something that leads to deep thinking about Black identity, history, and culture: "[As a teenager growing up during the early 1950s] I always watched how the Rasta people greeted each other, and how they talked to each other. 'Peace and love' was how they talked. But people mistreat and brutalize them. Those Rasta make me think different, want to be among them" (Brother Barody).

The water-in-the-face encounter experience has to be personalized; it has to be taken to heart in order for the substantial effort of the reworking of one's self-concept to occur. An encounter, even if it is not negative, can arouse anxiety, confusion, and anger. It is a very powerful experience to realize that "one's frame of reference," worldview, or value system is "incorrect," "dysfunctional," or more to the point, "not Black or Afrocentric enough" (Cross Jr., 1995:105). Cross provides little empirical detail on the encounter experience in his writings, but I found many accounts of them in my interviews. The key point is that the encounter must provide the disruption that leads to dislodging the old primary identity and makes the person "receptive" to identity transformation (Cross Jr., 1991:159; 1995:105). Otherwise, the experience is simply one of many upsetting or instructive racial moments.

Deviating from the nigrescence model, I contend that personalization of the encounter is likely not only to signal the beginning of the cultural and identity work that Black identity transformation requires, but also the work of internalization. The experience is one that is revisited many times.[6] It becomes a part of internalization, though it reflects a moment in time past. For identity transformation to begin in earnest, a person must learn about the new identity that he or she is moving toward and must be able to denigrate or even deny the identification that they are moving away from. This transition bristles with challenge and anxiety because it requires that a person inhabit a space of liminality. Not only may they have much to learn about the new identity and referents; they may not know where to turn for "proper" learning and thus must tussle with trying to subdue or erase the old primary identity without having yet established the new one. For the person's friends, family, and others, perhaps the perspective is different. She or he may still be seen by them as the "old" person but losing their grip on "reality" or "brainwashed" by malcontents.

Anger, bravado, romanticism, militancy, and zealousness are some of the first tools commonly used to tackle miseducation, deracination, and internalized Eurocentrism. Alone, these emotions will prove completely inadequate to the identity tasks at hand, but they serve to "keep up" or stoke a person's interest. During this period of searching, people commonly cast blame on a "system" of oppression, other races, and even one's own race. They might become militantly aggressive, although typically the bluster is rhetorical: talk against "Pope Paul," "Pirates," "Whitey," or "Uncle Tom" represent efforts to specify systems of oppression and relate them to particular people and behaviors. The bluster also helps to disguise a person's thin grasp of the new identity and parry the blows of critics. Ras Burrell moved toward identity transformation because of his existential questioning about the identity of God. However, during this transition his family and friends ridiculed his new beliefs. He found comfort in defending his beliefs despite having much to learn. He felt a greater zeal when in the company of other emergent Rastafari, and sometimes they put on theatrical performances to communicate what they were feeling and learning: "I show them [anyone] too man. . . . His Majesty is the true man, the true God. You know it is like I get in a spirit [fervor] anywhere I go three or four of us [Rastafari] and we smoking we herb, it's just preaching and lecturing [we do]."

Nigrescence theory defines this post-encounter process of identity transformation in terms of immersion and emersion. This is a monumental task, and it should be recognized as such. A person must resocialize himself, and this resocialization calls for immersion in situations that allow for learning about the new identity and referents. It is important for a person in the process of Black identity transformation to seek out and observe those people and groups who represent what he or she imagines becoming. This is a pathway to learning cultural practices, fathoming the knowledge surrounding the symbols, obligations, and rewards attendant to the new identity. This quest, if you will, for information and referents is important because the experience also provides the tools for sustaining an identity (building community, ongoing learning and interaction). At some point, the person "emerges" from the shadows of the old primary identity and ideally dispenses with or has renegotiated the sociocultural and psychological baggage connected to it.

Identity transformation is complicated. As we shall see, separation from the old self may come with costs, leading people to weigh the issues of loss and gain. Such thorny predicaments make the transformation less than smooth sailing, and dramatize the gravity and risk involved in the effort. Thus, during immersion, a person begins to busy himself with the cultural and identity work needed to reconstitute the social relationships and to rework the boundaries and content of their RGO. They may continually revisit the encounter because doing so reminds them why they must change their identity. Even though the person has much to learn, internalization processes are coterminous with the actions involved in immersion and emersion.

Another complication of the ideal depiction is that following an encounter, even a personalized one, a person may not continue to engage with the identity into which he or she has begun to invest. Psychologists, counselors, and educators, for example, name fixation, unhealthy identity development, and regression as examples of undesirable outcomes of Black identity transformation. These terms connote premature arrest, stunted-ness, illness, and deviance. Nigrescence postulates that some people never move past a fixation of Whites or Blacks as inherently "evil," or "corrupt," a sign of stalled identity development in a trajectory where the "right" path leads to comfort with and pride in Blackness co-occurring with be-ing at ease in interactions with other races and ethnicities. In this particu-lar account of nigrescence, those who are poor and suffering are deemed the most likely to fixate because of their inability to escape oppressive situations or to have access to people with "progressive attitudes" (Cross Jr., 1995:112). This speculation exemplifies another shortcoming of nigres-cence theory: a lack of an empirical cross-cultural and cross-class ground-ing, a point to which we will return. In fairness to Cross, his formulation of nigrescence refers in particular to inflexible Black nationalists whose concern for others does not extend beyond Blackness or anti-Whiteness. Cross (1991) sees bridging across difference as enhancing a person's open-ness to new ideas and technologies, while bigoted and provincial perspec-tives are less responsive to change or social concord. Nonetheless, the life stories which inform this book bring into question such assertions be-cause most of my narrators were poor (some exceedingly poor). Based on my observations, however, all were "progressive," if being so is defined by being able to bridge racial difference.

A person's emergent identity must be internalized, and the principle of immersion and emersion points to the sociocultural and psychologi-cal identity work a person must carry out in order to fashion and sustain the new identity. These efforts are concurrently personal and social. The identity must be internally and externally carried, enacted, and continu-ally revised in order to become a routine part of who one says one is. And, this cannot be done without the involvement of other people, who are important to affirming and challenging this reformulation process.

At first glance, the nigrescence formulation of internalization ap-pears to consist mainly of cognitive operations, and even on this score it is vague about what the internalization process entails. I suggest that internalization involves explicit cultural and identity work. Internalization may begin during the process of personalizing the encounter and during what the revised model describes as immersion and emersion processes, rather than afterward or toward the end of it. The emotion roused by the encounter may actually catalyze internalization because emotion is associated with sustaining memories. This possibility of overlapping processes is one reason for my disavowal of the stage formulation. Immersion implies internalization. My Rastafari interlocutors, for example, were internally assimilating the new information and relationships in which they were immersing themselves. They were learning as they explored, and even mistakes and gaffes that exposed their naiveté provided (possibly painful) learning opportunities. "You see," said Ras Brenton, "As a young [fledgling] Ras, I listen to the elder ones' reason. I never really interrupt them. Because if you do not know what you are talking they will embarrass you, show you that you do not know what you are talking of. So, I just hear them out, take outta it what I want take outta it." In line with established nigrescence theory, however, internalization describes that process where the person is working toward becoming comfortable with the new identity, relationships, and RGO.

The processes of internalization-commitment signal the capacity for individuals to focus on other concerns beyond Black identity. The equivalent of maturation in nigrescence theory involves processes of internalization and commitment. What these processes draw our attention to is how and when a person is comfortable with his revised or new orientation toward Blackness and is able to nurture and nourish this state of awareness. The identity formation game, however, is never done. Nigrescence theory does not ossify commitment but acknowledges a person must maintain this identity over the life course and will likely have experiences that raise anew a person's commitment to the new identity. People may thus "recycle"[7] through identity transformation processes, in particular those associated with immersion (Parham, 1989; Cross Jr., Smith, & Payne, 2002), which some Rastafari, in their own terms, seem to recognize as well: "You don't accept His Majesty one time. It is a gradual process. Of [evolving] understanding" (Ras Chronicle).

Nigrescence theory and Cross's formulation, despite their contributions, remain in need of extension. Three important and interrelated concerns are relevant here. First, nigrescence theory is based primarily on the experience of African (or Black) Americans, and its empirical basis is that of college-going and college-educated Blacks, even though the origin of the theory can be traced to an interest in what was happening in particular Black communities and social movements. Cross (1995) is probably correct in arguing that the nigrescence model can explain the identity transformations of Nat Turner, W.E.B. Du Bois, and Marcus Garvey, as well as C.L.R. James and Stokely Carmichael. Nonetheless, we need more cases showing the explanatory capacity of the nigrescence model in places outside of the United States, especially in situations where Black people are the majority. We must be attentive to how race relations develop in a given location. For example, does it matter much that slavery was abolished three decades earlier in Jamaica than in the United States? Equally important, we need to know more about Black identity transformation among those whose access to privilege, technologies, travel, and wealth are limited or severely curtailed, both within the United States and beyond.

Second, silent in the nigrescence model are the sociocultural specifics of identity transformation—how do people, for instance, maintain their new identities, processes nigrescence theory describes as internalization and commitment? This silence may be a function of disciplinary divisions of labor in which field research, ethnographic approaches, or biographical strategies such as the life story interview—cogent techniques for getting at identity—are treated as the province of anthropologists, sociologists, or oral historians. Cross, for example, dropped participant observation and field studies from his review of 41 years worth of academic writing on Black identity (1991:48). He reasoned that these studies contributed very little to documenting either self-hatred or the rise in positive salience placed on Black identity (1991:48). Field-based biographical approaches offer a means for situating the sociocultural and personal dimensions of identity transformation, in addition to other means such as surveying.

Third, attention needs to be given to how Black identity transformation process states coexist. Personalization of the encounter, for example, might signal the beginning of internalization, and internalization might be reconsidered in terms of intensity and intentionality of effort. Parham (1989) and Helms (1995) have raised similar questions, questions that are well-suited to a biographical and field-based approach to Black identity transformation.

Religion and Identity Transformation

Theories of religious conversion offer insight and strategies useful to theorizing Black identity transformation. Blackness and religion in the Americas have entangled and politicized histories, the latter providing hope, inspiration, resiliency, recovery, and even strategy, for the former.[8] Think of our Black insurgents like Sharpe, Bogle, and Bedward, who embedded together race, religion, and political action. As Lincoln has observed, "Religion is not race, but is often made to function as if it were" (1993:219). The emergent Rastafari were not only engaged in racial identity transformation; they were simultaneously experiencing religious conversion. The experience of Rastafari suggests that the similarities between racial and religious identity transformation are many. Cross recognized this early in his thinking about nigrescence, taking inspiration from conversion models such as Anthony Wallace's (1957) theory of revitalization movements. Many of my Rastafari interlocutors began their identity journeys during an activist cycle of the evolution of Rastafari. Thus, racial identity transformation, religious conversion, and social movement formation—and the cultural production involved in these—are all crucial aspects of the ethnogenesis of Rastafari.

Religious conversion is a type of identity transformation, although it is rarely explained as such. Conversion experience is likely to be explained in terms of an epiphany (which operates like the nigrescence encounter by generating a quest for religious information and community), a search for answers to "big" or existential questions, divine or paranormal intervention, the influence of an actor's social network, or some combination of these. As with nigrescence, there are recognizable patterns of religious identity transformation, and people sometimes cycle between them.

Religious conviction, like identity itself, can operate as a fundamental social anchor, positioning and locating people in relation to each other and the world around them. People use religion to alleviate doubt and uncertainty, and it influences social action. It provides affiliation, community, and values; it helps people interpret their experiences, problems, and successes; and it furnishes a framework for understanding the world. It provides ready answers to existential questions: "Why are we here?" "Why is there injustice?" It provides means of coping that may augment or supplant other alternatives. Like nigrescence, religious conversion involves problem-solving and resocialization, a gradual process that is never really finished (e.g., Rambo, 2003:217–218).

Conceptualizing Conversion

Kilbourne and Richardson (1988) have categorized analyses and studies of conversion into old and new paradigms. The old paradigm constructed people as passive agents and emphasized impersonal but potent forces working within or upon a person through their inherent needs, facilitating conversion. The new paradigm emphasizes people's agency, volition, and search for meaning and community. Research into conversion began at the end of the nineteenth century. From the first studies through the 1950s, there was a tendency to emphasize the mystical and dramatic aspects of conversion (Gillespie, 1979), although a few interpreted conversion in terms of problem-solving and change in attitudes and self-concept (e.g., James, 1929; Coe, 1917; Boisin, 1936; Allport, 1950:13–20; Sorokin, 1954). By the 1960s, perspectives emerged that incorporated issues of socialization, decision-making, experience, meaning, and culture (e.g., Lofland & Stark, 1965; Heirich, 1977).

Analyses of conversion, like those of nigrescence, have over the past three decades given more attention to socialization, learning, and identity. Robbins (1988), for example, explicitly argued that conversion is a type of socialization. Snow and Machalek (1984) contended that conversion entailed change in identity, "one's universe of discourse," membership, worldview, and values, while Meredith McGuire raised the issue of meaning in conversion by asking us to interpret conversion as a "transformation of one's *self* concurrent with a transformation in one's basic *meaning system*" (1992:71, original italics). Rambo concurs that important aspects of conversion involve change in expectations, norms, values, and social relationships that require learning a new language and how to use that language (1993:120–122). Indeed, the focus on the social dimension of conversion is echoed by Cross: "With this change in salience [of Blackness] comes membership in new organizations, changes in one's social network, changes in one's manner of dress and personal appearance, changes in one's self-referents, changes in what one reads or views on television . . . that's why the person feels totally new" (1993:70). Other scholars, anthropologists in particular, emphasized the social and temporal aspects of conversion, how these interacted with disparities of power between different groups, and how people integrate new beliefs with their own (e.g., Horton, 1971, 1975; Fisher, 1973, 1985; Horton & Peel, 1976; Harding, 1987; Hefner, 1993; Austin-Broos, 2003). Another anthropological line of approach involves examining how people work on combining the narratives of particular religions and religious proselytizers with their own life stories, in effect personalizing the religious story (Stromberg, 1985; Harding, 1987).

Identity-Relevant Religious Conversion Themes

From these wide-ranging explanations I want to extend our analysis of Black identity transformation by incorporating "seekership," crises, sociocultural context, relationships, and the potency of religious ideas.

Tropes of journeying and searching are frequently evident in religious conversion discourse, and aptly so. Saul of Tarsus' conversion is widely told and occurred while he was traveling to Damascus to stamp out the Christians (Acts 22). Struck blind by an awesomely brilliant light, he heard the voice of Christ speaking to him, which led him to convert to Christianity, change his name to Paul, and become a disciple of Christ and one of the foundational authors of the New Testament. While Saul was literally on a journey, some people may set upon a quest for understanding religiosity, race, or other identity-related concerns, and may come to involve themselves in identity transformation. Those seeking community or searching within a religious (or racial) framework for satisfactory explanations of fundamental questions about life, truth, righteousness, and justice can be called seekers. Yet, a person might not recognize that he or she is "seeking" until he or she reflects upon or is asked to tell his or her experience. Ras Burrell epitomizes this for my Rastafari narrators:

> [As a teenager] I see big people and I say to them, like my uncle . . .
> "what happen? What happen to the man God? How is he not among us?
> How we cannot see him?" And my people tell me that he live up in the
> sky. . . . so, I turn to answer them. . . . "How he live up in the sky and
> leave us down here? I would like to see him. I would like to know him. I
> would like to talk with him" . . . anyway, I don't know the true God [as a
> teenager] and [then] I start to use the Bible now. And I am studying the
> bible, studying the bible, studying the bible, 'til one of the day that I buck
> [came] upon a Psalm showing I, that, a man shall come in the world,
> crown King of Kings, Lord of Lords, Conquering Lion of Tribe of Judah,
> Elect of Himself, and Light of this World. So, when I buck upon that part
> in the Bible, I close up the Bible and look inna [the] world [around me].
> For I hear the youth there talk about this man say he is the King of Kings.
> So, then I look inna myself, and look on His Majesty. His Majesty is the
> King of Kings. He is the true one . . . from that day 'til now I don't leave
> him . . . I start to serve him. . . . I know now, as a Knotty Dread.

Seekers engage in activities that support identity transformation; they investigate different faiths, study texts, and talk with people whom they believe to have useful information. Nigrescence theory explicitly points us to the importance of immersion and internalization for Black identity transformation, but it does not make clear that a person can be a seeker prior to or concurrent with an encounter experience. In such a case, the encounter becomes entangled in things already in motion. The seeker has not yet consistently begun the work of identity transformation, but is open to changing his or her self-concept. Snow and Machalek suggest that some people's personalities or proclivities are such that they are seekers-at-heart, deeply interested in "self-transformation" (1984:180). Another value of the idea of seekership involves the role that big and existential questions can play in a person's identity transformation. Many of my Rastafari interlocutors were enthralled by inquiries about God, race, and justice, and the ideology of Rastafari answers to these questions.

TURNING POINTS

A turning point is a transition in one's roles or life that generates gnawing anxiety, insecurity, self-searching, or tension. Given religion's utility in problem-solving, it is unsurprising that some people seek it out during times of anxiety or stress. The idea of a turning point does not encapsulate the same processes as the racialized encounter, but both concepts point us toward emotionally laden experiences that unsettle a person's worldview, self-concept, or social relationships. For example, in the Americas, misfortune is well-known for leading people to try to change themselves. Even though Ras Burrell was already in the process of identity transformation, fateful things happened to him that made his transformation more urgent and relevant:

> "I went to prison," said Ras Burrell. "At that time I already had the concept of His Imperial Majesty, but though my heart good man take advantage of me. I had to defend myself. I charge[d] with 'aggressive wounding.' I never wanted to be a bad man. . . . In prison His Majesty come visit I inna the cell . . . he stand there but don't say anything. . . . I want to weep, but I cannot because I am in prison. Man cannot weep in prison. I know that I have to redeem myself."

Powerful emotions attached to particular experiences make it easier to internalize those experiences (Strauss & Quinn, 1997). Indeed, the encounter that is personalized is itself a turning point, a change in beliefs and behavior as a result of particular experiences, and the narratives of our Rastafari interlocutors encourage this interpretation. People who are satisfied with their situation and identity-related frameworks (even if blissful ignorance is the case) are unlikely to engage in identity transformation. Everyone experiences tensions—including persistently nagging ones—and there are many possible solutions to tensions and crises. Religious and nigrescent identity transformations are only two options.

SOCIOCULTURAL CONTEXT

The more we know about a person, the places they circulate through, the interactions in which they engage, and from whence they draw their cultural resources, the more thoroughly we may speak to identity transformation. Situating identity transformation within a historical, cultural, and socioeconomic context can bring into focus the acts of practice and interaction that relate to personal or interior experience. Glazier (2006), for example, who has studied conversions of Spiritualist Baptists and Rastafari in Trinidad, calls for such an approach (like what this book offers). Combinations of self-reports (such as biographical interviews), participant observation, and other ethnographic and methodological strategies offer a range of means to get at the interior and social dimensions of identity transformation. We may show in detail, for example, how and why coming into contact with a charismatic person [or persons] precipitates a turning point (or encounter). For example, I could better situate Bongo J's identity transformation because of some details he offered about his childhood. Bongo J was on his way into "town" (he lived in the country and rarely got to visit Kingston), when a relative suddenly made him turn around and return home. Bongo J badly wanted to make the trip, and his feelings were hurt by the abrupt change in the plan. He had to walk back home. Dejected, he dawdled his way back, in no rush to reach his less-than-happy home. While walking he came upon a gathering of people. He said:

> Me see some people them [they were Garveyites] . . . so me stand up out-side at the railing [of a fence] looking in on them, saw some nice old lady and old man, black, green, red, the flag right there . . . not red, gold, and green as Rasta flag. . . . when everything work out, Jah send some people come love me [the Garveyites spied Bongo J peering at them across the fence], [they said] "little boy, oh, what a nice little boy" . . . they take me in and they give me money too, and they give me food, but they don't give me no strong drink. Good. This was 1938.

Both of Bongo J's parents were dead and he was living with relatives. He came regularly to visit the Garveyites that he had watched through the fence. This experience did not lead to any immediate change in Bongo J's understanding, but later in life it provided the context for framing Blackness and his identity transformation. Those Garveyites became a baseline for his evaluation of Blackness. Without such sociocultural details, we might miss an important part of Bongo J's identity transformation.

Friends and kin can influence a person's conversion. Therefore, we must pay attention to the social relationships in which a person is involved. Willfully or unwittingly, friends and kin can introduce the potential convert to ideas and feelings he or she might not have considered without their influence. They provide the potential convert with a glimpse into the norms, values, and beliefs of a different way of being and relating. By virtue of being familiar to the potential convert, they potentially legitimate the new way and in some cases can provide a convenient path into the social network affiliated with the "new" beliefs. Nevertheless, friends and kin can also create problems for an emergent convert, especially if it is a transformation they do not approve of. Intimates may view the convert's transition from the familiar to the unfamiliar as indicative of their having been manipulated, fooled, or brainwashed into accepting new beliefs.

POTENT CULTURAL IDEAS

The major world religions and their derivations consist of central ideas about suffering, redemption, catastrophe, and evil. These ideas facilitate sensitivity to injustice, inhumanity, and culturally constructed ideas of malevolence. As such, they provide master frames that come with assumptions and values, perhaps submerged, that people employ in their narratives. The themes of these ideas may be dramatic and vivid: good versus evil; the last shall be first; renunciation of materiality; the frailty of the human body. These potent ideas may be integral to religious-oriented identity transformation, but should not be overlooked in regard to racial identity transformation. Tropes of redemption, "wickedness," and justice permeate the race and religious talk, justice motifs, and identity of the Rastafari. One lesson here is to be sensitive to the influence and role of racial and religious master frames in identity transformation.

Potent cultural ideas circulate through texts and stories, and either or both may be implicated in identity transformation. Brother Bongo's interest in Blackness, for instance, was greatly influenced by a copy of the paper *Voices of Ethiopia* that he came across during the early 1950s.[9] Literature and stories involving potent ideas and familiar cultural resources play important roles in the process of identity transformation. They serve as mediating artifacts. Again, potent ideas, as expressed in language, symbols, and other cultural artifacts, ask us to listen to what people are saying and how it relates to what they are thinking.

Patterns of Rastafari Identity Transformation

The encounter was an experience common to all of my interlocutors. However, at least three of my narrators (Ras Sam Brown, Brother Barody, Rasta J) were raised by parents who were adherents of Marcus Garvey's UNIA. They were socialized from a young age into positive conceptions of Blackness. They did not harp on their own miseducation, but spoke instead of the miseducation of other Blacks in ways that made it their own concern. The three Rastafari of Garveyite parents were among other emergent Rastafari interested in big and existential questions about the racial identity of God, the suffering of Black people, and what they interpreted as the positive behavior of the Rastafari. These concerns were related to their encounters and subsequent pathway toward becoming Rastafari. Thus, their becoming Rastafari was not unique compared to others who became Rastafari. They all embarked on a journey of discovery, learning, and resocialization.

The encounters of my narrators manifested in several recognizable forms: culturally framed sources of information and inspiration such as dreams and visions; curiosity and concern with existential questions related to race and God; experiential witnessing—personally experiencing an act of injustice or chancing upon a Rastafari who embodied charisma; and learning new information through textual and other sources. Through the encounters we get to see how peoples' worldviews were challenged, how they reacted, and how they took the challenge(s) to heart.

Emergent Rastafari described many sources of tension that they faced as converts, especially the ties to and images of their "old" identity and a pursuit of clarity on the various norms, history, and cultural meanings associated with their new reference group. They engaged in acts of denying or destroying vestiges of the old self but did not cleanly escape tussling with the remnants of their old identity. Sister Pear told me how people still bring up the person she used to be, often in conversations drawing on memories of the past. Sister Pear, however, did not like to hear too much about that woman from the past, the woman she was, that woman who privileged Whiteness over Blackness, unless it was to indicate how much better the woman was now.

Among my Rastafari interlocutors, militancy and symbolic aggressiveness were common to identity transformation, and it was not only males who acted thusly. Rasta Ivey, for example, showed me how she could shift into militancy when faced with injustice. Sisters Ecila, Amme, and Mariam also told stories that suggest they too went through zealous phases of identity transformation, and are still capable of shifting into militant mode. However, Sister Pear's recollections of her identity path were cool, and emotion was subdued both in her stories and her countenance as she told the stories. This suggests to me that the revised nigrescence model is probably right on the score of post-conversion change as not happening at the level of personality, even though being a neophyte Rastafari provided a context for militancy. This is partially because the surrounding public "pushed" the Rastafari in ways that made symbolic aggressiveness a defense as well as an identity-confirming practice (militancy could also mask naiveté). What we can say though is that recourse to symbolic aggressiveness became more situational as the Rastafari aged and their identity matured.

Peers and relatives were important in the narratives and were involved, even if peripherally, in the identity transformations of emergent Rastafari. That Rastafari identity was stigmatized in so many ways made many peers and kin wonder if the emergent Rastafari had "lost their head." Such contention was the source of animosity and anxiety, increasing tension for my narrators during their state of liminality. We must not overlook, though, how my narrators were not making things easy for themselves. They were professing a heretical faith and critiquing systems and people responsible for deracination, miseducation, and oppression. These touchy subjects were specified: churches; educational frameworks; dysfunctional and vindictive legal systems; exploitative industries and businesses; bigoted elites. They saw Black people (suffering from "mental slavery"), Browns, and Whites as part of the problem. And while they believed Rastafari to be the solution, they understood that the long list of oppressors at times took out a revengeful wrath on the Rastafari. We shall explore some of the personal details of Rastafari identity transformation in the following two chapters.

4

Encounters

For my Rastafari narrators, identity transformation serves as a means to address oppression, miseducation, nagging existential questions, and deracination. The justice motifs that permeate the discourses of my interlocutors—righteousness, truth, Black redemption, and Black liberation—help to create a living past, animate their identity, and inform their interpretation of the world and its history. Rastafari identity can serve as a radical challenge to oppression because it demands that reform begin with oneself. The Rastafari emphasize their ability to "see" things and do things differently, which is a way that they distinctively mark themselves and evaluate their authenticity. For the Rastafari, the power to see and know "the truth," to embody the past, and to radiate righteousness are pathways to liberation, undoing internalized oppression and gainsaying injustices past and present. What leads people to contemplate such ideas and to drastically change their identity, beliefs, and practices? We shall see that their journeys into the identity, and their expression of it, are diverse though woven with commonalities. It is through personal experience, especially encounters, that we are able to trace the beginnings of identity transformations and the reasons for them. The personal formation of Rastafari identity relies upon emerging Rastafarians being aware of and engaging with cultural resources such as Ethiopianism, the moral economy of Blackness, and other repertoires of antecedent social movements and associations.

In the following, I draw on the stories of the Rastafari themselves to reveal why and how they became Rastafari, and how they utilize the justice motifs. The justice motifs function, among other ways, as ideas which provide a foundation for articulating grievances and framing alternatives. Truth, for example, can speak directly to Rastafari concerns with miseducation or deracination, and how these are wrongs. As such, the justice motifs have aroused the indignation of several generations of Rastafari, contributing to the longevity of the movement's orientation and to its wide appeal. Our Rastafari interlocutors imagine themselves to be living memorials and embodiments of injustices past. For them, injustice and the past continually intrude upon the present, and it is through their identity that they address these intrusions. My attempt to discern adherents' motivations and explanations for becoming Rastafari has been aided by situating their life stories within the streams of social history that they navigate and that we have visited in previous chapters.

Something Is Not Quite Right with the World

The idea of cultural dissonance has been used to claim that the Rastafari represent efforts to reconcile living in a predominantly Black society in which Eurocentrism flourished (Barrett, 1988). The Rastafari suggest personal dissonance in their emphasis on self-remaking, alignment of self-conceptions with action, and their critique of oppression.

Another approach concerns the idea of relative deprivation. Poverty and a sense of lacking what others have also become primary explanations for the emergence of collectivities like the Rastafari. Both dissonance and relative deprivation theories are limited accounts, however. They tell us little about what makes people consider aligning self-concepts and action in the first place, why identity is involved, and how social history and cultural infrastructure shape experience and action across generations. Ideas of cultural dissonance assume relations between identity, deprivation, and poverty which are not confirmed by the accounts of people I interviewed. Before we delve further into the personal experience of identity transformation, I must make clear that none of the Rastafari I interviewed were unhappy or dissatisfied with their prior identity. However, in reflecting on the past, some of them voiced criticisms of their old self, especially in terms of miseducation. To the extent that the Rastafari voiced dissatisfaction and dissonance, it was with the world in which they lived and not with themselves:

> I used to attend church like other youth, but my mind was not there. My mind and heart was not in these church. It kind a come to me like a drone situation. I don't see no militancy and no uplift in the church. The looks of the church from I was a boy . . . is like it is associated with death . . . I did not too fancy the church, but as a youth, I was under the control of my parents. I had to go. Sometimes, I had planned with other boys and don't bother go a church. (Ras Sam Brown)

Ras Sam Brown was never dissatisfied with whom he "was," but he had no interest in the church even though his parents were devout religionists. What my interlocutors did tend to express about their pre-Rastafari identities were feelings that they should have been "more" than they were; that they should have been more righteous, just, or better informed. "Incompleteness" better describes these accounts than "dissatisfaction." Their explanations indicate a widespread Rastafari idea of being able to discover or create a "real self" consonant with Rastafari understandings. Statements by Cashmore's Rastafari interviewees, such as "I now look at myself as a proper person," "I wasn't myself before [converting to Rastafari]," and "We didn't know ourselves . . . now we're making positive steps to find our true selves" (1979:313), are reminiscent of what I heard from informants.

The discovery or creation of a "real self" simultaneously involves cultural and identity work, as attested to by the identity transformations of the Rastafari. Cultural work includes learning new symbols, meanings, and practices, and identity work entails creating and internalizing a new identity.

Diffusion and Awareness: Sowing Seeds of Rastafari Identity

A person cannot intentionally become what he or she is unaware of; a person must have some sense of identity options, even if they are vague. Awareness of identity options is a fundamental requirement of identity transformation, but awareness does not make it more or less likely to happen. Awareness of identity options is analogous to planting a seed: it may or may not germinate, and germination does not guarantee a plant will mature or bear seed.

As we have seen, people learned of the Rastafari through news stories, and prior to the early 1960s the preponderance of stories was negative. Other early and significant sources of information diffusion were street meetings and the traveling evangelism of the first Rastafari leaders, such as Howell and Hinds during the early to mid-1930s. Others followed in their wake. Rastafari like Rasta Ivey spread the beliefs as they traveled between town and country in the central and eastern parts of the island, selling and buying goods like "ganja" (marijuana) and produce. She took time during her travels to disseminate the message to those who would listen about the beliefs of the Rastafari. She recalled that "some do not like hear it and some like hear it." Already familiar with cultural activities such as street meetings and traveling evangelism, people in different locales got a firsthand introduction to the Rastafari through these practices. They also witnessed new and potentially threatening claims, such as the controversial argument that the Messiah had returned in the form of an African King. As Rasta Ivey noted, some people were fascinated by the ideas while others rejected them. Ras Brenton occasionally traveled across the island during the 1960s, talking about Rastafari to those who would listen. Rasta Ivey and Ras Brenton were not formally recruiting but sharing and pronouncing their conviction in their travels.

The experience of reading about and listening to the Rastafari planted alternative identity seeds in the minds of many of my narrators. Brother Woks, for example, became aware of the Rastafari during his teen years because he lived in Trench Town, where Rastafari actively assembled. Although Brother Woks was not initially interested in the Rastafari, their presence, such as their ceremonies welcoming the return of prisoners to their community, made him aware of their existence and uniqueness:

> From the early days as a little boy when I lived in Trench Town . . . Rasta used to come around me. . . . It is a ghetto and a lot of Rasses were living there. . . . whenever one was coming from prison, for example, police raid and may find a man smoking weed, and him may go [to] prison, when he is coming out as a Rasta, they always give him a welcome with drumming, a kind of chanting-like. (Brother Woks)

He paid attention to the details and symbols that identified the Rastafari, because they distinctively marked themselves:

> I can say he [Rastafari] has some form of identity because as a little boy I saw them wear a pom-pom . . . woolen material . . . with the green and the red and the black border and things like that. Like a little ball. . . . Some of them carry it on the top of the tam. The pom-pom could also be worn on the shirt with the button of His Imperial Majesty.

Years later, Brother Woks summoned these memories to internalize the intricacies of Rastafari beliefs and practices as he became socialized into the identity. These few examples suggest the import of the actual presence of the Rastafari, in various ways, to the spread and growth of the group. Indeed, people unconsciously transmit their "behaviors and attitudes" when others are observing them, communicating social memory between each other in an asymmetrical fashion (Crumley, 2002:39). The corporeal presence of the Rastafari, as suggested by Rastafari narratives, sometimes played a catalytic role in inspiring identity transformation.

I-Sight: The Power of "Seeing" and Being Visionary

Motifs dealing with seeing—visually, prophetically, and perspicaciously—are central to Rastafarian identity and ideology. The Rastafari emphasize their discerning faculties, which reveal "truth" in a world where obfuscation is the norm. Mediums that aid the Rastafari's capacity for "higher" understanding include dreams, visions, reasoning, reflection, and smoking cannabis (Forsythe, 1983).

To "sight up" refers to recognizing Haile Selassie I as a divine figure (divinity is variously defined, e.g., God-in-Flesh or Christ returned).[1] "I" is a privileged term of self-reference and can connote all the qualities associated with the eye and seeing. The plural of I, "I n I," extends the metaphor to the visionary qualities of the collectivity.[2] The final syllable of Rastafari is sometimes construed as "Rasta-Far-Eye,"[3] marking the capacity of the Rastafari to "see" (i.e., to know) things invisible or unknown to non-Rastafari (Brother Bags). This self-elevation marks the Rastafari as special in their own eyes, enlightened and superior compared to the non-Rastafari, who are considered blind and ignorant. The seeing motif is expressed in terms of deconstructing false or misleading beliefs, such as portrayals of Christ as a blond-haired and blue-eyed man, or the Christian belief that God is a spirit that resides in the heavens.

Brother Yendis gives an example of how the idea of "seeing" is involved in becoming Rastafari. Searching and discovery are the subtext to Yendis's emphasis on dispelling myths, of peeling away the layers of miseducation that have taught his contemporaries to look to the sky for a spirit who on occasion visits earth:

> Rasta is a concept, Rasta is a religion, Rasta is a faith, Rasta is you. You make yourself to be a Rasta. And in order to be a Rasta, you have to seek first the Kingdom of God, and all things shall be added. So when you find out the Kingdom, if you want to go on to other things [you can] . . . I man sight up Rastafari [through] I read I Bible, and I a talk 'bout other things [with elders], and when I read certain things what Christ say and certain role what Christ rule his disciples, me start to understand that Christ was a man who walk upon earth like we. We were taught that that was a spirit, but when you start read you Bible and we see what Christ do, and Christ break bread, and walk with his disciples. . . . We [Rastafari] keep away from this concept of spirit now, and a look for action,

practical framework. We find out say, you know something? The Pope and the Jesus what them a tell you 'bout, is not real, you know?

Brother Yendis's account gives example to the various ways race, religion, and grievances inform each other as a part of Rastafari identity.

Internalized Oppression and Black Divides

The Rastafari have their own theories of race. They critique both White hegemony and its role in Black oppression, and the oppression Black people visit upon themselves and others. Academic theories of Black identity acknowledge variation in how Blackness is imagined and lived; concepts such as the "anti-Black Black," the "pre-encounter Black," and the "West Indian" and "colonial settler" Black (e.g., Cross Jr., 1995; Henry, 1982) attempt to explain the racial discourses that Black people create for and about each other. For example, the anti-Black Black loathes Blackness and is scathingly critical of Black people. The pre-encounter Black may acknowledge being Black, but Blackness holds no special significance. The West Indian Black identifies as West Indian, and even as Black, but privileges British values and avoids confronting Whites and racism. The "colonial settler" Black pursues—even prizes—assimilation into British society, and seeks interaction with Whites while avoiding Black institutions. Similar ideas inform Rastafari understandings of Blackness but constitute an axis of their differentiation from other Black Jamaicans because the Rastafari see themselves moving away from, or being the antithesis of, ambivalent and self-abusive enactments of Blackness. Among the Rastafari, there is a widespread view that slavery and colonialism culturally, intellectually, and psychologically enfeebled Black people in ways hostile to their own well-being and autonomy. In support of their conceptions, Rastafari point to Black people's reliance on cultural beliefs defined by Whites, the failings of Black people's efforts at governance (because they keep up the practices of the oppressors they replace or answer to), and an apparent inferiority complex that enables Black-on-Black oppression. Ras Brenton, for instance, emphasizes race and governance:

[O]ur people never have much management in government in the fifties. It was the Europeans who was running things. And some people a say it was better [than today]. . . . Some people say it [late 1990s] is the roughest time them ever see, but them never see those times when the English man used to rule us down here and do us all manner of things.

Ras Brenton expressed the hostile feelings that colonialism evokes for some Black people, even in postcolonial Jamaica. Even in the early twenty-first century I could still find Black people who were nostalgic for the perceived sense of security, control, and order during colonialism, compared to Jamaica's violent and disorderly environment at the time. Yet, for my narrators, remembrance of past injustices revives/animates indignation and feeds into their grievances regarding White hegemony and Black oppression.

Race figuratively and literally colored the worldview of my narrators. Black, White, and Brown, as races and colors, served as contrastive metaphors to talk about the world. British rule in Jamaica facilitated Black deracination through its emphasis on its own history for instance, providing the context for making the privileging of Blackness a radical position. That Whites oppressed Blacks colored the imagery of everyday conversation and common analogies: "Look when them throw coconut milk in black coffee, it loses its potency. The coffee no strong again, and coconut milk always rises on top to keep black coffee down. You have to keep stirring to keep it on a balance to make black coffee have any strength come through. So, be Black and be proud" (Ras Sam Brown, 1998). The ordinary act of making coffee with coconut milk is used to demonstrate how Whites oppressed Blacks—the milk rises to the top, covering and keeping the Black "down." This can be read to imply that without the force suggestive of stirring or mixing, "Black" is more powerful than "White."

We saw that by 1865 a perspective that condemned White *and* Black oppressors had developed in Jamaica. The Rastafari tapped into and reworked this complex of cultural resources. The colonial settler Blacks, West Indian, or anti-Black Blacks were viewed as lacking primary loyalty toward other Blacks and lacking the courage to condemn White society as oppressive. Such Blacks took care to chastise or even to discipline those Blacks who deviated from British-defined social and aesthetic norms. Intra-black contentions over "proper" Blackness in Jamaica were a source of conflict and a means of in-group racial boundary creation: there were those Blacks who worked against racial solidarity and those who favored it, such as the Garveyites and the Rastafari.

Rasta Ivey and other Rastafari averred that during and after colonialism Black authorities were even harsher and more vindictive than Whites toward fellow Blacks, especially if they held contrary political and religious views. Arrested in the 1940s for preaching about Rastafari in public, Rasta Ivey recalled how twice she went before a White magistrate for whom a Black court official urged harsh discipline, and in both cases the White magistrate ignored the Black man's exhortations and dismissed the case. She said:

> If police get me, a White man might charge all 10 or 20 shillings; a Black man might charge all 1000 or 1500 shillings . . . if it [is] jail, White man might hand out a 30 day, six month, or one- or two-year sentence where Black man might pass all [of a] ten-year sentence.

While ten years strikes me as exaggerated, the point is that my narrators had many examples of how Blacks sought to harshly discipline other Blacks. For one, they could show Whites that they were able to avoid surrendering to the racial camaraderie that suffused the messages of the Black movements such as the Bedwardites, Garveyites, Rastafari, and some sections of the nascent nationalist movement. The Rastafari recognized Blackness as having both liberating and oppressive tendencies, and the latter was imputed to those Blacks whose reference frames depended on emulating or gaining the approval of Whites.

Contention among Black people over what constituted "proper" Blackness showed itself in different ways, such as in conflicts between the Rastafari, law enforcement officials, and legal institutions. The representatives of these institutions ridiculed and disciplined the Rastafari for their racial and religious transgressions of "proper" Blackness, which meant adherence to British-defined norms and rules. Rasta Ivey stressed race in her stories about "dirty Babylon," the police.[4] She related how under colonialism the police, especially in Kingston and surrounding areas, were Black while their superiors were White. Black officers were seen by the Rastafari as the frontline guarding a corrupt set of institutions that oppressed Blacks and upheld a class that gave advantage to Whites and a few Browns. "Corruption," in its many forms, became something for the Rastafari to stand against, to resist, and to tackle through symbolic battle because corruption was determined to be responsible for the plight of Black people in Jamaica.

Brother Yendis elaborates in detail about intra-black conflicts and a fundamental position of many of those who became Rastafari between the early 1950s and early 1970s: to separate themselves from what they viewed as a corrupt, "Babylonian" system. I quote him at length:

When me was a youth, me used to see White governor . . . White police officer, White, you know. . . . And . . . anywhere Black policeman see him [White] officer . . . he have to salute him, and me see them things wiped away. . . . Me don't even see no White people 'bout here. Black man a run the regiment, Black man a run the police force. Black man a Prime Minister. Black man a this, Black man a that. Black man a Governor General . . . Black man a everything. But what happen with them Black man here . . . [is] them is the house slaves. There is a difference between house slaves and field slaves. . . . The field slaves is the one what get the pressure all the while. . . . Always under the pressure. So him no too like that one [house slave] and that one no too like him. Well, the house slaves always have something good to tell the boss, and keep upon that attitude right now. Well, the house slave what a rule we here now . . . what him a do, him just a show the boss say him can keep the thing in place for him you know. To show I better than you. I can keep the thing in place you know. Because from 1962 [the year of Jamaican independence], you look in a any of them . . . and see what change? Nothing don't change. The only thing that change . . . we change the White man and say White one go siddown [sit] one side. And we sing [a Nyabinghi chant] "Wonder why them [White man] no go way, We want go home a we yard [Africa]." So we only a sing say the White man them to leave here, so we a go home. Them [Black] man a workers for the White man only so them can keep we in order you know. Them man a do the thing politely . . . [but] we know is must good [that wins] over evil.

Brother Yendis's trenchant critique of race and internalized oppression is historically, sociologically, and psychologically informed: Blacks have continued the work of the White colonials, even without their prodding. The Nyabinghi chant that Brother Yendis referenced above (also see the Preface) is still widely sung by the Rastafari, a testimony to their threatening rhetoric and intense desire to dismantle White hegemony in Jamaica and Africa. Dissolution of White hegemony through culture and identity is part of the solution the Rastafari are pursuing. Another aspect involves contesting racial oppression, including Black-on-Black oppression. Their emergent awareness of miseducation and racialized oppression stoked recognition of the benefits of Black solidarity and well-being. These recognitions and factors were also key elements propelling identity transformation at the individual level.

Inborn Conception: A Rastafari Theory of Identity Transformation

The Rastafari theory of identity is based on ideas of what we can call "anciency" and "latency." Anciency describes Rastafari conceptions of time, especially how they connect themselves and the present to the past. Latency describes how the Rastafari explain their identity as something fundamental to human consciousness, waiting to be released. One of their widely known identity theories is called (in their terms) "inborn conception." The idea of inborn conception conveys their idioms and cultural frameworks for understanding why and how people become Rastafari. As we shall see, the theory positively preordains Blackness, while allowing some contingency. This essentialism works as a bulwark, if not battering ram, against counter-essentialisms that denigrate Blackness. By essentialism, I mean the view that Blackness is a "natural" and real phenomenon with central, recognizable features such as the justice motifs. However, this type of essentialism is malleable because it also recognizes the absence of such features, which therefore are worthy of pursuit.

One of the first things I asked Rasta Ivey when I met her was how long she had been Rastafari. She replied, "I been in the battle since 1918." I was puzzled because her answer meant that she would have been a pre-adolescent during Alexander Bedward's last years and only 12 or so when Haile Selassie was crowned Emperor. As I got to know Rasta Ivey better, the more puzzled I became because I was learning that she was searching out different messages of Black redemption, such as those associated with Bedward, during the mid- to late 1920s. I asked her about her age in different ways and repeatedly received answers along the line of "I am in the battle since 1918." While reading *Alas, Alas Kongo* (Schuler, 1980) and contemplating the understandings of indentured African laborers brought to Jamaica during the mid-1800s, I realized that Rasta Ivey's reference to 1918 referred to her earliest memories of self-awareness and *not* when she was born. By my estimate she was born in the month of November sometime between 1906 and 1912.[5] For Rasta Ivey, "birth" was traced not to parturition but to her earliest memories of life, and her life as she remembers it had been one of struggle—a battle for liberation and against injustice and miseducation. As I learned about her life, I grasped exactly what she meant by this. She had been, by her own self-representation, a fighter from 1918 to the present because *she was born that way*.

My narrators imagine Blacks like themselves to be a vanguard of the race—and indeed, of humankind—beholden to actualizing an emancipatory practice focused on transcending oppression enacted through race, class, and religion. They believe that people are socialized into accepting and promulgating oppression and inhumanity, fostering interpersonal and structural violence. To abandon and destroy these behaviors and the systems that they sustain requires resocializing and disembedding oneself from that system and creating a "higher" one. The self-remaking of the Rastafari has been dressed in the cultural infrastructure and resources that they have continuously reworked over the decades. The Rastafari, through identity transformation, have embodied a critique both of a predatory capitalism that thrives on alienation, racism, and poverty and of Christian and indigenous religions that fail to encourage racial solidarity and uphold cardinal tenets of brotherhood and sisterhood.

The Rastafari themselves do not talk of "converting" to Rastafari, though they recognize the processing involved in "sighting up" or becoming Rastafari. Hypothetically, anyone, regardless of race, can be a Rastafari if he or she acknowledges what the Rastafari consider to be truths. Regardless of what precipitates or catalyzes a person's manifestation of Rastafari identity, the Rastafari say the seed was already there. The person has simply discovered and engaged his or her higher self. As Smith et al. (1960:24) noted, "The brethren do not speak of people joining their cult. In their view, the doctrine is in them at birth but unfolds and comes into consciousness when they recognise the Emperor as God and themselves become fully conscious." Kitzinger (1966:38) also detected the importance of the idea of inborn conception:[6] "A man may discover it [his Rastafari/Black identity and "heart"[7]] in himself after living the major part of his life in dissolute unawareness. . . . It was there all the time, but he did not know it." To manifest "heart" or to be "heartical" is to be an upright or moral exemplar.

Ras Brenton's recollections of the highly respected Rastafari leader Mortimer Planno illuminate his view that there is something innate to Ras Planno that makes his identity and understanding "natural":

> Mr. Planno was great in every way in Rasta business. He just knows it. He just born with it. He told me that he used to be down Foreshore Road sleeping in an old car for four years. . . . He slept in an old car for four years and read the Bible from Genesis to Revelation and interpret it for himself. Whatever he did not understand, he asked other brethren along the way still until he overstand almost everything that he read.

Ras Brenton identified study, reflection, questioning, and dialogue as important factors involved in Planno's becoming Rastafari, dimensions of identity transformation we will explore further in the next chapter.

The idea of inborn conception relies on an essentialized past that each person must engage and take responsibility for:

> I and I prophesy that we were born that way [as Rastafari]. It is an inborn conception to be a Rasta man, and when you check it out, all Black people is Rasta because Rasta means peace and love . . . Freedom, justice and I-quality [equality]. For these high qualities, we need to have a doctrine, but we need to also have peace and love among ourselves . . . our doctrine was from ancient [times]. . . . once your knotty [dreadlocks] is alright man, it is your countenance and your covenant. We have made a covenant with Jah, according to Numbers, chapter 6. We have made a vow of a Nazarene to fight against barbarism and all those barbaric sys tems. You figure me? So, because of this, we are just born to be Rasta. Jah just made us this way. We are a special and peculiar people, they say. We don't bow to everything. (Ras Brenton)

Ras Brenton's conception of Black identity and inborn conception presupposes that Black people, especially Rastafari, are predisposed toward peace, freedom, justice, and equality. In his view, these inherent and supremely humanistic qualities have been disrupted by hallmarks of modernity such as the Atlantic slave trade and racial oppression, and thrust deep within the psyche, necessitating awakening and release. And, it is Rastafari identity, as a moral, religious, and racially defined mode of being, that makes it possible to gain the liberation, justice, and redemption that the Rastafari feel they and others have been denied.

Ras Brenton's language is saturated with imagery of fighting against injustice and "barbaric systems." The recurrence of such themes, as well as efforts to enact these ideas, are suggestive of the use of Rastafari identity to address particular challenges such as those of Blackness and oppression and liberation in Jamaica. The identification with the past and with ancestors provides an emotionally laden sense of empowerment, something that people could feel and wield. Brother Yendis, with his fists clenched and his dark face intensely fixed with determination, related to me how he felt this power, how this power was connected to his past heritage, and how this power affected people:

When I back up a chant [sing a Nyabinghi hymn], I could feel that power. I could a feel the rhythm of the ancestor there, you know, and it direct me . . . that chant was something you would sit there and meditate and feel the vibes, feel the African vibes in a you. It is an authentic thing and it was there, and people welcome it.

Inborn conception involves incarnation and a recycling of life. Nothing is new in this perspective:

So as in the beginning, so it is in the end. You fool the people some of the time, but you cannot fool them all the time. What is hidden from the wise and prudent, is revealed to the babe and suckling. Whatsoever is yours a man cannot take it away because you have it from the beginning and you will have it in the end. Nothing is new. . . . Things can only go and come. A man cannot fool you . . . Yes, some [people], but not all. What is for a man, you cannot take it away. The Emperor was from the beginning and he will be to the end. From creation. Nothing new . . . Look at the little baby who is born. He should have a flesh fresh as a ninepence, but he looks as if he was here before. Look at the baby who just born. Look if he looks new. Look [and see] if it is not the same old flesh he has on. (Rasta Ivey)

Rasta Ivey draws our attention to a Rastafari conception of time that involves a recycling of experience and events. The Rastafari, like the metaphorical babe or suckling, are privileged because they have deciphered what is hidden to the non-Rastafari. Rasta Ivey invokes the Ethiopianist redemptive tenet that what Blacks had in the beginning they shall have in the end, that what they have lost they will regain, and that ultimately justice will reign. Being a Rastafari involves learned acts of reclamation which entail using a racially constructed past for present purposes that project a future where the last shall be first and oppression upended. The discourse attendant to these acts and identifications "sounds" millenarian in how it refers to a reversal of power relations in favor of the oppressed (e.g., Taylor, 1990), and it is understandable why the Rastafari have been deemed a millenarian movement. If the Rastafari are millenarian, however, then so are many if not most of their Black Jamaican contemporaries. The Rastafari are expressing views that draw on symbols and ideas common among Black Jamaicans, such as the biblical connections between beginnings/alpha and endings/omega. The Rastafari interpretation of time, for example, constructs Haile Selassie I as a part of a continuum traced to antiquity. In Rasta Ivey's view, Selassie I is a re-embodiment of God cloaked in new raiment and wearing a bejeweled crown of gold instead of thorns. Her interpretation is bound up with the official discourses on Haile Selassie I which place his lineage on the same tree as the Biblical King David. The Rastafaris' privileged knowledge is suggested by Rasta Ivey in her recognition of the recurrent workings of time. Thus, you can fool some people some of the time but not all of the time, and the Rastafari are those who can no longer be fooled. Inborn conception provides a conceptual framework for explaining and privileging the Rastafari, and to grow into Rastafari identity offers a potential antidote to oppression, miseducation, and deracination.

The elder Rastafari's idea of inborn conception informs their image of themselves as living embodiments of the injustices, struggles, and triumphs experienced by their Black New World ancestors. Recall, for instance, Rasta Ivey's calm disclosure that she was involved in the Myalist War of 1831–32 (chapter 1). Ras Sam Brown, for example, explains why he is Rastafari by situating himself as a link between the past and present:

> I was called to this [Rastafari]. Same as Jesus Christ called his followers. And I was one who walked with Jesus Christ in that day. And this day when he return in a new name [Rastafari], the sheep hear his voice and hearken unto it. So, that is why I am a Rasta man because I walk with Father from the foundation of creation. [It is] Not a thing that you really learn. We have been here for a longer time and through the inspiration . . . through inspiration, this may arise again [faiths and identities like Rastafari].

Ras Sam Brown points out that the convictions that gave birth to the Rastafari and its movement character, and the oppressive forces that helped shape it, still exist and inspire the transformation into Rastafari. The "inspiration" that Ras Sam Brown refers to is felt and experienced, something not easily explained. Yet, according to our identity theory and that of the Rastafari, one does learn how to recognize the experience even if it is not easily articulated.

Encountering and Seeking

How do people get onto the path toward becoming Rastafari? Common to most narrators was a particular experience or series of experiences that challenged their normative understandings of the world and themselves. They were introduced to ideas about Black Jamaican ancestral connection to Africa, for example. Or they witnessed injustice, or had dreams or visions that informed new understandings of self and society, or they made racialized connections between biblical scripture and actual occurrences. Drawing on nigrescence theory, I describe these experiences as *encounters*. The encounter is the catalytic experience that leads a person to *personalize* an event in terms of race, resulting in identity transformation reflected in changed attitudes, perceptions and understandings (see chapter 3).

However, Black identity theories such as nigrescence do not focus on how some people are open to entertaining novel ideas and beliefs *before* they experience an encounter, so that the encounter becomes enmeshed with already existing concerns, orientations, or pursuits. The focus of some of the religious-conversion literature on people's subjective and objective states prior to and during identity conversion is particularly useful in extending Black identity transformation. This broadened conception of identity transformation is able to incorporate the ways in which the narrators were grappling with existential questions, the ways in which they internalized experiential witnessing, and the intellectual inquisitiveness they expressed in matters of religion, history, and politics.

I have identified three primary categorical types of encounter experiences involved in the identity transformation of my narrators: dreams and visions; curiosity and engrossment with existential questions, which includes engaging texts (and the quest for answers); and experiential witnessing.[8] Each category depicts a set of patterns identified across the experience of diverse individuals. The categories, however, are not mutually exclusive and sometimes overlap, as with the curious seeker whose worldview is unsettled. An encounter is typically fortified by study, reflection, observation of actual Rastafari, and dialogic engagement with what it means to be Rastafari.[9]

"Sighting Up" His Majesty: Dreams, Visions, and Insights

Dreams and visions, and the insights drawn from them, are common ways in which emerging Rastafari experience an encounter and enter into a state of seekership (e.g., most of Chevannes' Rastafari interlocutors mentioned dreams and visions as a part of their conversion narratives [1994:111]). I define a dream as images that a person experiences while asleep, and a vision as a supernatural experience of images that occur while awake or asleep. The dreams and visions related by the Rastafari were rich in Biblical imagery and symbols (see Homiak, 1987). These dreams and visions provided cues and clues for action, and played a vital role in identity transformation. Several of my narrators claimed to have envisioned or communicated with Haile Selassie I, himself. These dreams and visions of His Majesty all draw on similar symbols: the Emperor is usually riding a white horse, carrying a sword, well-dressed, and wearing a crown or helmet. The Emperor is dreamed in ways consistent with the pictures of him that the Rastafari have seen, and consistent with many biblical images, especially those of Revelations. Jamaicans do not always assume that experiencing visions or hearing voices talking to oneself, especially in the context of religion, is a sign of abnormality. In some situations visioning and communication with the supernatural are understood as exceptional talents.

I asked Brother Bongo if he remembered his first vision, and he vividly recited the story. As he recalled his experience, his eyes glazed, as if he had entered a trance that was helping him summon and relive the story:

> [I saw] His Majesty in his khaki suit in command like he reminding that you have a work to do. . . . [It] Just appear. . . . I was seated on the beach. . . . It was night because on the beach we would sit and watch the moonlight and watch the planes over Palisadoes Airport. . . . So it was down there the revelation came from. . . . So, it was there it developed and I started to read. That is what get me. I took to the Bible a lot and at nights, read myself to sleep.

Brother Bongo, during the same interview, recalled another vision, its motifs similar to those expressed in the above quote. In this vision he saw "His Majesty in the vision [dressed] in military suit, coming across the heavens. More than once [I saw it], and it gave me strength," he said, speaking with the kind of conviction that could be used to persuade a person of the forcefulness of the experience. Brother Bongo's visions were a part of his encounter and move toward embodying Rastafari. His visions, study, reflection and dialogue with other Rastafari were together integral to his identity transformation.

Prophetess Esther's life story illuminates how visions and the supernatural define encounters and fuel identity transformation. I first cast eyes upon Prophetess (the name she uses and asked me to use when referencing her) during an annual Rastafari Federation meeting in Kingston in

1998. The afternoon program for that day allowed an "open mike" for Rastafari to make statements or announcements to the audience. Many Rastafari, male and female, took to the stage to announce upcoming events, read scripture or poetry, or to deliver discourses on issues of concern to the Rastafari, such as repatriation. When Prophetess took the stage, she immediately caught my attention. She was seventy-one when I met her (born 1927), but she looked ten years younger. She had olive-brown colored skin, stood perhaps not quite five feet tall, and was wearing a white dress and white headwrap. Because she was dressed in white, I wondered if Prophetess was a revivalist. I expected her to be shouted off the stage by Rastafari intolerant of "backward" religions. Prophetess launched into a fiery tirade against "corrupt Babylon," authoritatively using Rastafari language and imagery. Unlike many of the Rastafari present, however, she did not have dreadlocks and she was not sporting the red, gold, and green of Rastafari. I wanted to know more about her. I noticed that she had gained the attention of the audience more so than most of the speakers before her. I asked Ras Tee "Who is that sistren?" "That is Prophetess," he said. The focus of Prophetess's brief sermon was the endemic corruption in Jamaica and how the Rastafari had to get ready to leave Jamaica, immediately. She was invoking a narrative common to her generation of Rastafari, and she predicted that a ship would arrive in August 1998 to deliver all Rastafari ready to leave Jamaica to Ethiopia. I walked to the stage in order to introduce myself to Prophetess when she stepped off. I greeted her, and barely had I finished saying "I would like visit you and learn more about your work" before she agreed and began telling me about her life's work.

Prophetess is the epitome of the spiritualist tendency among the Rastafari. The spiritualists emphasize supernatural intervention as the solution to their concerns, while the pragmatists emphasize practical resolutions (Price, 2001). As we shall see, however, Prophetess's journey into Rastafari identity and her techniques for telling her story are unusual among the Rastafari life stories I have recorded. She liberally mixes Rastafari, Christian, and other Jamaican religious symbols and ideas in unique combinations.

When I arrived at the home of Prophetess about a week after the conference, she greeted me at her door projecting an aura of urgency. She said to me, "He wants to know if you will stand up to be a leader to those [Rastafari] that are over there [in America] that separate and don't have a leader to lead them and to teach them?" I asked, "Who

Prophetess Esther, born in 1927, in the parish of Hanover. Prophetess exemplifies the mix of Rastafari and Revivalism. Note her white garments and that she wears no dreadlocks. She unequivocally defines herself as a Rastafari.

is 'he'?" She declared, "The spirit." Surprised, I asked, "What spirit?" (I knew that revivalist and other indigenous religious practices had been purged from Rastafari discourse and practice before the 1970s; thus I was puzzled by her talk about spirits). She said, "His Majesty and Jesus." Curious, and feeling challenged, I nodded affirmatively and said, "I will speak to them. I will gather them and I will teach them." Prophetess said in response, "I will speak to him and let him know, because he says it is what he wants to know, and he is very, very anxious to hear or to see the representing of the land [Ethiopia]." She continued, as if to let me know the seriousness of the matter and how legitimate her communication was with these supernatural entities: "Who will stand up and say they will take that responsibility to look about the land for those that want to go ["home" to Ethiopia]?" After some small talk, Prophetess and I sat in her sanctuary and began a tape-recorded interview where she launched into a mesmerizing story about her encounters on the path to Rastafari identity. Her story flowed effortlessly. She rarely paused to collect her thoughts or to ponder what to tell. The memories and stories gushed forth. Only occasionally did I need to use prompts that helped to keep

Prophetess Esther displays evidence of her visit to Shashemene in Ethiopia during the early 1970s. She returned to Jamaica to "gather up the children" and to return to Ethiopia.

her focused on discussing her life and how she came to be Rastafari. I struggled to find moments to interject follow-up questions because her monologue was so continuous. It was a barrage of detail, and I did not want to interrupt her. A striking story emerged. Prophetess constructed a retrospective story about her encounters, perhaps an idealized account, which is not uncommon with the telling of life stories. It was *her* story about her coming into Rastafari, however, and I wanted her to tell it as she saw fit.

I began my first interview with Prophetess by asking when and where she was born. She answered, but did not linger on her beginnings. She wanted to get directly to her concern, which involved "the spirit" and preparation for leaving Jamaica for Ethiopia. In doing this, though, she did tell me about her life. Prophetess began hearing and communicating with voices (the spirit) around the age of nine. She also had visions and dreams in which she communicated with spirits. Her encounter is so compelling that it deserves to be treated at length.

When I was 9 years old, I was sitting in the class one day, and I heard somebody speaking to me. I turned around and looked all over the school. I don't see anybody, but when I come back steady, and sit in my seat, I heard the voice speaking to me. . . . I start to look on the teacher. Teacher not saying anything. Teacher sit at the desk. I look around on all the children them. I see everybody doing them work, but I continue hear the voice saying to me, "I come to speak to you. I come to speak to you." So I [am] looking to see who speaking to me. [the voice repeats] "I want you to listen to what I am saying. I want you to listen to what I am saying." I get up and look all under the bench to see if is anybody [there]. I see nobody. I get back in my seat and start to write what the teacher give us to write, and the voice still saying, "I come to speak with you . . . " And for a whole day until school over in the evening, I hear the same thing.

Prophetess shared her encounter with her father, who seemed unsurprised to hear that his young daughter was hearing voices. Prophetess:

Me say, "Dad, the whole day in school somebody speaking to me, but it is not a woman. It's a man, and him keep telling me say, I come to speak to you. I want you to listen to what I am saying to you." Daddy say, "You hear that baby?" Him [daddy] say, "this is a spirit being speaking to you. And him don't say anything else?" Me say, "No, Daddy. Him only telling me that him come to me, and want to speak to me, but him want me to listen to whatsoever him saying to me."[Daddy said] "God want you, me dear. God want you, and you see, Him send the spirit to speak with you, and if it's not Himself speaking to you, it's an angel. Listen carefully [to] what him say to you and come back and tell me." [That] Night I went to me bed. I wake up next morning alright. I didn't get no dream.

Prophetess animatedly related her narrative. She used different voices for each spirit and she ducked and bobbed as she told me about how she was looking for the voice. She sometimes stood up and regularly gestured with her hands. I felt like I was watching an actor perform.

[The first spirit] Him say, "I tell you yesterday that I come to speak to you. . . . I am coming far from a place name Africa, and my people is in slavery in Jamaica, and I want to deliver them, and I want to take them out of slavery, and I want to free them." Me say, "Then sir, who must I say speaking to me?" Him say, "You ever hear anybody talk about one man name Jesus?" Me say, "Yes, sir! For the church we going to teach us all the while about Jesus." Him say, "Well, I am Jesus speaking to you and telling you that I come from far, from Africa, and I come here to speak with you. I want you to hear me. I want you to listen to me. I want whatever I am going to tell you to do, I want you hear me. I want you to do it." Me say, "Yes, sir!" Him say, "I want you to stand up and to teach my people what I going to teach you."

The first spirit is Jesus, and Prophetess has located him in Africa, making him relevant to Black people connected to the continent, which is a marked deviation from prevalent narratives about Christ. The spirit is also teaching Prophetess and revealing unknowns, since she tells me that she knew nothing of Africa before the spirit's visit. By inquiring into the narrators' earliest memories of learning about Africa, I found their learning of Africa and their connection to it to be an important part of refashioning their self-identification. Although Prophetess's claim to be unaware of Africa before the spirit told her about it strikes me as unlikely, I recognize nonetheless that in her narrative she is stitching together Africa, Blackness, and biblical figures. She continued to elaborate on what this first spirit is asking of her:

> "Tell your father, say my name is Jesus and me come from Africa, and ask him if him know a place name Africa." Me say, "Yes sir!" Him say, "My people is in bondage; my people is in slavery taken away from the land of Africa and bring to the Western Hemisphere by the British Government. When you going to speak to your father, ask your father if him know anybody in the world name British people . . . [and] British government. They are the ones who take away me people from Africa and bring them here and turn them into slaves. I come to deliver them and I come to give them deliverance." Me say, "Yes, sir!"

Slavery and injustice are pivotal themes in Prophetess's narrative, especially in the parts of her story where she references Jesus and Selassie I. Slavery and injustice are racially situated in ways that can be read as grievances against Whites, "British people" in particular. The Jesus that Prophetess describes is different from the one who is familiar to most Christians and who is silent on issues of slavery and Africa and on his relationship to Black people. The Jesus speaking to her is absorbed by the issue of slavery and its effects on Black people and wants it completely abolished and his people sent home to Africa. As Prophetess speaks for the "spirit," it seems they both agree that slavery is not yet abolished. As the story unfolds, her critique of "the system" becomes sharper, and more Rastafari, and she employs Ethiopianist imagery and ideology, pointing to how themes of thievery, oppression, bondage, and freedom are embodied in her identity:

> My father say, "You know who is Jesus? When you go to church on Sunday morning, what parson teach you say?" Me tell him say him say Jesus died for us and shed his blood for us. Him say, "Then a him come to you and tell you say him name Jesus?" Me say, "Yes, Daddy, him say him name Jesus and him come to free Him slave people them . . . for him people the British people take away from Africa and bring them come here and turn them into slaves." Him [daddy] hug me up and him kiss me and him say, "Dear D [Prophetess's nickname], Dear D, Lord Jesus [has visited to you] through you in your baby stage, and him tell you say him name Jesus and him tell you say him a come from Africa?" Me say, "Yes, Dad, him coming from a far place name Africa, and him coming here because of the slaves. Him say if the slaves was not here, him wouldn't have to come here, but because the people who come here come from Africa is his people. British people thief them away from Africa and carry them come here so him have to come here now to do a work. To save them." Me father say, "This is great! Dear D, you born for this purpose, and if Him is Jesus, Him is the Son of the Creator being. Through you, who is nine years old now, and Him telling you those things?" Me say, "Yes, Dad . . . Him want me to stand up and see to it that me deliver the people and bring the people out of slavery." Him hug me up, him kiss me and him say, "Make me pray fi you baby."

Around the age of 11, Prophetess began hearing a second voice, one that elaborated upon Ethiopia, slavery, and injustice. This voice is that of Haile Selassie I, himself.

> When me complete 11 and going up now to 12, I hear another voice speaking to me and say . . . "I would like you to know who speaking to you." Me say, "Yes, sir, the first gentleman that was speaking to me tell me that his name was Jesus. Who you is now? What is your name? If you want to speak to me . . . Jesus [is also] speaking to me and telling me that he come to free his people." Him say, "Is the same thing that Jesus want you to do

to free his people, it's the same thing I want. I want the people them free. I want the people them come home." I say, "Come home where?" Him say, "Africa." Me say, "You come from Africa too?" Him say, "Yes." Him say, "I am a king, and I am sitting in a place name Ethiopia." Me say, "Ethiopia? You is sitting in Ethiopia?" Him say, "I am King Haile Selassie." Me say, "Sir, Jesus is different from you?" Him say, "Jesus is Jesus. And I am King Selassie, but the two a we moving together. So the two a we come to speak with you because Jesus want you to lead His people and me want you to stand up and lead the people. For the people for Jesus is my people and my people is Jesus' people. For all my people is taken away from Africa and come here as slaves. So me want them to come home to me. . . ." [I asked my daddy] "You ever hear any name like that . . . [Haile Selassie and Ethiopia]?" Him say, "No . . . me never know anything about Ethiopia."

In Prophetess's narrative, the theme of going home to Africa takes on greater urgency as she ages; the second voice, the King of Ethiopia, Haile Selassie I, is now speaking directly to her. The King concurs with what Jesus is asking her to do: help redeem the slaves and deliver them home. Prophetess sees Jesus and Haile Selassie I as connected, the ancient past and the twentieth century, concurrent with the Rastafari version of the Order of Melchisidec, which conflates priesthood and kingship, and in which both Christ and Selassie I are Redeemers, at different points in time, and now simultaneously. Rasta Ivey held a similar view. She concluded during the 1930s that King Jesus and King Selassie were not two separate entities, but related to each other—incarnations of each other. Prophetess's interpretation differs, though, because of the prominent role she gives Jesus in her narrative.[10]

Prophetess is a remnant of the Rastafari who combined revivalism, Ethiopianism, and Rastafari (see Chevannes, 1994). She is a product of the cultural traditions of Bedward, the class leaders or shepherds, and more specially, Claudius Henry. Prophetess is a country girl born into rural life, claiming that she knew nothing of Africa or Ethiopia—and neither did her father and mother—before being instructed by the spirits. My probes to determine the veracity of her claim suggest this could indeed be the case. I asked the same question in different ways: "So you never learned about Africa in your schooling?" "Just through the spirits come talk to you, you know it?" She replied "Only when the voice come talk to me. . . . The first in my life me ever know say one place there 'pon the earth name Africa. And it is the same spirit tell me about Kingston."

That the young Prophetess was hearing voices and relating her experience to her parents created problems for her. This is a recurrent aspect of my narrators' identity transformation: Negative reaction from friends, family, and strangers. Prophetess's post-sixth standard teacher decided that she did not want to teach a precocious child who was hearing voices talking about Ethiopia. While her father had been lovingly supportive of her visionary experiences, her mother did not believe her. Prophetess reminisced how her mother would say, "She don't know how pickney [child] at that age can talk say something a talk to her, and she hear man a talk to her. Then that mean say she a get off her head. She no right." To compound an already out-of-the-ordinary situation, the voices began threatening to take Prophetess away from her parents because her mother was too inattentive to her "special" power: "Me say, 'Daddy, Lord Jesus say him going [to] take me away from you and me mother, and the King which is Selassie say the two of them [are] going [to] join and take me from you because my mother can't understand what me saying to her! She can understand, but she don't want to understand!'" Does this part of the story reflect a ploy by Prophetess to grab the attention of her parents, to persuade her mother to accept her stories, or is she literally assuming the role of the prophet who must leave family and friends to spread the word? I believe it was a combination of both.

Prophetess's route to Rastafari was lengthy and circuitous, driven by her continuing encounters and communication with two primary "spirits," Jesus and Haile Selassie I. She supernaturally received her mission, directly from the spirits, and took it to heart:

I say, "Mama, nothing going to stop me [from reaching Kingston]. . . . I must go, because Lord Jesus have a work for me to do. Not in this country [rural place], but in Kingston." His Majesty come back and say, "I have a work [for you] to carry through but not in this country." So I say, "Beg you pack me grip." That is how I get to come into Kingston.

Prophetess, in actuality, probably knew little about the people and history of Africa. However, she showed familiarity with Ethiopia and Africa-in-general through references to it mentioned in the Old Testament, and through the symbols and imagery of Ethiopianism. And she did travel to Ethiopia during the 1970s to inquire into repatriating herself and other Rastafari to Shashmene (she returned to Jamaica to "gather up the people" and return to Ethiopia). As a young person, she probably heard stories that pertained to Ethiopianism and Africa, and over time pieced them together, as did Rasta Ivey. Prophetess's narrative is highly stylized, suggesting she has told it many times. Her account illustrates the diversity of experiences and practices that characterize the Rastafari of different historical moments, as well as the commonalities that they share in terms of the themes that define their identity and beliefs: slavery, justice, redemption, a profound affection for Ethiopia-Africa, and an association of truth with these beliefs.

Brother Bongo and Prophetess Esther illustrate two ways that visions, dreams, and the supernatural function as encounters that open the pathway to becoming Rastafari. The experience shakes up or challenges a person's extant understandings of self and her world, and opens a window onto an alternative identity path. But the encounter only opens the window; it does not mean that a person will or must change identity. For the identity transformation to begin, the encounter has to be personalized.

Truth, Miseducation, and Redemption: Existential Questions

By disrupting a person's customary framework for making sense of the world, the encounter can create the context for a person to explore existential questions about the world and their relation to it. At the same time, curiosity, inquisitiveness, interest in existential questions, and searching for answers can precede or mesh with an encounter. Why have Black people experienced the kinds of oppression they have? Why are some people poor? How should I imagine God? These existential questions reflect a person's awareness, no matter how vague, of the ambiguity, instability, and indifference of the institutions around them and of dominant explanations for the way things are. The questioning also implies a person's awareness, no matter how vague, of alternatives, and perhaps even the authority to craft more personally compatible meanings and arrangements. The ways that emerging Rastafari deal with big questions about purpose, justice, God, and history are important considerations. This kind of interest in such questions suggests that what a person currently knows is insufficient, if not wrong.

Sister Amme began her journey toward Rastafari sometime around the time of the visit of Haile Selassie I to Jamaica in 1966. The reaction of tens of thousands of Jamaicans to Selassie I's arrival led her to seriously wonder if he was truly the Conquering Lion of the Tribe of Judah mentioned in Revelations. She wanted to know "the truth." Selassie I's visit and questions about the visit's significance can be considered her first Rasta-fari-related encounter. A second encounter experience occurred one night, a year or so later, while she was sitting by an open window. In the distance she could faintly hear drumming. To hear it better, she went out onto the street. She found the rhythms captivating and decided that she wanted to know more about the activities surrounding the drums. She said:

> It come in like the drums them was calling me–pulling me. I said to my-self "I want to go [to] where those drums are." I hail a bus. I don't even bother go upstairs and tell nobody. I get on the bus and say, "Driver, you hear the drum them?" Him say, "Yes. Over a Bull Bay the Rasta them hold a 'Binghi [Nyabinghi ceremony].'" I say, "Put me off there." I reach and follow one little path in [to] some bush near to the sea. I see a heap of Rasta people. Them is chanting and beating the drums. I just watch and listen. I never join them. But I was captivated. . . . Late in the morning I go home.

Twelve years elapsed between Sister Amme's initial self-questioning about the identity of Haile Selassie I in 1966 and her next step of declaring her faith and commitment by growing dreadlocks in 1977. This attests, despite observers' assumptions, to the sometimes lengthy duration of these iden-tity transformations.

After being confronted with Rastafari as an identity option, Sister Amme began to question people knowledgeable about the Rastafari and to engage in serious study. She sought out literature on Africa and Ethio-pia; she spent hours in the Institute of Jamaica reading "historical docu-ments." She began to read the radical literature of that period, such as the writings of Guyanese historian Walter Rodney. During this period she not only began to identify as Black, African, and Rastafari, she began to *see* certain things as "unacceptable; just wrong." Through her new eyes, Sister Amme was finding injustice everywhere she looked, and this awareness further radicalized her. She began to pay attention to the efforts of Third World nations attempting to overthrow colonialism and became angry be-cause she did not "know better" all along, and that so many people failed to see the injustice that she now saw as systemic. Sister Amme's struggle to grasp what "truth" meant in the context of her identity change involved coming to think of Selassie as God and becoming conscious that misedu-cation and deracination were at the root of her "blindness" and that her inability to see the problem worked to maintain systems of oppression.

Perhaps the key dimensions of "truth" for the Rastafari revolve around recognizing Haile Selassie as divine and addressing the distortions surrounding Black history and culture. To discover the possibility that God has taken the form of a Black man and to then come to confidently believe and profess this, along with the ability to explain why this is the case, contributes to their sense of themselves as privileged and "peculiar" people who see and know what others do not:

> You must know that the White man painted Jesus as a White man using one of the Pope's images to portray the Christ that they [are] now worshiping . . . [some have called him] Jesus Christ of Nazareth,[11] Jesus Christos in Amharic, Jesus Christ in English, but it is the said man and [he] is a Black man. There is certain parts of his life that they did not tell us. (Brother Bongo)

Rastafarian concern with truth of the divine, though, cannot be separated from their other chief concerns, especially those of justice and liberation. Sister Amme, for example, discerned that important parts of what she had learned of the history and political economy of Jamaica and the Third World were not the full story. Hence, justice, truth, and even liberation were subverted because elites and oppressors had made their versions of culture, religion, history, and politics the "natural" and "real" version.

Rasta Ivey said it was her interest in the truth that led her to Rastafari in the early 1930s. Her search was a lengthy one. She had been attracted to Africa-oriented movements since she was a teen during the 1920s. She listened to the messages of Alexander Bedward, Marcus Garvey, the Salvation Army, Bishop Brown, Leonard Howell, and others (see chapter 1). She settled her early Rastafari affiliation with Robert Hinds, whom she referred to as "our leader," and who is described in much of the literature of Rastafari as one of its founding leaders. During the time that Rasta Ivey was listening to these messages, she noted, in her own words, how she was "searching" and "listening." "What were you searching and listening for?" I asked. She replied that she wanted to know about the "Black Christ . . . [and] Black people. . . . I want to know when redemption was coming." Rasta Ivey investigated the various religious and racial organizations in and around Kingston. Slowly, she began to eliminate them as she concluded that they were not satisfying her thirst for knowledge about Blackness that spoke to the justice motifs. She eliminated the Pocomanians and Revivalists. They were not dealing with the past, especially slavery, in a way that appealed to her. Ethiopianism made much more sense.

> I don't business with them. It was not something sensible . . . So I just put them together, and it is not right. See the right thing here. Rastafari in Ethiopia. Ethiopia is the right land. Not Jamaica. I understand from I was born that I was a slave. I know slave was here [in Jamaica] . . . Some did not come as slaves, but when they came here, they became slaves. Some came to see their families because if you have family you want to see them wherever they are. (Rasta Ivey)

Even when put all "together," the other religions did not make sense to Rasta Ivey. She concluded that Ethiopia and Rastafari were the "right thing." Rasta Ivey joined her analysis of the messages of the early Rastafari to her understanding of and concern with slaves and slavery and—seeing herself in these terms—to stories transmitted to her by her elders, such as those told to her by her grandmother (who Rasta Ivey says lived to the age of 116 years). Given some of the memories that Rasta Ivey related to me, it is possible that her grandmother was one of the indentured African laborers who came to Jamaica during the mid-eighteenth century. Statements such as how some people did not come as slaves but became slaves (she did not know what indentured servitude was but classified my description of it as slavery), or came to see their families, resonate with Schuler's account of African indentured laborers in Jamaica (1980).

Brother Barody traced his interest in Rastafari to a very tense moment in the evolution of the Rastafari, right around the time of the Prince Edward Rastafari convention in Kingston in 1958. Brother Barody recognizes, in retrospect, how he had been concerned with existential questions about race and God since early in his life. He tells a story of how at the age of seven or eight, while attending a Catholic school, he asked an abbot if God were Black or White. The abbot refused to answer his question, but did suggest that God has "no color." Brother Barody was born into a family in which Blackness was a salient identification (his parents and grandparents were Garveyites), and he wanted an answer from the abbot because he was supposed to be knowledgeable about religious matters and because the Garveyites were arguing that Black people should view God through the "spectacles of Ethiopia." He, however, refused to talk about race and God.

Years later, through study, dialogue, analysis, and reflection, Brother Barody concluded that Haile Selassie I was God embodied and, hence, Black. Crucial to Brother Barody's identity transformation were the questions and sentiment that arose from his scrutiny of the mistreatment and scorn he saw directed toward the Rastafari. He saw injustice in how people that he interpreted as peace-loving were needlessly abused, and he was confused by the mistreatment of the Rastafari for beliefs he found to be reasonable. Brother Barody sought to comprehend what made the Rastafari outcasts. He was searching for answers to questions about race and God, and neither the churches nor educational institutions provided him with satisfactory answers. Brother Barody slowly came to identify with the Rastafari's "sufferation" (tribulation, poverty) and belief in a Black God and King who had returned to redeem Black people. Even though Brother Barody was already race-conscious before these encounters, he vicariously personalized the indignities he recognized the Rastafari as enduring.

Ras Burrell described how as a youth he was driven to seek knowledge about "truth and rights." He felt he could not articulate the questions but felt them "deep within me." He paid close attention to different ideological competitors: the revivalists, the Pentecostals, Garveyites, and Rastafari. Like Rasta Ivey, he determined that it was the Rastafari who were representative of truth and righteousness. To experience an encounter is not enough, as I have emphasized. In terms of identity transformation, the person must also interiorize the experience, and pursue and absorb cultural resources and information requisite to becoming competent from the standpoint of the new identity.

Witnessing the Personage of Rastafari

Experiential witnessing, a memorable and emotional experience of meeting or observing the Rastafari, can function as an encounter leading to identity transformation. The actual observation of or contact with the Rastafari is one way in which identity seeds are planted. Rastafari poet Mutabaruka hints at this by pointing to how attractive a symbol Rastafari has become for some people: "People does look on Rasta and does love Rasta, and does want to look like Rasta. This is really something, this is a phenomenon. . . . 'Bwoy, me like how you look,' and you start get up one morning and you try to look like him. This is a phenomenon" (2006:36).

Many of my narrators were drawn to Rastafari identity because they sought to grasp why the Rastafari were so persecuted. Their identity and cultural work involved observation and investigation and in the cases studied here, led to conclusions that there were no good reasons for inhumanely treating the Rastafari. They harbored something important and powerful, something that offered an antidote to miseducation and deracination. Some observers came to admire and wonder about the Rastafari for reasons as diverse as appreciation of their stances against injustice, the appeal of their doctrine about miseducation, or the contrast between the humble countenance of particular Rastafari and the power of their message. They were enticed to learn more about the beliefs and practices of the Rastafari.

Brother Yendis's encounter, like some of the experiences discussed above, was sparked by witnessing what he interpreted as an act of injustice committed against a Rastafari. I relate the story in detail in order to illuminate experiential witnessing as another primary pathway into Rastafari:

> [in 1947] me and my old man walk between Mullings Grassyard . . . and Tivoli Theatre . . . There was this Rasta man a push him cart coming up and we was going face him to the east. . . . I see a police man stand up and do so to him [gesturing wildly with his hands] turning him back. The police want him turn back. "I tell you to turn back," said the police. And the Rasta man say "Why you a turn me back for? Me a go 'bout me business." The police lift up him cart and turn it over. I was a little youth, and say to my father, "Papa, what him do that for?" and my father say, "Is Rasta," and we gone. I go inna [into] myself and say something wrong.

Brother Yendis, a young boy at the time, did not understand what had transpired and why the policeman had mistreated the Rastafari, and his father did not explain what happened. Yendis, however, sensed that something was wrong about what he saw. This vignette points out the cruel capriciousness suffered by the Rastafari of that time. Certainly, other people witnessed discriminatory and violent acts committed against the Rastafari, but how many were moved, like Yendis, to continue contemplating the experience weeks later? Or, to eventually change their self-identity and beliefs as a result?

Brother Yendis could not forget what he witnessed. He disclosed how

> About two weeks after that [encounter near Tivoli Theatre], I talk to my aunt's friend . . . I said "You know me and Papa go a town and a

policeman come up to a Rasta man wearing short pants and shirt and do him somthin' [assaulted]" . . . and she say "A Rasta that." That kinda get me shaky and make me feel something must wrong with Rasta.

The answer provided by the friend of his aunt further confused Yendis while also arousing his curiosity. He discerned the injustice but had no framework for making sense of what happened. Yendis was impressed by the Rastafari man's composure in the face of abuse from authority because he did not become enraged at what happened to him; he picked up his goods and moved on. The vague answers that Brother Yendis received from family members, however, implied that there was something wrong or bad about the Rastafari. Yendis wanted to know what was problematic about them. He received no satisfactory answers from others, so he began to investigate for himself. Truth became an important concern for Yendis. He began to believe that the institutions and authority figures such as schools and churches, teachers and parsons were obscuring more than they revealed about race, religion, and history. Yendis became disenchanted with these institutions and their leaders.

> Every Sunday morning, we go sit down beside the radio because me say one a them day ya [there], the parson man a go tell me the truth . . . Yes, we say one of these fine Sunday mornings, one of the parson man a go tell the truth. Them youth here lucky now, because them have the chance to say little things . . . Them don't get to understand the pressure [experienced by the older Rastafari]. Them don't get to understand the strain. Them don't get the chance to understand the holocaust what I and I have to go through. Rasta lose them life for this [faith and identity], my brethren. Sistren get beaten. Sistren have to take up them things and run with it.

He expected to find the truth in the revered institutions and people that his parents patronized. Yet, these institutions were not providing information relevant to Yendis's existential questions. After listening to many sermons in light of the encounter he had experienced, he came to believe that miseducation was inherent in the operation of these institutions. So many of them had absorbed and disseminated the hegemonic beliefs and values of elites and those who rule Jamaica. Nonetheless, it was the struggles and triumphs of previous generations of Rastafari that opened spaces of opportunity and acceptance for contemporary Rastafari.

The Rastafari man in Brother Yendis's account is significant in another way. Some Rastafari tried to be conspicuous bearers or exemplars of their identity, as a way to "help others recognize the Rastafarian in themselves" (Tucker, 1991:109), to germinate that "inborn conception." And this sometimes had the desired effect. Douglas Mack, one of the Rastafari who traveled with the Mission to Africa, related how as a youth during the mid-1940s, a charismatic Rastafari known as Brother Lover enthralled him with his "peace and love" messages and commanding bearded countenance. Even though the Rastafari were feared by many, Brother Lover had the opposite impact on him (1999:19).

Brother Dee, a first-generation Rastafari born in August 1912, attributed his path into the identity both to his curiosity about big questions of race, god, politics, and oppression, and to experiential witnessing. For Brother Dee, it was Leonard Howell, a Rastafari founder, who precipitated his move toward Rastafari. He listened to Howell's discourses on Haile Selassie I, Black redemption, and communal living, and wanted to learn more about his teachings. This led to intensive study of the Bible (and intense debate) with Rastafari he had met in the streets of Kingston and Spanish Town. Like many of those who became Rastafari between 1931 and the early 1970s, Brother Dee spoke using language that conflated Whiteness with capitalism, colonialism, and imperialism. He equated wealth and the power to control with being White. Rasta Ivey, of the same era, used similar language and allusions.

Organic Intellect and Curious Dispositions

Many of the Rastafari I consulted showed themselves to be organic intellectuals—poets, thinkers, writers, singers, organizers—who critically analyzed their situation and the world around them and challenged the prevailing common sense. Born to a family in which both parents were Garveyites and Seventh Day Adventists, Ras Sam Brown was socialized into Ethiopianism and Black nationalism from an early age; as with Brother Barody, racial awakening was not a fundamental catalyst to his coming into Rastafari. He met or knew all of the founding Rastafari. He met Marcus Garvey at the age of five and this made a permanent impression upon him:

I go Eidelweiss Park with me old man and from the gathering there to the little house [porch] that Garvey and his lieutenants was sitting on. . . .

I say to me father, "I want to talk to Marcus Garvey." Them say, "Sit down and behave yourself. [You are] Too rude." I say, "I want to talk to Marcus Garvey." Me mother say, "I will spank you," and start to screw [wrinkle her face to] get me quiet. Me father look 'pon her and say, "Make him go on." Thousands of people in that place [and] . . . it look to me I cannot see how I would find back myself to go back to my parents. I walk, I come down the balcony beneath and reach the grounds. I walk from cross the grounds . . . go up on a little three-step place. Marcus Garvey and some more man upon the verandah behind a desk and I go up there and I stand up at the table. Me head can barely catch the table. I stand up at the table. I don't know what to say now. I see a short man [Marcus Garvey] come out a inside room . . . him come righta the table to me. Other dignitaries sitting round the table you know. Him say to me, "Son, what do you want?" I say, "I would like to read that big book, sir." Him put him hand upon me head and say, "You will read it one day son." And I really read it you know.

Ras Sam Brown's account of his life emphasized his precociousness, both as child and adult. By his parents allowing him to accompany them to Garveyite meetings, Ras Sam Brown developed a keen interest in the condition of Black people and in Africa:

It was an inspiration that was in me. When the teacher a teach, showing us geography, I was more enthused with the map of Africa than any other map in the atlas. So, I had a conscious opinion of Africa. My daddy was a Garveyite. My mother also because she had to go along with him. So, from a little boy I was conscious of certain things. I went to Edelweiss park [where Marcus Garvey often spoke] with me mother and father.

The study of Africa was not a part of Jamaica's educational curriculum. As Ras Sam Brown moved into his teens, he increasingly became disinterested in the status quo. He felt that the church of his parents was unsatisfying. He said he "sensed the Rastas had a message and I was attracted to the way they did things." He began to listen to the messages of the itinerant and Rastafari street preachers of the early 1940s. The emphasis on Black redemption, Ethiopia as home, and the return of the Messiah as a Black King were provocative and engaged Ras Sam Brown. He studiously read any material on Africa and Black history he could find; he combed through the Old and New Testaments to check and double check the claims being made by the Rastafari. Gradually, Ras Sam Brown took up the faith and became one of its most impassioned defenders, articulators, and teachers.

Ras Brenton, unable to escape living in dire poverty, has maintained a sense of wonder and questioning throughout his life: "I was always thinking," he said, "'Why is it Black people have to be suffering like this?' You see me? So that is why I actually become a Rasta man, because me come see the Rasta man a cry out against the sufferation and me have to cry with them too because me see say it right." While it was unclear exactly what first led Ras Brenton to sympathize with other impoverished Black Jamaicans, he came to identify with and internalize the Rastafari critique of the injustices endured by the "sufferers."

The belief that ultimate truth(s) can be known and acquired is important to affirming the emerging Rastafari's investigation and pursuit of the new identity. Rastafari identity is partly an antidote to how Blacks have been socialized into absorbing hegemonic White versions of religion, history, and culture, all of which have been presented as "common sense" and natural truths. Rastafari identity provides a means to deep re-socialization and offers Black people a culturally framed psychosocial medicine for racism and discrimination. Nevertheless, overturning common sense and building a new identity do not happen automatically. The encounter is a powerful experience that opens a person's eyes and challenges their thinking.

The differences between the Rastafari and other Jamaicans, though many-faceted, hang less on biocultural phenotypic markers such as untrimmed hair, or cultural signifiers such as red, gold, and green, than on Rastafari "seeing" and "knowing" contrasted against the blindness, ignorance, falsehoods, and victimization associated with the non-Rastafari.

5

Acts of Identity Work

[O]nce ago, them used to tell we say Africa is the dark continent
and no man can go there and survive because is only lions there to
eat you . . . And now we a get to realize say that no real. . . . A lie,
as you say, them a tell upon Africa.

(Ras Brenton)

Some Black people internalize the negative tropes of Blackness
and Africa that Ras Brenton has come to recognize as hypocritical myths.
Getting away from such beliefs is part of the Rastafari identity transformation process. Beliefs, such as those about race and culture, are not totally
consistent or logical, and no matter how wrong, they can unproblemati-
cally dwell in people's minds unless seriously tested (Toch, 1965:117–118).
The connections that Ras Brenton has made between miseducation, race,
and oppression contribute to making his old beliefs untenable and his
new ideas and identifications potentially viable.

One summer afternoon, while Ras Brenton and I sat on the broken
porch of his tiny two-room shanty, he told me stories that illustrated how
his curiosity and interest in existential concerns about oppression and
race were actualized in ways that led him to desire to know more about
the Rastafari's views on these issues:

I remember, we use to use [Mortimer] Planno's yard . . . I used to go
there regularly to get counseling there and that is where I get to learn
most [about Rastafari] because I used to go to him yard, where him is.
And when we go there, chalice¹ a burn and me was a chalice man, so I
had to sip chalice because I used the same chalice to get to them too, to
get reasoning out of them. Seen? So when the chalice a run, I was always
pronto . . . I just sit back and watch what is happening and take it in. I

did not do anything more than take in the reasoning. Now and again, I would make a point because I know man loves to embarrass man. Sometimes I feel like they will want to embarrass me too. I sit in and listen and be a good learner.

The encounter, metaphorically, is a door. Once it is opened, a person does things which determine whether he or she will look inside the door, and if so, whether to cross the threshold and continue investigating what lies beyond the door. Ras Brenton crossed the doorstep not only because he found the Rastafari cry against injustice fascinating. He decided to listen and learn from the Rastafari, even though he assumed a passive role early in this process. Ras Brenton could have decided the Rastafari were of no interest, however, and therefore would not have begun the work required for identity transformation. In retrospect, I know that by the time Ras Brenton began spending time at various Rastafari yards, he had already begun his identity transformation: he was becoming Rastafari. The decisions attendant to walking through the door opened by the encounter also open up a person to unforeseen challenges, tensions, and satisfactions, and these, as we shall see, shape the experience of identity transformation.

Creating a Rastafari identity for oneself involves many challenges. A person must decide how to deal with whom he or she was "before" and how to deal with the relationships attendant to the "old" self. He or she must also "construct" and maintain the new identity. Thus, processes involving investment, sacrifice, renunciation, mortification, and reward are set into motion. These actions almost invariably generate tension and insecurity, along with feelings of achievement, in creating a new self and kinship with the newfound family of Rastafari. Identity transformation turns into an ongoing project, always subject to being undone or stalled because it requires continual negotiation and regular maintenance.

Identity transformation presents itself as a solution to the questions, tensions, and concerns of our narrators. They focused on seeking information related to their new identity and group, making an intentional effort to learn what they could about the new group. In the case of the Rastafari, study of print media (especially the Bible, and when available, literature on Ethiopia, Africa, and Black history and culture) took precedence along with learning from already acculturated members. Gradual participation in activities associated with the new group referent began during or after personalization of the encounter. During this phase, many of them were aggressive and defensive in asserting the new identity, swaggering to conceal any shallowness in their knowledge about Rastafari or to present themselves as respectable members. While this was a part of erecting their new identity, militancy and symbolic aggression were also used for other purposes (see chapter 2).

Renunciation involves ending or renegotiating relationships that compete with the new identity (Kanter, 1972). Family and friends questioned my narrators' decisions to change and sometimes estranged themselves from the convert. These experiences of persecution may have been painful to emergent Rastafari, but they also served to inform practices and understandings of sacrifice, investment, and reward, all being important dimensions structuring the edifice of Rastafari identity formation. These emerging Rastafari were also challenged by the wider public. To continue on their identity transformation path, they needed to muster conviction in a view of themselves as a chosen and special people who *must* sacrifice and endure maltreatment because of their beliefs, thus enacting a self-fulfilling prophecy.

As an emerging Rastafari learned more, he and she came to see the world in a different way, frequently invoking moral superiority vis-à-vis the non-Rastafari. The fact that my interlocutors became comfortable with their new outlook and identity did not necessarily suggest that their identity-related tensions ended. Instead, they had to maintain and negotiate their new identity over time. For example, with the ascendance of the Dreadlocks Rastafari, it became an issue for one not to wear dreadlocks. Rasta Ivey, for instance, tells me she did not grow locks until the early 1980s. Sometimes the Dreadlocks criticized Rasta Ivey and other Rastafari who did not wear locks (the "Combsomes"), marking them as not totally committed to Rastafarian identity because they had not taken the step of making physically tangible their "covenant" (dreadlocks). This critique, though, had little effect on Rasta Ivey's decision to grow her locks when she did. Comfortable in her conviction, she believed that she did not need to grow locks to indicate her identity and commitment.

Miseducation and Socialization: Keys to Rastafari Identity Formation

Moving through the door opened by the encounter requires "identity work," the activities attendant to creating and internalizing a new identity. A central thesis of Cross's nigrescence model asserts that deracination and miseducation are what make possible the positive valorization of

Black identity. For my narrators moving into Rastafari identity, hunger for information about Black history and culture showed itself. Information about Black history and culture, in its various forms—books, pamphlets, news stories, tales passed from one person to another—became integral to informing their new identity.

One way I learned how my interlocutors came to exalt Blackness and Africa was to ask how they learned about Africa or Black history. For instance, I asked whether they learned of Africa or Black culture during their schooling in Jamaica. Invariably, they had not been introduced to Africa or Black history and culture in school, at least not in any substantive way. Brother Bongo emphasized how "No African literature was distributed in school." What Brother Bongo did come into contact with were stories of "Bomba the Jungle Boy." "We had a literature," he said, "with a story about Bombo [sic],[2] African boy, a boy in the jungle. That was the only story about Africa. Most of the times . . . colonial slave masters was the main history. Sir Francis Drake, Christopher Columbus . . . Henry Morgan . . . [and] John Hawkins." Instead of education about Africa and Black history, Brother Bongo's formal learning was filled primarily with teaching about Europeans important to modern history whom he referred to as "slave masters" and "pirates," whose exploits were canonized. Brother Bongo and his peers sought to reeducate and remake themselves as "Ethiopians" proud of their African heritage and association with the Messiah who also hailed from that continent: "We develop ourselves through reading. This man will get a literature and pass it on to that man, and we sit and reason" (Brother Bongo). Because his formal education taught Brother Bongo to give prominence to Europe and its influence in the world, he was not learning about the culture and history of his ancestors. This suppression of Blackness is simultaneously a source of miseducation and deracination and a starting point for the Rastafari quest to resuscitate and validate Black culture and history and analyze oppressive practices. Identity in many ways is an able vehicle for moving their project.

My narrators developed their Rastafari identity primarily through interiorized conversation with oneself and participation in dialogue and interaction. Interpretation of public perception and reaction were also crucial sources of information for identity transformation. Brother Bongo's early experience of identity transformation, for example, involved a coterie of people whose interaction with each other provided support and conviction:

We always seek to reason on the higher level of reality. My clique. That is when we touch 18, 19 [years of age]. So we find ourselves gathering, start working out [mentally and physically] you know. About 1958 into 1960. During the '60s, I was working at a woodwork shop by Norman Road . . . where they made big settees, big furniture for export. At midday, we used to go by the beach and burn the herb and reason, follow up in the evenings; we go and reason touching the works of His Majesty. We started to penetrate the history of His Majesty and Africa generally and go right up into our history to know who we are and where we coming from. At a time, we realize that working out there in Babylon just keeps our minds enslaved to the Babylon system. It does not give us any time to think of ourselves and think of the future. So, I come to the conclusion that I would leave the work. But, before we leave the work, the consciousness start show on us as we start to let the hair grow now, and beard started to spring up.

For Brother Bongo and his brethren, growing into the new identity required moving away from the routines and relationships associated with their existing identities. In nigrescence theory, pursuit of information about Blackness is referred to as immersion. Immersion, as an experience and a process, is about a person's exploration of the norms, beliefs, and practices of the new identity and reference group, while better developing a rationale for why identity transformation is necessary. Growing into Rastafari identity in the company of like-minded people affirmed the choices of some of my narrators.

One of the preoccupations of the Rastafari between the mid-1950s and mid-1970s was learning Amharic, an Ethiopian language. They reasoned they needed to learn the language in preparation for repatriation to Ethiopia. Learning Amharic supported their identification as Africans and drew borders that differentiated them from other groups in Jamaica. Most Rastafari of that era used at least a few words of Amharic in their communication with each other. Rastafari like Brother Bongo sought to become fully competent in Amharic:

We got acquainted with Amharic language. We got a document with the alphabet and he [another Rastafarian], having a book shop and in the literature circle, came upon a dictionary for interpretation of Amharic to English–translating Amharic to English. The first word we find is "Wadada," meaning love; second word is "satta amasagana"—give thanks. We go on and find "Kibbilahamla"–glory to God. Then we started to put word and word together. First of all, we ran down the alphabet of Amharic . . . We go as far as that we could recite the whole 276 characters by heart.

Knowledge of Amharic was a means by which to gain respect from fellow Rastafari and to show commitment to Rastafari identity.

An important experience of the emerging Rastafari involved listening to and studying what seasoned Rastafarians do and say. As Ras Brenton put it, "me move amongst the Rasta them, and go all 'bout them there and try to get argument [insights, lessons] from them, and [I] study them more and learn more from them because me a study them from before me put on me knotty (dreadlocks)." Ras Brenton learned much about the Rastafari through studying their exemplars, and he sometimes prodded them to share their understandings so that he might better grasp what he himself was on the path to becoming. His participation during the early phases of engagement was on the fringe. He "moved" among them, but discreetly. Ras Brenton did not make his vow to become Rastafari until he grasped the fundamental norms and practices of the group. "Putting on" one's "knotty," "covenant," or dreadlocks, had by the late 1970s become a primary means of publicly displaying or symbolically conveying one's identity and commitment to Rastafari (Many of my narrators became Rastafari when there was no obligation to grow locks).

Study of the Bible is fundamental to Rastafari identity transformation. It is the pivotal authority informing Rastafari conceptions of the justice motifs, and a key way in which the Rastafari come to identify with the past and make it relevant to the present. Paradoxically, the Bible has also been used as a medium for miseducating Blacks about religion, culture, and history. But through subversive techniques, the Rastafari use the Bible as a tool for reeducation. The Rastafari read the Bible through "new" eyes, employing a racial and critical analysis that gave biblical characters living, contemporary analogues.[3] Through such practices the Rastafari drew radically different conclusions from the same text that serves mainstream Christianity.

On another summer afternoon, Brother Woks and I sat on a bench beneath a cottonwood tree in an open, parklike area known locally as "racetrack," talking at length about his memories and knowledge of Rastafari. Brother Woks was familiar with the politics of Rastafari. Few in-depth conversations between Rastafari continue very far without reference to the Bible, and soon we were talking about the Bible and how it related to his becoming a Rastafari:

> The Bible is the thing that bring me stronger to the light because the Bible is like a compass. It is the spirit that holds you firm. As His Majesty says, "a person without a religion is like a body without any soul." We have to have a religion though government does not recognize the Rastafarians, who over the years, are agitating for recognition that the government should recognize us as a religion. Notwithstanding, we still know that this is a direct religion and it is religiously political.

I asked Brother Woks, "How does the 'political' come in?" He replied, "Through Black Nationalism. From the mere fact that you really fly a flag, that is politics . . . [Then there are] . . . the atrocities committed against our ancestors, and . . . they raped Africa and it is the reason why we are here." In grounding his grievances *and* identity in slavery and the spoiling of Africa, Brother Woks offers perspective on how the Rastafari do not organize governance, religion, race, and grievances into separate compartments. The Jamaican government refuses to officially recognize Rastafari as a religion, and he feels that part of the reason is because both "fly a flag," raising questions of national loyalty. The Ethiopian flag is an important symbol for the Rastafari because in their minds it outwardly marks them as a nation and a nationality that foregrounds race, a race committed to the idea of Africa and a Black God. Perhaps Garvey and his UNIA were influential in this regard:

> Now, when Mr. Marcus Garvey talked about a king shall be crowned in Africa . . . they check with the Bible. So, on checking with the Bible and reading Revelation, chapter 5, there is a question asking "Who is worthy enough to open the book and to loose the seven seals thereof? No man in heaven, nor on earth, nor beneath the earth is found worthy to open the book and to loose the seven seals thereof." So John, in his vision cried. He wept and a spirit said to John, "Weep not. Behold the lamb who was slain. The Conquering Lion of the Tribe of Judah shall come, and he is the one who is found worthy to open the book and to loose the seven seals thereof. Look on his gesture and look on his thigh and look on his style and it is written that no man knoweth but he himself. King of Kings and Lord of Lords. The Conquering Lion of the Tribe of Judah. Elect of God and the Light of this world. Out of his mouth has cometh a sharp

two-edged sword. With it, he shall smite the nation." So the brothers said, "This is Him that Mr. Marcus Garvey is talking about. This must be the man that Mr. Marcus Garvey is talking about." . . . That is the basis from which we all come to the acknowledgment that His Majesty is the returned Christ seated on the throne of David. (Brother Woks)

Brother Woks offers us here an illustration of how the Rastafari reinscribe the meaning of biblical narratives as a part of dismantling the negative effects of miseducation and deracination.

Through You, I Am: Babylon and Christianity as Reference Groups

Be ye not unequally yoked together with unbelievers: for what fellowship hath righteousness with unrighteousness? And what communion hath light with darkness? . . . For ye are the temple of the living God; as God hath said, I will dwell in them, and walk in *them*; and I will be their God and they shall be my people. Wherefore, come out from among them, and be ye separate. (II Corinthians 6: 14, 16, 17, original emphasis)

Rastafari identity, as a social construction, is contingent upon the identities of other groups. In particular, their identity depends on their trying to be what others are not, of having what others lack, of clarifying their identity by excluding others (Hall, 1996:4). Through their recognition of other groups, the Rastafari socially define and position themselves. In thinking others, we also think ourselves (Holland and Lachicotte, 2007).

Christians play an important recognition role for the Rastafari, helping them distinguish and position themselves. And, their differences notwithstanding, the two share much in common. Historically, they have drawn adherents from the same pool. Further, they both rely on the King James Bible and draw upon many of the same discourses and symbols. The Rastafari, however, actively construct themselves as different from Christians, and as suggested in the Corinthians passage cited above, they symbolically separate themselves from those who do not hold to their beliefs. The Rastafari mock the Christians because they are waiting for God to return, to enter the physical plane through the firmament. For the Rastafari, however, God has already returned to mingle among humans in a physical form. Belief in a physically embodied God is consistent with older beliefs held by some of the African slaves and their descendants in

Jamaica (Turner, 1982). Although a direct connection cannot be made between the beliefs of these Africans and their Jamaican descendants, the beliefs are strikingly similar. The Rastafari call Jamaica a living hell. Hell, for the Rastafari, exists on earth, not under it. In their estimation, it is a human creation, a product of oppression and exploitation, and through identity transformation they expect to free themselves from contributing to its perpetuation.

The Rastafari denounce Christians for their failure to walk the path of righteousness. For the Rastafari, the Christian mission is not about justice, liberation, Black redemption, the remembrance of slavery, or resistance against mental slavery. Only the Rastafarians are carrying forward the crusade:

> When one says Christianity, we have to differentiate in this time because you see a Christian out there and his actions are that of a barbarian and he claims that he is Christian. He may say he is a Roman Catholic, he is a Baptist, he is a Pentecostal, but his behavior is Satan. So, you cannot prove him to be a Christian, and you know Christianity is righteous living. So, His Majesty see that we [Rastafari] are righteous people, because all Ethiopians are righteous people, originally. We only break away through captivity and through slavery and learn the ways of alien nations and become aliens, and some of us lust and get lost along the way. (Brother Bongo)

Modern Babylon, the Rastafari conception of a reincarnated ancient system of injustice and wickedness, includes the Christians. Black people, in the Rastafari view, were originally a righteous people, but lost their innocence and purity because of ancient sins and the tribulations they have since experienced, especially slavery and the class system cultivated on its foundation. Rastafari is a collective effort to reclaim that imagined innocence and purity, a racialized moral vision of society. This separates the Rastafari from those who they see as "barbarians," rendering a sense of superiority: they are emancipated. Emancipation from mental slavery means to cast away the shrouds of miseducation and deracination, to step away from and criticize the political and economic institutions that pit people against each other. Emancipation also means not being driven by material desires to accumulate or to lust. Like the Christians, though, some of my narrators struggled to faithfully embody and enact the ideals of their faith.

Identity Work: Tensions and Challenges for the Emerging Rastafari

I listened to a youthful Rastafari, Ras Desmond, whose scarce facial hair and unblemished smooth dark skin suggested he was in his early to mid-twenties, solicit advice from Ras Grantly, who was perhaps in his late forties. Ras Grantly, an imposing figure with his stern visage, piercing eyes, and single large lock folded onto his shoulders, had been seasoned by years of activism. Rastafari and non-Rastafari alike respected him for his quick intellect, rhetorical skill, and straightforward manner. Ras Desmond walked in the Rastafari Federation seeking advice; he sat in a large and sparsely furnished room with Ras Grantly, Brother Yendis, and me. Folded up in one of Ras Desmond's hands were several articles about the Rastafari. Ras Desmond wanted advice on the hyper-zealousness and aggressiveness of some of his youthful contemporaries. Known to some as "fire bu'n" Rastafari, Desmond's contemporaries were antagonistically calling for "burning" of Jesus, literature, and even the Bible. To invoke "fire bu'n" ("fire burn") is to damn or denounce a person, thing, or happening. Desmond's problem was that he saw such confrontational condemnation as being abused, and, as a result of his ambivalence, he attracted the ire of his fellow Rastafari. With a confused face, Desmond asked Ras Grantly, "How them a go bu'n book? How them a go bu'n Jah?" Certainly, Ras Grantly, once a "fiya" (fire) man himself, would have an answer, I thought. During the 1970s, Ras Grantly was a militant and zealous Rastafari enamored of his faith and identity, a vocal critic of Jamaica and capitalism. Methodically, arms folded across his breast, Ras Grantly walked to a cabinet and retrieved a book consisting of a collection of Haile Selassie I's speeches. He began to read from a speech delivered by the Emperor to the Trinidadian Parliament during the mid-1960s. The speech emphasized the importance of tolerance and spiritual progress. After slowly reading the speech, often pausing on and repeating for emphasis key words like *tolerance,* Ras Grantly offered his analysis:

> Those who are so quick to bu'n everything are not following His Majesty's words, which for example in His Majesty's speech on material and spiritual progress, he asks that people be tolerant of other faiths and beliefs. Second (now speaking very loudly for emphasis), it is important that we allow for difference as we do not seek unity of ideology. Third (now holding up the index finger of his left hand), [Selassie I asked us to] organize and centralize.

After Ras Grantly's oration, we continued to analyze some of the issues confronting Desmond and his generation of Rastafari. A fundamental disconnect existed between the younger Rastafari and Ras Grantley's generation. Desmond's generation of Rastafari was ignoring how Ras Grantly's generation had grappled with and moved beyond questions such as how to address "europeanized" interpretations of the Bible, or whether they should completely abandon books that in any way reinforce White and class hegemony. A similar disconnect, however, had been experienced by Ras Grantly's generation as they rejected the beliefs and practices of their Rastafari elders such as the Combsomes. How Desmond's generation will resolve this issue is an open question because their experience and context are different from that of previous generations of Rastafari. We shall return to this issue in the next chapter.

Given that an emerging Rastafari has so much to learn about a new identity, it is unsurprising that a fledgling can be exceedingly zealous, defensive, or romantic about his or her identity. Such displays both mask and expose the personal insecurities about not being thoroughly familiar with the norms, practices, and beliefs associated with that new identity. When people immerse themselves in Black history and culture, combativeness and outright anger toward Whites, anti-Black Blacks, and the status quo may define their general attitude (Cross Jr., 1995, 2001). As emerging Rastafari become increasingly competent in and confident with their identity, aggressiveness and anger shift from regular to situational behavior. Ras Brenton, for example, moved beyond his confrontational stance long ago, and his experience suggests that both Ras Grantly's and Ras Desmond's generations are dealing with the same problems at different points in time, although Ras Desmond's generation has not acknowledged this:

> I been trying to show them [young Rastafari] these things, you know, but sometimes they don't accept it. Me no bother bu'n them with no fire. Me just allow them. Me pass them stage there now. . . . me just allow them, and next time me an them can either reason it out or otherwise. Them hold on to what them hold on to . . . I am holding on [to my beliefs] the same way too . . . I ain't going to let you take me off my track because me come here like a king, priest and prophet. (Ras Brenton)

During earlier phases in his Rastafari identity development, Ras Brenton would have been likely to condemn verbally anyone uninterested in what he had to say about his beliefs or society or anyone who ridiculed his identity. He had "mellowed out," so to speak, accepting differences of opinion and faith without being overly zealous.

The Rastafari must be prepared to defend their faith with each other and against an unsympathetic public. A Rastafari's capacity to forcibly articulate his identity is valued by other Rastafari because

> when one can really defend his philosophy to a certain level, the fighters [challengers] realize that this is not a person whom you can ask any and every kind of question except those questions are based on an intelligent manner. But if you are going to ask him some stupid question, then you will find yourself in trouble. (Brother Woks)

Not all Rastafari revere the practice of belligerent argumentation and hyper-zealousness. Many of them value prudence and humility, indicating the many variations of ideology and practice that characterize the Rastafari. Brother Woks's criticism illustrates this point:

> When I was coming on from a youth, a lot of [passionate] sentiment usually were expressed during those times. Them burn literature, them burn everything. If you even have on clean clothes and things like that, they would burn you too. You even wear a watch and things like that, a pen pinned to your pocket, they would burn you. Looking clean, they burn you. If you speak with a female, they did not too much like that because they feel that you fleshy. . . . That is part of what set back the movement.

Brother Woks is referencing the struggle for ideological and ritual hegemony within the Rastafari by the ascetic and combative factions of the Dreadlocks. As we saw in previous chapters, these Rastafari moved beyond rhetorical critiques to disengage from Jamaican society and reject material trappings. They were zealots and at odds not only with Babylon, but their moderate brothers and sisters. Brother Bags, for example, stopped wearing clothing, donned a burlap bag, and moved into the hills of Wareika. He gave up using "manmade" tools and ate only what nature produced. He too pursued a "prehistoric" lifestyle, like Ras Jayze. These prehistoric Rastafari imagined themselves as wandering saints. Brother Woks believes that the aggressiveness of some of the Rastafari agitators of the 1950s and '60s expedited the repressive reactions against them, reifying the already negative representation of them.

Getting Away From the Old Self Is Easier Said Than Done

Identity transformation, as experienced by my narrators, tested their re-lationships because their change contested people's inflexible understand-ings of the convert. The past of the emerging Rastafari haunted them into the future, depending on what relationship stresses they had to deal with and on how far disengagement and renunciation were taken. The emerg-ing Rastafari's pre-existing relationships conjured the issue of old loyalties and how to alter (or even completely eliminate) them in ways that ap-pear consistent with the new identity. Ras Brenton early on in his identity transformation found himself trying to "satisfy" a church woman whom he had loved as a child by letting her try and comb out his dreadlocks. She appealed to his affection as a way to "undo" his locks because she be-lieved he should be a Christian:

> Me remember one time, me Dread, and a church woman what me know name Miss Grant. She was a good friend of mine because she had a son and me and him was good friend and through that we have to love her more. . . . the woman never stop till she influence me and tell me 'bout make she comb it out [the dreadlocks] for me . . . and through me a try to satisfy her feelings, me dissatisfy myself. . . . The woman pressure me to comb out the locks . . . me have to stop her part of the way you know, and see how me a give this woman her heart's desire. . . . When she done comb it out Rasta, the whole of my scalp in a fire. So, me take a oath and say, me would never make a woman do that again because she come like Delilah upon me.

Ras Brenton's attempt to please an adored female figure had the effect of making him more resolute and committed to his identity; former loyalties did not trump his emergent faith and identity. He remained regretful that he allowed Miss Grant to persuade him to shed his locks.

Other kinds of relationships created tensions for the emerging Rasta-fari. The ascetic Rastafari forswore employment of any kind and moved into the hills or bush to live hermitic lives. Other Rastafari continued with status quo conventions such as wage employment. For those individuals already growing into Rastafari, wage employment and its relation to the old self was sometimes problematic and a source of hostility, and this ill feeling could affect family and friends. Brother Bongo reflected on how

At the work place, they said they could not tolerate the loose hair, so we have to trim and shave to continue the employment . . . management told I that personally. . . . "You have to trim. If you don't trim, Monday morning, you cannot come back." That was the Friday evening after pay. Well, it was between getting another pay bill and keeping the covenant. By that time, we developed full consciousness. That pay bill cannot help us. We want to research and know whom we really are. Monday morning, I just went for my tool box and left the work. That time, I was living by Cambridge Street in Franklin Town. It was my family's place and they, too, started to take resentment for my faith and the growing of my hair. So there was a policeman in my aunt's husband's family . . . and being a policeman, he was strictly against Rasta and said he did not want any Rasta on his father's premises. So, I had to leave the home at Cambridge Street. I thought it over, and that time, I had a girlfriend . . . I say to myself, I will have to leave this place and I am going to build a tatu [a makeshift dwelling]. . . . My girlfriend said, "Anywhere you go, I am going to follow you." I said, "You go back to your parents, because this life that I am going to take is not for you this time. It is a rugged life . . . I am going to make a trod right now." . . . Eventually, I had a brethren who we worked same place and he took on to the faith too and we linked together, and the both of us moving in the same direction, and we built a tatu down by Charlotte Street.

Mortification consists of actions and thoughts that involve a person's willingness to submit him or herself to the norms of a larger, valued group (Kanter, 1972) and is a part of disengaging from the old identity and its referents and relations. Mortification has as its complement the inculcation of new personal standards of meaning, value, and reward, along with different referents and relations attendant to the new identity. While identity-related collisions with family, friends, and others can cause a person tension, anxiety, and uncertainty, there is also the potential to resolve this stress through developing new relationships and referents. Mortification and identity transformation entail investment, sacrifice, conviction, and the *promise* of reward:

We have to keep the faith. The faith is peace, perfect peace and . . . perfect love . . . from we have the love of Jah, miraculous things can happen. So, we just have that faith of love. [Mortimer] Planno used to sing a tune,

"We leave our homes and families just to travel with the chord of love."
(Ras Brenton)

The reminders of the old identity may never completely disappear, depending upon how an emerging Rastafari goes about constructing his or her identity. A few of my narrators suggested that they severed all of their ties to their old identity, although most were more discriminating in distancing themselves from relationships connected to their old identity.

Displacing or erasing the old self was for my narrators easier said than done and rarely as impersonal or uncomplicated as their accounts sometimes implied. Commonly, the old self was devalued through identity work that disparaged or rejected the previous identity. While self and group identifications were merging through mortification, other processes, such as renunciation or the repudiation of some aspects of the social and material world, were also at work. Through mortification and renunciation, the emergent Rastafari symbolically and socially distanced themselves from their old selves and their ties to the world while creating new relationships and referents. They were redrawing and strengthening identifications related to their RGO.

During the 1960s, Brother Bongo and many of his fellow Rastafari were adamant about completely renouncing Jamaican nationality in favor of Ethiopian nationality. They invested a great deal of time and energy on renunciation, efforts which spilled over into the world of formal politics.

Our program was "Ethiopian Nationality Claim for Resettlement to Ethiopia." So, we decided to draft a resolution with the provision, by law, of our rights to claim our Ethiopian nationality. . . . the Jamaican Constitution also makes provision for us to claim any nationality . . . we endorsed the resolution at a meeting, a street meeting . . . which was very well attended.

The work of political Rastafarians like Brother Bongo toward formal identity recognition ratcheted more tightly the tension between them and unsympathetic Jamaicans. In 1964, Jamaica had recently gained its independence from Britain, and here were the Rastafari demanding a distinct identity and independence from Jamaica. Collective confrontations such as those referenced by Brother Bongo reflected, among other things, how personal identity meshed with collective identification in creating a distinct identity. The individual Rastafari were in a larger sense actively carving out an identity space in Jamaica through collective efforts to re-frame identity boundaries between themselves and other Jamaicans. By the 1960s, renunciation had become a phenomenon present across the world, forcibly expressed, for example, in the national liberation, inde-pendence, and Black power movements that rejected the hegemony asso-ciated with colonial and Eurocentric-oriented national identities.

Another dimension of establishing a Rastafari self and renouncing the old identity involved changing one's name. As the Rastafari grew into their identity, many changed or revised their name, drawing attention to and emphasizing the new identity. Honorifics such as Ras, Brother, Sister, Queen, Princess, Bongo, or Congo were common titles adopted by the emerging Rastafari. People baptized into the Jamaican Ethiopian Ortho-dox Church have been required to take on a new name as a part of the Church's process of creating new members and bringing them into the existing community.[4] Brother Bongo, who joined the Ethiopian Orthodox Church as a way to deepen his affirmation as an Ethiopian and a Ras-tafari, explained why he changed his name, and why it is important for Rastafarians to change their name:

> I man can declare I self as an Ethiopian national abroad because my name . . . [is now] "Servant of the Trinity." I renounce "John Brown" which is my slave name; that is my slave master's name. I come of age and to the consciousness to my ancestral rights, my original rights, my original identity as an Ethiopian.

Before joining the Ethiopian Orthodox Church, Brother Bongo had as-sumed "Bongo" as a part of his name and identification. By taking on the name Bongo, he employed a familiar subversive act of racial conscious-ness. Bongo, like "Nigger," or "Blackheart man," can be used pejoratively to denigrate and caricature Blackness (Bongo as fool or brute). The Ras-tafari took Bongo (and Blackheart) and made them into honorific titles signifying Black pride. In explaining his new name, Brother Bongo em-phasized his effort to destroy the lingering vestiges of slavery at the most intimate level, that of his personal identity.

'Damn Fool Turn Rasta'

Ras Sam Brown's mother was displeased that he had begun to grow his hair and beard, a sure sign that he was moving toward Rastafari. Cleverly,

Ras Sam Brown evaded discussion of his identity transformation by evading ("bobbing and weaving") her:

> After me father died, I start grow me hair tall. Me father always a give me money to cut me hair when him was alive, and I bob and weave him out. Me always comb it and pat it down and all them things there. After me father died, me mother she did not like to see me face hairy up so, but . . . me know how to bob and weave her. And although she became proud, one a the time she say she didn't know she was going bring a ram goat into the world. Afterwards, when she see her son and see them lock courtroom door and try I behind lock and have to open the courtroom door and let me out, she feel proud of me, man.

Recalling the memory of his mother calling him a ram goat led Brown to laugh loudly. I laughed too. "You know 'bout ram goat?" he asked me. "Yes," I said. "Ugly. Rank. Tall beard." I could have added "dangerous." Non-Rastafari intentionally invoked "Ram goat" as a way to denigrate male Rastafarians. The idea of the Rastafari as dirty and dangerous was expressed in many ways, and Jamaican cultural tropes such as the ram goat provided identity fodder for Rastafari and non-Rastafari alike. For the non-Rastafari it provided a way to ridicule the Rastafari. However, for the Rastafari, such tropes applied to them provided evidence of how people unreasonably maligned them.

Even gradual moves toward Rastafari could discombobulate family and friends. The stigmatized status Jamaicans created for the Rastafari made it difficult for them to grasp why anyone would identify as such. These situations led some emerging Rastafari to seriously ponder whether Rastafari was worth the loss of family and friends. My interviewees took the risk and came to privilege Rastafari over other identifications and worldly concerns. In actuality, though, they were unable to completely avoid either family and friends or worldly concerns. Sometimes critics of Rastafari softened or became tolerant of them, something which the emerging Rastafari had to consider. Brother Yendis told how his father reacted as he slowly grew into the new identity:

> When the brother yah [speaking of himself] a turn Rasta you know, my father say, "Heh, heh, heh. See the boy a turn a damn fool, man?" A him friend him a talk to, you know. "See the boy a turn a damn fool, man?

Look at the boy . . . You no see!? You no see him!? Look [at the dread-locks] upon him head!" The man say to him say, "Tell me something Brother D. Him a do something wrong? Tell me what him a do. Him a walk round and make trouble? People a complain to you?" "No, no, no, no. But him no Rasta?" [said the father]. The man say to him . . . "if what him doing is not committing any problem, allow him now man." And from that my old man is a changed old man, you know.

The contempt that Brother Yendis's father expressed toward the Rastafari exemplifies what so many of the Rastafari were asking of themselves and society: "If we are doing no wrong, but simply following our beliefs, why are we being mistreated?" It took a trusted friend of Yendis's father to sug-gest the bigotry of his position and to drive home the point that Yendis was not doing anything wrong.

Ras Brenton reflected on some of the social and interpersonal conflicts his identity raised for him. On one side, he felt he had disappointed his mother by not becoming her "Christian son," though he was not at all remorseful. On the other, he had to deal with a public who abused him because of his identity. He sometimes defensively reacted and "burned" them with "fire":

[I] get a lot of bad names being a Rasta, but my mother never curse me. My mother tell me say she know I was going to be her Christian son . . . me never even know 'til when me turn big man and put on my dreadlocks. She a look upon me and a say to me say, "Boy, me know you was going be my Christian son, you know, but you no know, it is just life all over." She no fight me down, and me daddy no fight me down either [about becoming Rastafari]. A just old Nayga ["Nigger"] a fight me down, and me have to fight them forward. You no see it? Me no stop burn them with fire, and ease them off a me . . . Because me realize say me come with the God power, and is it me a defend, and me no make the heathen turn me back.

Ras Brenton, like Brother Yendis, did not completely alienate himself from his family as he moved toward Rastafari. However, the identity transfor-mations of both men precipitated conflict with relatives. Ras Brenton's mother was unhappy with his identity transformation, but given the pov-erty of her family and the lack of financial support from other children, she needed his assistance, possibly explaining why she did not completely reject his new identification.

Similarly, Brother Bongo's mother could not afford to become estranged from her son even if she disagreed with his identity transformation, even though many other family members did reject him:

> When they saw me as Rasta, my mother was not in a position to fight the faith. I was on my own, and I was helping her at the same time. She was in England for a good while and when she came back, she saw me and my brother. I am Rasta and my brother was not. We had no cause to fight.

In these cases, we see that becoming Rastafari can alienate family and friends. But this does not doom the relationships to drifting apart. Many complicating factors suffused the relationships between the emerging Rastafari and other people, such as whether or not there were people sympathetic to the emerging Rastafari or what role they played in familial and social contexts. Even Rastafari such as Brother Dee and Brother Bags, who took the ascetic Rastafari path, eventually reconnected with people associated with their old identity.

Commitment and Internalization

Specifying the exact point when a person feels sufficiently comfortable in their Rastafari identity is an elusive endeavor, but it is an empirical condition that people experience. At some point, the new identity becomes internalized, operating as a regular and central part of a person's identity repertoire; they have become comfortable with who they say they are. The actions and activities associated with earlier phases of identity transformation are not completely abandoned, but are now deployed differently, and perhaps less consciously. Acquisition of information continues, for example, but ritual and quotidian interactions may provide the information as opposed to a focused pursuit of information about the Rastafari. The uncompromising rhetoric and posturing common to early phases of identity transformation are situationally employed rather than regularly used. Rastafari and non-Rastafari come to acknowledge the new identity, confirming what the Rastafari believes he or she is.

For the Rastafari, commitment and internalization are vital to group maintenance because there are no enforced participation requirements.

The lack of coercive participation practices may help explain why the Rastafari were originally thought to be a short-lived millenarian-messianic cult. What has been overlooked is the personal commitment the authentic Rastafari have made to their identity and the ways in which they go about maintaining them. Commitment can take various forms, but sacrifice, investment, and culturally constructed rewards work together to imbue the identification with value. Threats of violence, ostracism, and forfeit of material gain are hardships, and hence, they are sacrifices. But they also work as investments in being Rastafari. Other kinds of investments are made in relationships with other Rastafari, participation in ritual and community, and in inscribing one's self with the knowledge and beliefs associated with the identity. The rewards are culturally constructed and interpreted through the lens of the identity itself: "I am part of a chosen people"; "I know things that others do not"; "We have achieved things that show that I have made the right decision." Together and over time, sacrifice, investment, and reward are things that decrease the likelihood of rejecting the identity. They facilitate commitment.

The people I interviewed have identified as Rastafari for between approximately 25 and nearly 70 years, implying serious commitment and thorough internalization. This is not to say, however, that they never experienced doubts about their identity as Rastafari or perhaps even considered abandoning it. However, such doubts did not surface in formal interviews or informal conversation. These doubts may have been hidden because of the lengthy period of time that the narrators had to work through the challenges their identity posed for them. Perhaps people who are actually emergent Rastafari, rather than devotees thinking retrospectively about their identity, would construct their narratives differently. Nonetheless, we must not overlook how some Rastafari probably never reached the internalized identity "comfort zone" of our narrators, or perhaps they completely renounced the identity they constructed. For example, Ras Grantly used as examples two internationally famous reggae performers, a man and a woman known as Rastafari, who converted to Christianity during the late 1990s. Ras Grantly believed it was the charisma and influence of Bob Marley that lead these two people to profess Rastafari identity and that "them heart never really in it. When Bob dead them start to move offa it [Rastafari]." Ras Grantly and Brother Yendis pointed out that the conversions received news coverage, and were titled in a way to suggest that the Rastafari were in a state of crisis, swiftly growing irrelevant to the people of Jamaica. Neither Ras Grantly nor Brother

Yendis saw such repudiation of Rastafari as especially troublesome. None-theless, even for those Rastafari who reached an identity comfort zone, there will always be experiences that encourage or necessitate reexamina-tion of being Rastafari.

Self-Commitment and Persistence

Scholars, politicians, and non-Rastafari leaders believed that the Rasta-fari were a "passing fad" that would slowly disappear as Jamaica "modern-ized," ultimately dying a "natural death" (e.g., Murrell 1998:1). The Rasta-fari did not directly recruit adherents, and they wanted to leave Jamaica for Africa. Certainly, elites reasoned, Rastafari identity and ideology would become unappealing to younger generations living in an independent and modernizing Jamaica. Nevertheless, the Rastafari have persisted, and their identity and beliefs have proven appealing to people the world over. Their justice motifs and messianic convictions have continued to provide attrac-tors that support affinity and community.

What keeps the Rastafari vigorous as a collective is each person's com-mitment to his/her vision of the justice motifs and moral economy of Blackness. As suggested, this commitment involves sacrifice, investment, and reward, and these practices and experiences are internalized and ex-ternalized in ways that keep the Rastafari viable. They have no prescrip-tions for how much time a person must give to the group nor for how much money should be tithed, although there are cultural expectations of selflessness and sharing. This is consistent with their ideology of free-dom and liberation; no Rastafari has rights or authority over another (this does not mean that there are no internal squabbles or transgressions of these ideals by individual Rastafari). Each must be responsible for himself in the service of the identity, faith, and collectivity. Groups such as the Rastafari that dislike central authority and bureaucratic prescription must rely upon a commitment to a given set of beliefs so strong that individu-als take it upon themselves to internalize and maintain them. This does not mean that interaction, interpersonal relationships, and communion are not vital components working to ensure that traditions and ceremo-nies are kept alive. It does mean, however, that the individuals must hold themselves responsible for participating in the life of the larger group.

Theories of Black identity do not explicitly address identity commit-ment and maintenance, although this is likely to change as theorists continue to grapple with the complexities of racial identity formation.

Personalization of revelatory experiences and identification with Rastafari alone can ensure neither the endurance of the group nor a person's commitment to it. My narrators' stories communicated how they and other Rastafari parried the challenges competing interests pose to identity commitment. For example, they could distance themselves from non-Rastafari or avoid the obligations attendant to wage labor or politics. The success of such strategies, however, depends on how well and for how long this distance is maintained.

Commitment and maintenance strategies that rely upon separation and distancing apparently become less important to Rastafari identity once internalization of the identity is well-established. Several elders, such as Brother Dee and Brother Bags, were once fire-burn Rastafari who lived as hermits, but they eventually relinquished these practices and became self-employed. Such transitions were not necessarily the result of the harshness of self-abnegation, though such living may have taken a toll on some Rastafari:

> Man mash himself up, you know. He move into the bush and do himself all manner of things. Man put all one hundred scotch bonnet [a blistery hot pepper] in a pot . . . man dash away him clothes and put on sack . . . sometimes him don't eat nothing but banana. Now he have stoppage of water [urinary problems], arthritis, him is sick now because of all them things. (Brother Barody)

Another explanation is that, as the Rastafari internalized the identity and reached a "comfort zone," the urgency of spiritual and ideological zealousness declined. Brother Bongo realized self-employment and part-time employment were not violations of core Rastafari principles. Indeed, self-reliance is a core value of classic Black Nationalism. Brother Bags eventually set up what has become a busy enterprise treating people with herbal remedies. Brother Dee took to vending.

My narrators agreed that "putting on" one's "covenant," or growing dreadlocks, is a sign of commitment, that a person is willing to bear the "cross" of Rastafari. This act was especially significant in the 1970s because it meant they were exceedingly willing to endure the ostracism and marginalization of being a Rastafari by publicly identifying themselves as such. Although today many Rastafari of the various sects and Orders continue to view locks as a sign of commitment and identity, the popularity of wearing locks among non-Rastafari has complicated how locks, as a symbol of "Rastafari-ness," are interpreted. Some Rastafari see the popularity of growing dreadlocks as a vindication and legitimization of their beliefs. Other Rastafari see secular non-Rastafari locks-wearers as disrespectful cultural thieves who profane their faith by popularizing something that many have suffered, even died, to express. We pick up these concerns in the next chapter.

"No Cross, No Crown": Persecution and Commitment

The Rastafari are a prime example of how ostracism and persecution can have the paradoxical effect of strengthening group and personal identity. Being singled out for ridicule, scorn, and verbal and physical violence strengthened the commitment of my narrators when they were still "new" to the faith. Even some of those who became Rastafari can remember when they too held the Rastafari in contempt:

> One of the things about coming up in those days as a youth [during the 1940s], I used to see Rasta as something to scorn. . . . They were barefooted, they wore a piece of pants, no shirt, onion bag, and so on, tie 'round them, going about their business. Sometime they identify and sometimes they don't . . . but I know them is Rasta still. (Brother Woks)

These elder Rastafari have viewed adversities related to their identity and beliefs as tests of their faith, an indication that they are a chosen and special people. It is a part of their sacrifice for and investment into the identity. Paradoxically, tribulation built conviction rather than weakening it. Rasta Ivey recalls how she suffered great brutality during the 1930s for her beliefs and identification: "Yes man. Them [non-Rastafari] beat me up . . . , kick [me] up . . . [me] gone to jail, [me] get lick [hit] down, and all those things." But such challenges were insufficient to stop her from pursuing her beliefs and maintaining her identity. Rasta Ivey has a reputation for standing up for what she believes in: "They say I am a fighter. Whether I am a fighter or not, they say I am a fighter. They know I can fight." That Rasta Ivey suffered cruelty was less a matter of abuse at the hands of men rather than her uncompromising stance toward her identity and beliefs. Perhaps her fierceness coupled with being a woman Rastafari doubly irritated attackers, but this is not how Rasta Ivey related such stories. During the 1960s, Rasta Ivey was sent to the asylum because she got into an argument with a parson over repatriation. The police were called to quiet her. As a result, she ended up briefly confined to the asylum because of her insistence in arguing her beliefs. By asserting her identity and conviction, though, she was also displaying her investment, sacrifice, and commitment.

Brother Yendis believed that it is not simply the Rastafari that the authorities were seeking to suppress through persecution: it was also their doctrine that they sought to invalidate and stamp out. He was correct that the colonial authorities saw the Rastafari as a threat because of their anticolonial, antistate, anti-Christian, and racial messages. Yendis, however, emphasized religion:

> [W]hen we say Rastafari is God, it makes a difference to the world, and if we is a people who criticize . . . [the Christian's] God and find our God, what people want to get vex with we for? Why people don't understand say, well, "Seek ye first the Kingdom of God and all things shall be added?" So, we no say people vex with we only because we a Rasta [it is also the alternative Rastafari offers]. No, man. We no human being? We are God fearing, we are honest, and we love we neighbor.

Elites, though, focused on the potential disruptiveness of the Rastafari's ideas in a land known for its Black rebellions and millenarianism. For example, a White police inspector noted that " . . . any riot which is not promptly and ruthlessly suppressed at once tends to develop into a race war" (Thomas, 1927:28). Thus, the Rastafari incensed people protective of the status quo, even if they were moral exemplars. These tensions facilitated drawing boundaries for the Rastafari, because they saw themselves as trying to live righteously while being persecuted for it. Although the motivations driving the persecutors of the Rastafari were many, persecution had a cumulative and peculiar effect of reinforcing their identity.

Brother Bongo, thinking back to the 1950s and 1960s, recalled the scorn directed toward the Rastafari:

> You would be passing and sometimes you just have a fresh bath and come out and people going on the street and you passing and them say "Move dutty [dirty] Rasta boy." But that time you have man who resent your doctrine and is ignorant, and go on with even physical accusation and assault. He would want to assault you. You have to be wise and walk him out. You have to be clever. Especially in the city. . . . Sometimes you have to get dirty with them. Show them that you are a man.

Incarceration was no stranger to my narrators, and often it was some aspect of being Rastafari that landed them in jail:

> In a yard down Fleet Street, the policeman them raid. When they accosted me, I did not have a spliff. I had no herb, and them say, "Go into the jeep." They held about four men. Eventually, I was the only one who picked up a sentence. Eighteen months. . . . The other three was not Rasta. They were just normal. One was a Chinese. They had Barristers, and they were linked with the government in power at the time, which was Labour Government. They were politicians. So the Rasta man paid the sacrifice. (Brother Bongo)

In a wistful voice, Brother Bongo related how in prison:

> Everyone meets there. The good, the bad, and the ugly is right in the prison. It was a test, and all during those times, I had my gold medal [given to him by Haile Selassie I, in 1966] there with me in the prison. It was in safekeeping of the warden . . . I did one year flat. I did not lose one hour remission because Jah was with me, and I was well respected on account of my principle, and I was a tradesman and a man of Jah, and anywhere you say Jah-Ras-tafari, every man has to look on you officially, especially in trouble. So, I leave prison and come out, and I develop a stronger vibes in Rastafari. I went on, and I find myself visiting the Ethiopian Orthodox Church.

Brother Bongo saw his incarceration as a sacrifice and a test of his identity, and viewed his early release and fair treatment as a reward for his conviction (which strengthened).

Drawing on analogies to difficulty and crucifixion, the Rastafari equate their identity and beliefs with bearing a cross. While this comparison suggests burden, it is a burden they are prepared to bear:

> Well, you have people who will fight [you]. The scriptures forewarn us that when you take up the cross and start to follow Christ, we have to prepare for people to say all manner of evil against you. You must. That is a must. No cross, no crown. You have to bear a cross. [People will say] . . . watch how the good boy start to a mash up himself and all them kinds of things. All kinds of [depreciative] remarks are being passed. (Brother Woks)

Expecting ostracism and persecution, the Rastafari bear the burden that comes with their identity. Thus, there must be something in the way of personal satisfaction or reward to console them during and between contentious times. Awareness of the difficulty attendant to their new identity prepared the Rastafari for adversity. Rhetorics of struggle, such as those drawn from Scripture or the history of Black oppression, function as cultural resources. Sacrifice became an investment.

Relationships related to Rastafari identity constitute investments because it is through other Rastafari that each one recognizes and defines herself. Other investments include the effort involved in assuming and inscribing Rastafari identity with content, which involved learning new norms, language, symbolic content, and frames of reference.

Rewards are culturally constructed reinforcements and inducements. Constructing the Rastafari self and collective as a special and chosen people provided a framework for understanding adversity related to identity and why it should be endured. The cross (tribulation, burden, sacrifice) and crown (reward, divineness) are symbols, but such symbols are meaningful and powerful; they have the capacity to motivate people to pursue and commit to Rastafari identity.

Ultimately, the elder Rastafari now face a contradiction in terms of commitment and sustaining collective identity—currently that of being both stigmatized and popular (Blackness as an identity and ideology in Jamaica is in a similar paradoxical situation of simultaneously being accepted, trendy, but also deficient and inferior). Brother Yendis believes this contradiction can be resolved only through the ending of the exploitative social order: "If we don't change the system, we will forever tell the world that we are a set of no-good people, a menace to society, and all we do is smoke ganja, we no have no use. But anytime the tourist come, a we [Rastafari] them a ask 'bout." Despite their popularity, the Rastafari remain outcasts as far as official government and church relationships are concerned. They have yet to be recognized as an official religion, and even less probable is the possibility that the state will consent to decriminalizing marijuana as a sacrament for ritual use. However, the popularity brought to the Rastafari by reggae music, Bob Marley, and other performers has turned their identity into a commodity that brings revenue to the island and notoriety to Jamaica. Tourists buy Rastafarian art and crafts, come to smoke and export marijuana, and want to visit Rastafari communities. Jamaica is now known the world over for being home to the Rastafari. A striking example of the new contradiction is the emergence of a cottage industry called "Rent-a-Dread," which is comprised of mostly men who cater to the desires of White female tourists seeking excitement and exotic romance (Pruitt & LaFont, 1995). Popularity, though, threatens the vitality and survival of the Rastafari by commoditizing it and undermining some of the key investment, sacrifice, and reward practices exhibited by my narrators. Nonetheless, the contestation between the Rastafari, government, churches, and others, helps to maintain the us-them distinctions instrumental to group identification.

Identity, Communion, and Community

I sat in a large, open hallway of the Rastafari Federation, watching Brother Yendis call the assembled people to order. Approximately 20 people were present, mostly male Rastafari, young and old, but also a few women Rastafari and a few "baldheads" (non-Rastafari). The meeting, like all meetings convened by this organization, began with singing of the "Universal Ethiopian Anthem." Brother Yendis would recite a stanza—"Ethiopia the tyrants are falling, who once smote thee 'pon thy knee"—after which the audience would chant it. With their hands held to their hearts, the audience chanted the anthem in rough unison. Although Brother Yendis's call "told" the audience what to sing, I noticed that the "baldheads" relied upon reading from the light green pamphlet containing the lyrics. The Rastafari present were familiar with the routine and the lyrics. In countless small and perhaps far more mundane gatherings like this one, the Rastafari engage in identity work around building and maintaining community. Through cultural resources such as the Ethiopian anthem, they appeal to recollections of past injustices and achievements, summoning cultural sentiments that affirm who they are and what they believe in a space that allows for identity and relationship-building work to occur.

Ongoing group attachment is facilitated by continued interaction and communion, especially participation in rituals, ceremonies, and other activities that create a feeling of being a part of a moral community (not to be conflated with moral economy of Blackness). By moral community, I mean a sense of collective and recognizable identity steeped in particular values about responsibility, virtue, right and wrong, and the symbols used to reinforce these sentiments and provide a means of helping people feel connected to each other. Communion describes that sense of community that enkindles feelings of belonging to something larger and more important than oneself, based in fellowship and some sense of equality, reciprocity, and collective awareness. Communion is a reward because it provides emotional satisfaction.

Various rituals and patterned interactions provide context and means for transferring cultural information and engaging in identitiy and relationship-building work. For instance, the sometimes loosely planned act of "licking chalice" can provide a framework for an elaborate configuration of activities through which Rastafari identity and practices are performed and affirmed. One evening, after leaving a Rastafari meeting in lower Kingston, I was traveling with Brother Yendis, who stopped to visit some Rastafari he knew to "check them for some herbs." The front of the small single-story home was surrounded by sheets of tin that shielded the yard's activities from the eyes of passersby. Once inside the gate, I saw at least a dozen Rastafari engaged in conversation and preparing to "lick" (smoke, burn) the chalice. One Rastafari was finely chopping up an ounce or two of ganja; two other Rastafari attended to a boiling pot containing a vegetable stew; others were occupied with conversation. The chalice was brought forward, wrapped in what looked to be a pillow case. It was carefully, almost sensuously, uncovered, disassembled for cleaning, and reassembled. The bowl, a three-inch long thimble-shaped piece of clay, was inserted into a coconut shell containing some water. On the side of the shell opposite of the bowl extended a hollow, tubular piece of rubber, perhaps once a hose for a car engine. The youthful looking Rastafari who prepared the chalice took it to Brother Yendis. Brother Yendis laughed the quiet "heh-heh" he so often does, and took the chalice. In a loud voice that increased to a shout, he said "Let us give Ises [praise] to His Imperial Majesty, Haile I, Selassie I, Jah Rastafari." Those Rastafari wearing crowns, like myself, removed their knitted head covering. A series of prayers and offering of thanks ensued, and the chalice was lit with a fire taken from the wood and coal under the cooking pot. Ras Yendis gripped the hose and puffed as if siphoning air from a closed container. Soon, a dense cloud of smoke emerged from the chalice and the mouth and nostrils of Brother Yendis. The chalice was passed next to Ras Grantly, sitting on Brother Yendis's left, and the "cup" was methodically passed to all present. During the early part of this impromptu gathering, the collective discussion revolved around Rastafari affairs, such as preparation for the upcoming independence day, and around world affairs, including a critique of Jamica's financial affairs. The language used, the topics discussed, and the cultural signs and artifacts used together affirm and inform Rastafari identity. One had only to watch to begin to see contours of cultural protocol and identity work: Brother Yendis, an elder, respected leader, and guest, was given the chalice, to "bless" and light; ritual surrounding the chalice was revealed; the foods favored by Rastafari were present; and on display were the modes of food preparation. Communion was created and imbibed, but in ways that made the activities appear natural and routine.

Many recurring Rastafari celebrations typically mark dates of importance to them, such as anniversaries of Haile Selassie I's coronation, his "earthday " (birthday), his visit to Jamaica, as well as Ethiopian Liberation Day, African Liberation Day, and Jamaican Independence Day. In addition to the rituals associated with these events, Nyabinghi ceremonies may be convened for many reasons, ranging from the visit of "oppressors" such as Ronald Reagan to Jamaica in April 1982 (when an island-wide Nyabinghi was called to contest his presence), the freeing of Nelson Mandela in 1990, or simply to bring together Rastafari for communion.

Repatriation and Black redemption remain of primary significance to my narrators. In his mid-seventies at the time, Ras Sam Brown proclaimed, "I not going to feel good till I go home. But I going reach home. You see, I trod the way that the Honorable Marcus Garvey trod and the Honorable Marcus Garvey tradition is repatriation. That's why he went as far as to deal with the Black Star Liner ships." Those Rastafari who are most adamant about repatriating to Africa are often those who are least able, either because they are too poor or in bad health. This fact has led some observers to speculate that the Rastafari have moved from a literal to a symbolic desire to repatriate, or that repatriation is a symbolic cover for a desire to escape material privation. My Rastafari interlocutors, however, say they still want to go Africa, and are aware of the troubles and poverty that plague Africa (even though some of them continue to think of it as "Zion"). These Rastafari recognize that life in Africa will not be easy, but many of them still cannot imagine it being worse than their lot in Jamaica. Nonetheless, whether some Rastafari want to physically relocate to Ethiopia, or whether it is the idea of "returning home" that carries currency, repatriation is a cultural construct that evokes memories and feelings that connect past and present and that facilitate collective imagining and identification.

Discourses of enslavement, White hegemony, oppression, and pre-colonial Africa are culturally generated symbolic themes and stylized memories to which people can attach (and detach) themselves. These provide grounds for defining racial and religious commonality and communion, as well as explaining the importance of returning to Africa. For example,

Ras Brenton's description of why repatriation is important to him is embedded in his view of racialized exploitation:

> From the slaves come from Africa they been pondering to go back to Africa, and I come and learn that. I come and learn that the slaves did always want to go back. Some of them jumped overboard say them would try and go back [to Africa] and them never reach back. Well I come up as a young Rasta and say the same thing. Say it is right for Black people to go back to them continent because the White people treat us too badly, and because of this, they influence everyone else to treat us badly. Because me is a man who come to the conclusion say: Black man, Indian man, Chinese man, every nation organize against the Black man eventually to keep him degraded, to keep us down. . . . So, we must want go home forward where we can go build we own tabernacle, and build we own people, and build we own selves, instead of building other people everywhere. Because I man come to the conclusion say Black man build everywhere . . . and yet still when them [other nations, peoples] to help him build up now, them a murmur and a quarrel, and no want do it. (Ras Brenton)

During Nyabinghi ceremonies, chants such as "We want to go home a yard," which is about wanting to return to Africa, create the context for focused communion and affirmation of values "we-ness" within a larger framework of building fellowship:

> For every time I chant Nyabinghi I want to go a yard
> For the Rastaman tired to live in a Babylon
> there is pure victimization
> for through the Iwa [time, era] of the King of Kings, I n I wants to go a yard

Chants such as this evoke particular memories and symbols, in this case grounding the participants in valuing and longing for repatriation to Africa, and an escape from victimization.

Another way the Rastafari build and maintain group commitment is through formally and informally organizing themselves into units such as "yards," "houses," and "mansions." The idea of organization, or association, has always had some currency among some segments of the Rastafari. Some of the founding Rastafari, as we saw, created various kinds of organizations. In Jamaica, yard is a metaphor for many things—home,

security, cooperation, privacy, control—though home and the space surrounding one's home is perhaps the most common and literal meaning
(Chevannes, 2001). It is not uncommon for Rastafarians to create their
own living, gathering, and "pass through" spaces. For instance, one elder
Rastafari's yard—a cluster of walled-in living spaces on Church Street
in downtown Kingston—was widely known to Rastafari in surrounding
areas as a gathering place to rest, commune, and talk. The elder's yard was
especially a place for the meeting of those Rastafari who were activists
involved in one or another issue related to the justice motifs. The houses
and mansions, especially those with designations such as "Theocratic"
or "House of," represent intentional efforts to create associations and to
provide venues for interaction and action. Houses and mansions are so
named in recognition of Christ's proclamation: "In my Father's house are
many mansions: if it *were* not so I would have told you. I go to prepare a
place for you" (John 14:2, original italics).

The Rastafari houses and mansions are spaces of communion, identity and cultural work, and even activism. The Rastafari International
Theocratic Assembly (RITA), of which I am a member, was an offshoot
of some activist Rastafari affiliated with the Rastafari Movement Association, an explicit movement organization that eventually dissolved. The
RITA membership consisted especially of youthful Rastafari, male and female, along with some elders. The elder Rastafari provided the youth with
leadership in the ways of Rastafari and in discussing issues of concern to
the Rastafari. Through organizations like RITA, the Rastafari create space
in which to share knowledge and experience associated with being Rastafari, and to invoke, deploy, and reconstruct the cultural signs and resources central to their identity. The purposes of Rastafari organizations
are many (I have not, for instance, discussed the more spiritually focused
ones), but the chief concerns involve solidarity, communion, and promotion and protection of Rastafari interests through collective action. Even
though formal associations and Rastafari yards are familiar in Jamaica,
there persists a notion among some scholars and pundits that the Rastafari are loners and individualists. While this view has merit because individuality and autonomy are valued by the Rastafari, we should not overlook the culturally patterned forms of collective action.

Although the violence directed toward Rastafari has dwindled, it has
not ended. One leader of the Rastafari Federation had this to say about the
threat of violence and their organizations' perspective: "Make something
develop and the man them start disrespect Rasta and a do [all manner of]

things. Any part of Jamaica you live, [and] you a Rasta . . . in country or in a the town, any part you live [and] you a Rasta . . . man a bruck [break] you skin same way you know" (Brother Yendis).

The threat of mistreatment due to being Rastafari continues to be a real concern and, as such, remains a way in which Rastafari understand and relate to each other, thus substantiating their sense of being a "special" people.

"All a We a Rasta First": Community, Communion, and Reward

The fact that my narrators embraced Rastafari identity and maintained it for several decades suggests that it must offer some rewards or benefits. As noted above, a central satisfaction involves the feeling of being a "special" or "chosen" group, of being righteously superior, and of being part of a Black spiritual vanguard whose purpose is to set an example for others to follow. This reward, in turn, encourages motivation to continue identity work:

> I and I the Rasses have to stand up for the teaching of His Majesty, and I and I have to . . . [demonstrate] discipline to the nation, set example, be a model for the generations to come in righteousness, clean principles. You have some brethren going around burning [damning, denouncing] God, burning Bible, burning this, and burning that. In a sense, [these] Rasta come as a revolutionist, wordically [using words], and burn down all things that are not right in the sight of God. Now some of the youth say that they burn Caesar, in the true context, the churches preach Jesus, and it is the said churches that crucify the said Jesus. . . . They say they are Christians this day . . . but those who were with Jesus at that time, those are the ones with His Majesty in this time. (Brother Woks)

The satisfaction that derives from being a part of a chosen people also comes with responsibility, fortifying commitment and investment. Brother Woks's analogy, comparing the Rastafari to Christ's disciples, lends anciency to their identity while it critiques the Christians and privileges the Rastafari.

Ras Brenton's analysis emphasizes themes similar to Brother Woks's, although highlighting trial and tribulation. Indeed, strenuous effort and sacrifice in the service of identity and righteousness are naturalized and the reward is constructed as immense. It pays, figuratively, to be Rastafari:

So, they still have Jesus Christ in Ethiopia, but we have him as the Black one, we do not have him as the blue-eyed one. He [Christ] also said that he alone would not bear the cross. We will also have to bear it too. Every one of us will have to bear our cross. Rasta man says he has a cross to bear and a Jah to glorify. So, we go on glorifying Jah and go on bearing our cross. And we see Jah work out things actually for us because we are working with him. He says we must put him in remembrance and he will never leave us nor forsake us. So, we have to keep him in remembrance. He makes things work out. Rocky though things may be. (Ras Brenton)

Another expression of communion, community, and reward operates through a type of fictive kinship design in which all Rastafari are connected together through the father figure, Haile Selassie I and his Queen, Empress Menen. There is a view among the Rastafari that one can only know if one is an "authentic" (genuine) Rastafari through the signature of their works. While my narrators located authenticity in whether a person accepts the divinity of Haile Selassie I and whether they privilege a morally configured Blackness, there was great latitude in what was considered acceptable within this framework. Mutually agreeable definitions can be worked out through dialogue (for example, the standing of a White or Japanese Rastafari could be locally legitimized through this strategy). In the views of my narrators, however, locks, insignia, and invocation of Rastafari signs and language are insufficient to mark one as a genuine Rastafari. Also important are a person's deeds. Sacrifice, investment, and display of valued behavior—skill in word, sound, and power, righteousness, discipline, love, and communion—are highly valued. Therefore, being observed by other Rastafari is an important part of being Rastafari. "It take time to know one's heart and ways, to see their works, to see their righteousness" (Sister Mariam). It takes time to develop such a record. Thus, being accepted as more than nominally Rastafari—as being "authentic"— does not come automatically and, hence, is also a reward:

All a we is Rasta first. We have to say, His Majesty is the Almighty God and him is your father, then I and I supposed to be his son, and if I and I is his son, then me and you must be brothers. No? So it go. [If] Me father have two pickney, the two of us must be brothers or sister. . . . Me no want get into this little backwardness of division [factions]. From you say Rastafari, I and I respect you. Sometime, we respect one what we do not know of, you know. But because of the divinity of the love for Rastafari, we give that respect. Some man what we know out there, we shouldn't a call him Rastafari you know, but as we a say, we don't know the ways of the I . . . But since we cannot judge no man, he will be known by his works. . . . So, anything a man a do inna the darkness, must come to light. (Brother Yendis)

The faith the Rastafari have in the power of their identity and beliefs reinforces their commitment, strengthening their conviction that they have made the right identity choice. This too is a type of reward. Any Rastafari can be a testimony to the power of Rastafarian identity and ideology, and incredible occurrences are interpreted and explained in terms of self-identity. Identity itself can become a self-validating reward. Leaning over in his chair, staring at me through the thick lenses of eyeglasses with only one ear handle, Ras Sam Brown emphatically declared the power of his identity and beliefs:

Watch here, me get gun shot to me ass, man. Me go in a train crash, man. Is only the name Rastafari save me life. On both occasions, when I reach death. . . . is the name Rastafari I call upon. [Remember] The time of the gun shot when I tell you . . . the whole world go dark. It is only the name Rastafari bring back life to me eyes . . . Is Rastafari I say, you know. . . . a brother say [to me], "Sams, a word sound save you life, you know." A bear [pure] Rastafari I chant and I never stop because I know He is who have brought I through the gates of death many, many a time. (Ras Sam Brown)

Ras Sam Brown's immeasurable reward for his faith and identity has included his passage "through the gates of death" without getting caught. By calling out the name of the Messiah, his living God, he has been able to gain the protection of supernatural forces.

The self-validating dimensions of identity are successful because the Rastafari interpret their experience through the cultural constructs that inform their identity. Not only do the Rastafari say "we are a special people," or "I see what others cannot," but the older Rastafari also take pride in pointing out the fulfillment of their beliefs and prognostications. Brother Yendis, lecturing to me about the power of the Rastafari, convincingly argued:

Everything have to come to an end you know, me brethren. Because we here preach "free Mandela and free South Africa" . . . and then we see all them things happen. . . . Now, you see a youth as a Black man say that . . . [these things that we prophesy] can't happen. . . . [But it then] Come to pass. . . . Me know history, man. Me know a prophecy. A man say, "boy, look like the words a come to naught because nothing no happen" . . . still apartheid. That is why we . . . sing 'bout Botha. About three or four years ago. . . . White man have to go a prison go take him [Mandela] out and say: "Come, a your country, take it." You have 500,000 White people and we have six million Black people can't get up on them feet. Yes, man. Mandela, the first Black President straight from the prison to the Presidency. Power to Black people all over the world and them not even take that as a sign and understand. [Now is] The first time a Black man is head of United Nations. Secretary General of United Nations is a Black man, you know. Now, days gone by, that sound impossible. . . . It is these things that Rasta people call for long time before it happen.

In Brother Yendis's view, many of the things that the Rastafari have longed for and prophesied would occur have come to pass. They called for "Black man government," "Black man time," and an end to colonialism and "White man rule" in Jamaica. They argued the wrongness of apartheid and the imprisonment of Mandela, and concentrated much attention on his release and freedom from the grip of Whites on the government and people of South Africa. From Brother Yendis's point of view, their canniness has been confirmed. Calls for these changes were framed in the idioms of race and religion, chanted at Nyabinghi ceremonies, and discussed during reasoning sessions, illustrating what the Rastafari see as the "power of the 'Binghi" to effect change. Yet, as discussed in previous chapters, Black man rule, especially in Jamaica, has been a disappointment for them, so now they are talking of a Rastafari time to rule:

This is Rasta country. Rasta birth here you know, but Rasta not manifesting him authority. . . . Rasta don't have no authority round here. Rasta man come from any part of the world and them stop him from go a airport . . . and if contact not made with me and me make some noise and do certain things 'bout it, it no done there so [it is a done deal]. We want authority man. We must become a mass force to reckon with in a the world. (Brother Yendis)

6

Rastafari Nation on the Move
Identity and Change

"See," Ras Cee said to me:

It look like the elder them can't take Rastafari no farther. It is up to we youth now to take Rastafari to the next level. Look what them do. Them did lose control of Repatriation; them did visit Africa, and hold countless meeting since. What happen? What [come] of it? A few Rasta reach Ethiopia, but we still don't have no program [for repatriation]. His Majesty told we to organize and centralize, but that is not what happen. Enough Rasta want to hold his own corner [do his own thing]. And 'nough Rasta a get him education. Them no really see say the Rasta them a Barbados and England nah wait 'pon we. Them man a build up themself. Build up them [Rasta] people. But see we a lag. So, now, you see why the [Rasta] youth a gwaan ("go on") so? Them see the elder them not really making any progress. So, some a them rise up and make a militant noise. Say them want to burn everything. I do not approve of that, but I overstand it. So, you see, it is time for we youth to pick up the banner and carry it. But the elder them must release [their control] and not fight we.

Ras Cee related these thoughts to me while we walked down a crowded East Queen Street in downtown Kingston, one hot autumn afternoon. I met Ras Cee at a RITA meeting in 1998. We kept in touch and came to spend time together since Ras Cee lived in downtown Kingston, where I spent much of my time. Ras Cee was around 31 years old at the time of our conversation. His short locks must have recently sprouted from his head, not even beginning to touch the slender, long neck that rested on an equally slim and wiry tan-brown-skinned frame. Ras Cee had made the decision to grow his locks and "manifest Rastafari" a couple years earlier, he said. Even though Ras Cee was in his early thirties at the time, in

Jamaica, he referred to himself as a "youth." Youth in Jamaica covers a far greater age range than in the United States. Youth like Ras Cee are growing into Rastafari in an era very different from that of even a generation ago.[1]

Ras Cee's observations point to change and generational shift among the Rastafari. Elders such as those who populate this book recognize and acknowledge the vital role this younger generation of Rastafari will play in the continued development of the Rastafari in Jamaica, but the generations see many things differently. While Ras Cee recognizes that the elders have made tremendous contributions to strengthening Rastafari, he believes they have not successfully capitalized on some of their achievements. Older Rastafari like Ras Chronicle expect that the younger Rastafari will build on their sacrifice and achievements, even if those achievements are incomplete. "What we are doing now," said Ras Chronicle, "we a lay the foundation for years to come. You understand? Fifty or a hundred years or a hundred and fifty years or a thousand years. We [Rastafari in Jamaica] will have the history and we a carry the history. And the Rasta is the cream of this history for the next century." Ironically, Ras Cee's observation is evocative of the generational conflict between the first generation of Rastafari and those who became Rastafari between the 1940s and 1960s. This conflict had much to do with interpretation of doctrine and differences in experience and age. Many of those who became Rastafari between the late 1940s and 1960s worked to purge Rastafari of some of its Revivalist and Kumina practices and attempted to align the beliefs and identity of Rastafari more closely with their perception of the history and people of the Old Testament. They were willing to engage in belligerent and contentious acts as a part of enacting their faith and identity. That generation introduced new ideas and practices into the faith and identity, contributing to the vitality of collectivity. And perhaps something similar is happening with Rastafari during the early twenty-first century. This tension between the older and younger Rastafari is only one of the important issues confronting the continued ethnogenesis of the Rastafari.

The third annual conference of the Rastafari Federation (mentioned in the opening of chapter 1), convened in Kingston, Jamaica in 1998, is illustrative of how the Rastafari continue to evolve. One of the "official" leaders of the organization was a woman. There were Rastafari delegates from abroad, who came to Jamaica to give reports on Rastafari in their respective lands. These visitors to Jamaica hailed from Guam, Uganda, Cuba, St. Lucia, St. Vincent, Barbados, and the United States. The Ethiopian Orthodox Church had a strong presence at the conference. Thus, the Rastafari depicted in chapter 2 have continued to evolve in ways that remain inadequately conveyed in popular perception. Women Rastafari now project a very visible and active presence in Jamaica. The Rastafari now have a global presence which can be observed even in Kingston, a destination less frequented by tourists, and which can be seen in some of the most far-flung reaches of the planet—New Zealand, Venezuela, Senegal, South Africa, Japan. And, among the younger Rastafari in Jamaica, especially Kingston and Spanish Town, a new strain of militancy has emerged.

What Happens If God Dies?

In chapter 2 we saw how disruption and surprise was an integral aspect of the evolution of the Rastafari. Likewise, we witnessed the shift in social representation from outcasts to exemplars of Black culture and history. We also saw how elites repeatedly sought to discredit publicly the Rastafari and how they regularly announced the demise of the Rastafari. Elite pronouncements regularly failed to materialize, but the success of the Rastafari rarely blunted criticism or attempts to undermine the positive status they had attained following Selassie I's 1966 visit to Jamaica.

On August 27, 1974, the *Daily Gleaner* (8/27/74:2) reported that Emperor Selassie I had been "stripped" of power by his own armed forces, his advisors imprisoned, and his personal court disbanded. Many Rastafari were aware of what was happening in Ethiopia. Some, such as the Rastafari Movement Association, saw the intervention of the army as a positive sign of much needed change. They noted that there had been little bloodshed—the Emperor remained alive—and that the Emperor was actually calling the shots (generally, *Gleaner* stories did not take such an optimistic view of the Emperor's circumstances).

On August 28, 1975, the *Daily Gleaner* announced: "Selassie Dies at 83" (p. 23). The *Gleaner* article was critical of the Emperor, claiming he was out of step with his people and the modernizing world around him. Michael Manley and Edward Seaga, perhaps not wanting to offend constituents who revered the Emperor, straddled the fence and announced their "regrets" at his passing (*DG*, 8/28/75:23). Most elites saw this as the end of the Rastafari, at last. How else could they continue to profess a God who now seemed so mortal and weak? This surprise has not brought about the demise of the Rastafari. It shook many of them up and pushed them to reflect critically upon and interrogate their beliefs and identity. Ras Grantly, for example, noted:

Yes, man. The news shook up a heap of them [Rastafari]. It make I n I look deep into what I n I a deal with, what it mean [to] say that I art Rastafari. It separate the wheat from the chaff, the goat from the lamb, the puss from the Lion. Me hear all manner of things being discussed and reasoned. . . . Some of them, a good number, trim [cut off their dreadlocks, renouncing their identity]. Me hear some a them say Rasta must look to His Majesty son, rae, rae, rae (blah, blah). But some of we approach the matter with reason and calm. We come to see the pieces nah really fit. We see too many man rush to judge and don't really consider the power of God.

In Ras Grantly's view, the news of the death of Emperor Selassie I brought the Rastafari to a collective turning point and in doing so, thinned their ranks of many whose commitment was perhaps shallow or not deeply internalized. He also demonstrates the power of faith and millennial expectation to adjust and adapt to even the most jarring perturbations.

While I cannot explore here the many ways in which the Rastafari reconciled news of the death of Emperor Selassie and their own beliefs and identity, they continued to grow in numbers, in Jamaica and abroad. Elites, it seemed, could not draw lessons from what happened after Jesus Christ was crucified: Christianity flourished. Reggae music grew in popularity, more and more Jamaicans came to identify as Rastafari, and the Rastafari began convening national and international meetings in the United States, Canada, and the Anglophone Caribbean to organize a coherent entity able to direct Rastafari destiny on issues such as repatriation, religious freedom and civil rights, and legalization of cannabis. In 1995, the Rastafari Federation was born as the result of the deliberation of thousands of Rastafari. Following one of the Emperor's key recommendations, "Organize and centralize for your future development," it sought to organize the many houses and mansions of Rastafari within an umbrella structure. The Rastafari Federation achieved some success in its early efforts, but a lack of financial resources impeded its ability to build capacity, and by 2003, the Federation lost its headquarters lease and much of its membership, as well. These developments occurred within a wider field of change involving other issues of crucial concern to the Rastafari.

New Terrain for Rastafari Identity Formation

The penetration of new technologies into Jamaican society, the internationalization of the Rastafari, a shift in the role of women, new opportunities for education, and new sources of income and status, are some, but only some, of what make for a different context for the Rastafari. Jamaica at the turn of the millennium was vastly different from Jamaica during the 15 years following independence. Indeed, Thomas (2004) makes the case that since this period, the morally configured Black identity that I detail in these pages has been unmoored. It has been superseded by a new configuration of Blackness that looks toward the United States and England rather than Africa, and whose ethos is consumerist, individualistic, and nihilistic rather than austere, collective, and idealistic. What does this mean for becoming and being Rastafari? Will the Rastafari persist as a viable identity option, or will they slide into obscurity?

Jamaicans desire and have access to the kinds of consumer goods found in wealthy societies. They can travel internationally with ease, the main obstacle to doing so being a lack of money or the right connections. They have access to the latest items of fashionable popular culture from abroad and are in touch with popular culture the world over, and the world consumes Jamaican popular culture. There are new sources of income in Jamaica—some potentially lucrative and deadly—for example, ganja, guns, and cocaine. Information is much easier to come by. Technologies like the Internet, in the context of globalization, make a range of print and visual media accessible to all but the poorest and oldest Jamaicans. The earliest Rastafari had extremely limited access to texts about Black history and culture and very little information about their own people beyond what the newspapers told.

Today, though, a person does not need to attend a street meeting, Nyabinghi ceremony, or live near a Rastafari community to learn about Rastafari. Countless books, articles, websites, and other sources provide a bewildering array of information about the Rastafari. These changes generate possibilities that may compete with developing long-term commitment to Rastafari identity that my narrators found grounded in ideas of anciency, Ethiopianism, peculiar and chosen status, and symbols of the Old and New Testaments.

The post-1970s growth in the appeal and global spread of reggae music, the consumption of marijuana, and Rastafari culture, have in various ways influenced Rastafari conceptions of their identity and future. They have contributed as well to the international appeal of Rastafari identity. All constitute threats to group maintenance, especially the kinds of identifications constructed by the Rastafari focused upon in these pages. Marijuana and reggae draw many people to the identity and its panoply of beliefs and practices, and we can speculate whether their motivation and interest might connect with some of the key themes of morally configured Black identities. Nonetheless, my observations of "fresh" Rastafari in the United States suggest experiences involving reggae and cannabis smoking have created the context for their awareness of Rastafari identity. They might possibly serve as portals to becoming Rastafari. While these new situations potentially allow for a greater variety of encounter experiences, feelings of miseducation, deracination, and oppression will likely remain key elements of Rastafari identity formation.

Challenge and change are not new to the Rastafari. Leonard Howell, Joseph Hibbert, Archibald Dunkley, and others of the first Rastafari evangelists traveled abroad to work, and it is likely that they returned to Jamaica displaying differences in wealth and experience compared to those who became their disciples. Times change and so too do people's understanding of themselves and others. Many of my narrators recognize with clarity what is happening around them and to their identity, and some of them have come to embrace change by arguing for the importance of education and the use of technology—as long as identity as Rastafari remains central. A few though, are disheartened by the changes they see, and some of the oldest and poorest, like Rasta Ivey and Brother Dee, are nearly oblivious to what is happening outside of their gates.

Significant Shifts in the Rastafari Landscape, Population, and Attitude

Ras Brenton recognizes that "There are more Rasta youth coming into the movement now. Some of them are ignorant of the facts. . . . [Yet] we respect that [they are keeping the movement alive], and we have more conscious sistren coming up in the movement and more conscious brethren too. They help to make things easier for us." Brother Woks sees the continued growth of the Rastafari, in Jamaica and abroad, as "Good signs, because His [Selassie I] voice shall be heard throughout all generations and His dominion is stretched from shore to shore, and simply because of that it will have to spread because righteousness will have to cover the earth as how water covers the sea. No corner of the earth shall escape his voice." In Brother Woks's view the positive spread of Rastafari identity outweighs the negative trade-offs, such as people with superficial commitment to the identity. Brother Woks continues his train of thought, connecting the spread of the Rastafari to their need to develop an economic base to create opportunities for each other:

If Rasta was economically viable, and become strong from a longer time [ago], set up an economic base, we could employ these [young Rastafari] people. We would have them working with us. Instead of the society having them, it would be we who have them, but simply because of this tug-o-war thing [hardscrabble living], every man is looking through different eyes and all these kind of things.

In Brother Woks's estimate, it would be in the interest of the Rastafari to develop opportunities for themselves. Whether to work is rarely the issue for my narrators. The question is for whom and what purpose.

Most of my narrators see education as something positive to pursue. They do not mean the kind of education that involves the miseducation and deracination that they have sought to overturn. Rather, they mean an education which allows a Rastafarian to gain skills and experience that can further the collectivity's general interests without undermining the identity commitment of those Rastafari who acquire education within establishment institutions. I asked Ras Chronicle what he thought was most important for the youngest Rastafari. He repeated slowly, for emphasis: "Education is the main thing. Education is the main thing."

There is a growing number of college-educated Rastafari in Jamaica (and a greater number abroad). How will they balance their personal commitment to their identity and ideology with those of the collective and the requisites vital to group persistence: investment, sacrifice, commitment, and mortification? Renunciation may or may not become an impractical affair; old and contentious ideas such as racial oppression can be reframed for the twenty-first century. Education, though, will be a potential source of division and discord:

And the Black man and the Black woman them what got the education, they don't facilitate the truth about Rastafari, not even the least in this country. Seen? And, the average Rastaman, plenty of us cannot read, man. Seen? And those that can read try to make themself so big and gone on as if like them superior. See, if you don't stand up a way, a man don't see you. (Bongo J)

Bongo J sees some of the "educated" Rastafari as "full of too much pride." In his estimatation, education is not a solution but a problem to manage.

The younger Rastafari in Jamaica, male and female, live in a vastly changed land. Some of the challenges that their elders faced, however, remain for them to struggle with, in the new terrain. Even though the Rastafari are now exemplars of Black culture and identity, they may still find themselves denied opportunities because of who they are. While Brother Bongo decided to leave his job during his transition to Rastafari during the late 1950s, young Desmond, whom we met in the last chapter, lost his job in 1998 because of his dreadlocks and his identity. Rastafari identity has not completely lost its stigma.

Technology

Some of the ascetic and militant Rastafari garnered a reputation for rejecting modern technologies. They exalted simple, "prehistoric," if not hermit-like living. This rhetoric, though, had its limits, even among the radical Rastafari. While Peter Tosh railed against polluting industries and practices, and Bunny Wailer fiercely disliked the "iron bird" [jet plane] and touring, both found uses for technologies that could be rationalized as useful within their faith/identity complex. They, for example, put to work electric guitars and synthesizers in the service of Jah music.

> Price: "I have heard enough Rasta say 'fire burn Babylon tricknology' (tech-
> nology). Now, everywhere, I see Rasta using cell phone. That is Babylon
> tricknology, no?"
>
> Ras Brenton: "Rasta," directing his reply to me in a deeply direct and per-
> sonal way, "I n I control fire. Fire we control. The cell phone use energy,
> spark, that is fire. We fe control that. Anything what involve fire, we fe
> control that."

The Rastafari single out fire as a powerful symbol in their discourse and rituals. Fire cleanses, destroys, promotes new growth, and signals eternity, redemption, and salvation. This supple symbol, therefore, can be used to make certain technologies less problematic, and easier to incorporate into the Rastafari "world." Technology is a problem for my narrators when it is used to control, oppress, spy upon, and destroy, but they reconcile their beliefs with the realities of living in a highly mobile capitalist post-colonial society. This is not simply a matter of "routinization" or "accommodation" between the Rastafari and the society that they live in (as Edmonds [2003] might suggest). Ras Brenton, who still didn't have a phone or electricity in his dwelling as late as 2002, reasoned:

We are in the technological age, and Rastas will have to deal with technology because some of them are in it right now. Like Ralph would tell me that up in New York, most of the Rasta youth going to college now, and they are going to come out to be technologists. So, we have to appreciate that, we have to respect that. We love that. To see Rasta coming from Back-o-Wall, for instance, where he had to eat and drink out a burn pan, yes, and wear rubber tire shoes. Now he is wearing everything. He is wearing Clarks [a sporty British shoe]. He is wearing anything that he wants to wear, and you cannot fight against that because it is the age that we are living in. Okay. So, we have to respect everything progressive, going forward. We cannot fight it down because it is that we actually fight for. Rastas were suffering when we get the vibes to be like Rastas, and Jah say we must go this way to find it a little easier and a little better. Little by little, it will be because we want to go to Africa, but the time has not really come yet. We have to wait on His Majesty's time, and some say that we have to make it our own time now. His Majesty sets the pace, but we must carry it through. If we do not carry it through, we are keeping back ourselves.

Even though Ras Brenton had no phone or electricity in his home, he would if he could have afforded them. He would because they fall within his concept of fire. It is no contradiction, then, that he takes a positive view of change and technology and places responsibility for successfully managing change upon the shoulders of the Rastafari.

Among my narrators, even the oldest ones like Rasta Ivey, there were no grudges against modern technology, even though they themselves were not using it. Bongo J moved from advocating rejection of technology during the 1960s to a different position by the dawn of the twenty-first century: "So, to whom [Rastafari] have got the knowledge now [and] can operate technology, that nah nothing, that is great. That is great. To what the integrity him have."

How can we explain the greater tolerance for new technologies among the older Rastafari? We can refer to one of the claims of nigrescence theory for direction. As people become comfortable with their new identity and their commitment to it becomes thoroughly internalized, they are more likely to be open to new experiences and change because they are confident in and comfortable with whom they say they are. Or, hinting at a decline in the influence of the older Rastafari, as Ras Chronicle suggests, the old naysayers are dying off:

Them man deh wash out [done]. Some of them die. Some of them get old
. . . . [Today] some [Rastafari] man say just money him want; some man
say him no want no money him just want go home [Africa]. But we realize now, say, him have to have some education [emphasizing this point
by talking slowly]. Him have to have some education, him have to have
some money, him have to many things fe go home.

Elders like Ras Chronicle recognize a need to do things differently in a
different era.

Internationalization

During the 2002 Rastafari Federation conference that I attended (convened at the University of the West Indies), women, the different "sects"
of Rastafari, and "foreign" Rastafari were active participants and audience
members. Rastafari from Barbados and St. Lucia were especially well-rep-
resented (several women delegates represented them).

The Rastafari now have a global presence, which can be observed even
in Kingston, such as the four Japanese Rastafari wearing near waist-length
locks that I briefly met in a working-class neighborhood on Montgomery
Street in Kingston. On another occasion, at a celebration of Leonard Howell's Earthday (birthday), Rasta Ivey saw a stocky, twenty-something Japanese
man, dressed in white pants and tee-shirt, and wearing a head of puffed-up
jet black hair that looked to be transitioning to dreadlocks. He carried a tape
recorder. I marked him as either a journalist or a field researcher. Rasta Ivey
saw something different: "Look!" she shouted to me while forcibly yanking
my arm. "A Japan man! We deh in Japan!" For Rasta Ivey, seeing the young
Japanese man knocked her into a deeper if not new awareness: the ethnic,
national, and racial diversity of people influenced by Rastafari is staggering.
Rasta Ivey simply lived too isolated a life to really grasp how people around
the world were embracing and embodying Rastafari.

Other elders, though, were aware of the internationalization of Rastafari, perhaps because they had helped to initiate it. When I asked
Ras Chronicle whether the Rastafari movement had changed since the
early 1970s, he replied: "Yea man, [it] change a whole lot, a whole lot.
Now Brethren travel and go to Ethiopia, England, France, Germany, all
about . . . and the Rastafari nation is now a large nation." Ras Chronicle
elaborated on his statement when I asked him about the influence and
presence of Rastafari in the nations he listed:

That is why me say nation, Rastafari nation. Rastafari consciousness spread like wildfire. Because it come from up a Jamaica yah [right here]. Ya understand? And the message that Rasta carry is so dynamic with its forwardness . . . the future is in us. Because this whole Christian philosophy break down. It is Rasta philosophy that will be able to change the world.

Ras Chronicle recognizes how widely Rastafari identity has circulated across the globe and how appealing it is. The Rastafari are now a nation of diverse peoples. He does not view this as threatening or problematic. Instead, Ras Chronicle interprets the diffusion and embracing of Rastafari identity as an indication of its power and part of the fulfillment of the promise of Rastafari faith and mission: the bearers of tradition of Melchisidec, King David, Jesus Christ, and Haile Selassie I.

As more people began to view Rastafari as a powerful, positive, and appealing expression of Blackness, the numbers of people professing Rastafari began to markedly increase. Based on the stories my narrators related, I believe this growth trend began around 1968–69. From this point forward, it seems that it was cannabis and reggae music, along with the positive representation of Blackness and the rhetoric of justice, that attracted many during the post-1969 period. Examples of this trend were some of the young middle-class Jamaicans and the lawbreakers who professed Rastafari in the 1970s and the large number of individuals who were drawn to Rastafari through the influence and music of Bob Marley and the Wailers and other internationally prominent reggae musicians.

Anciency, Black redemption, repatriation, righteous living, and the Godly Emperor Haile Selassie I, cornerstones of the identity of those who came into the faith through the late 1960s, must now jostle with a movement in abeyance and a people who now position Rastafari identity in diverse ways within their self-concept. Selassie I, Black redemptions, and the moral aspects of Blackness may be less important to newer adherents of Rastafari identity. Even so, this does not deeply trouble Ras Chronicle:

You see all them what put on the knotty [dreadlocks], now, is a sign. Them don't really have the eyes of Rastafari, but some of them feel the power. And that is what is important. Righteousness must cover the land. Remember one time a man couldn't wear his knotty and not pay a great price. Now, everyone is wearing it and it is we bring it forward. We bring it in righteousness and recognition of we Black ancestors and we Black culture. And so, that what them is really dealing with, but some a them don't know yet. (Ras Chronicle)

Ras Chronicle hints at some disingenuousness on the part of people who are attracted to the symbols of the Rastafari but do not seem at all interested in becoming Rastafari. At the same time, his talk reminds us of another tenet of nigrescence: because people are now aware of the Rastafari, there is always the potential for them to become Rastafari. Although nearly all of my elder narrators saw the spread and popularity of Rastafari as a positive phenomenon, a few dissented. For example, Bongo J said, with disdain, "See how the Rasta them go to Europe and America and fuck around and come back buy big car? Them let foreign take them off their true sight [Rastafari]." Ras Chronicle offered a different view when I asked him if travel abroad and living in places like the United States lead to Rastafari brothers and sisters losing focus on their identity: "I don't see that [happening]," he said. Bongo J, in contrast, saw international living as a potentially corrupting force on the Rastafari because of the additional difficulties of being a practicing Rastafari abroad. Bongo J also described the wearing of locks by non-Rastafari as disrespectful. However, his greater concern was those people who falsely profess Rastafari identity: "You see them with big beard and tall locks, and them a lick [use] coke, eat pork, and engage in filthiness [e.g., sexual promiscuity]. . . . You see, them a play with God, man. Fire will consume all of the false prophets. Their portion will be a lake of burning fire." While Bongo J represents a dissenting voice, perhaps the experience of the two men might offer some perspective. Bongo J has never traveled abroad, while Ras Chronicle has visited several countries and has been instrumental in building international connections between Rastafari in different nations.

The internationalization of Rastafari identity, together with the new technologies, will generate new possibilities and new challenges. For instance, a person can experience Nyabinghi music or "experiment" with "being" Rastafari without needing to meet an authentic Rastafari, or grapple with internalizing the knowledge and norms attendant to being Rastafari. Such "experimental" Rastas are easily recognized by my narrators. Brother Yendis commented on a White Rastafari from the United States that he met in Kingston: "Them man strange. Them can't chant. Them can't beat drum. Them can't reason. So what is them? Them is in need of instruction." Brother Yendis's conclusion recognizes the centrality of what academics call "socialization" and "internalization" to the identity transformation process. Despite the surfeit of available information about the Rastafari and their practices, people must interpret and digest it which, as we saw, is a challenge for someone in the process of identity transformation. Without the interaction with living exemplars of an identification, the neophyte is never really sure whether she or he has gotten it "right." Why is green at the top of the flag displayed by the Nyabinghis, and red at the top of the one used by the Bobo Dreadlocks? How do I learn the intricacies of the rituals of the Nyabinghi ceremony? Do I need to be able to drum? As Cross Jr., pointed out, questions like these are addressed during acts of immersion, when a person intensely seeks out information about the new identity from many sources, including watching people who are models of who one wants to become. Regardless of how the future unfolds, the issue of what and who constitutes an "authentic" Rastafari will likely become more contentious where the centrality of Blackness and divinity of Haile Selassie to being Rastafari is challenged.

Female Rastafari

We opened chapter 1 with Empress Dinah making an impassioned presentation to a gathering of male and female Rastafari. Empress Dinah was not the only female to deliver messages to the assembled. "Princesses" (young Rastafari women) as well as "matriarchs" like Prophetess, delivered presentations, with some focused on women's concerns. Women are an unmistakably visible, if not a prominent, presence among the post-1980s Jamaican Rastafari. This trend dates at least to the end of the 1970s, when Rastafari women began to reshape some of the dominant cultural rules such as dress codes that stipulated women must cover their locks and wear long frocks in public. Such cultural revision was partially a result of the growing number of Rastafari women adherents, many of them younger and some of them employed or seeking employment (Rowe, 1985:19). Nevertheless, women have been an integral part of the evolution of the Rastafari from the beginning. Howell, and Hinds, for certain, had women devotees and many women in their listening audiences, and Rasta Ivey attests to being an active female presence among the early evangelists. During the 1950s, women Rastafari marched and demonstrated in protest with men and went to jail along with them. The space of participation was far less circumscribed for these early women Rastafari than for their sisters between the 1960s and early 1980s (Rowe, 1998:75 offers a similar observation). As I already noted, the ascendency of the Dreadlocks that restricted participation of women is perhaps better grasped as an interruption rather than *the* pattern of gender relations.

The Rastafari are widely described as a male-dominated collectivity. Their gender understandings are deeply informed by biblical prescriptions and cultural understandings developed over the centuries in Jamaica. Austin-Broos explains that Jamaican Pentecostal women are able to subvert the Pauline injunctions that circumscribe the role of women in the Church because they have access to the public domain, which she believes is denied Rastafari women (1997:241). Indeed, Lake (1994, 1998) views Rastafari women, for the most part, as participating in their own subordination by adhering to the scriptural and male Rastafari injunctions that require their subservience to "man and God." From Lake's perspective, we could view Rastafari women as quadruply oppressed: by Blackness, religion, men, and capitalism.

There is great variability among the Rastafari about what constitutes "proper" gender behavior, and my own experience and observation confirm this. There are male Rastafari who firmly believe in the Old and New Testament rules (e.g., the Pauline injunctions such as "Let the woman learn in all silence and with subjection," 1 Timothy 2:11). There are those who talk about rigid gender relations but don't actually practice them. And there are those whose gendered interactions are contingent, open to negotiation, and not steeped in understandings of sexual difference in ways that enforce subjugation. On the contradictory gendered practices of male Rastafari, consider the position of women in Brother Bongo's talk during a conversation with me:

> Brother Bongo: We go as far as that we could recite the whole 276 [Amharic] characters by heart. And up until that time, I had my sister [female companion] with me. She did not leave me, she still stood with me and supported me right up.
>
> Price: So, did she feel threatened by the fact that she was openly learning Rastafari among men?
>
> Brother Bongo: No. She still stuck with me until she could repeat Psalm 117 in Amharic. I had a concert at which she recited the Amharic prayer and Our Father in our interpretation. . . . It come now that we were on the beach and they called for a development of the beach, and the caretaker of the beach said we would have to leave. We had to leave from the beach and pitch tent up on Wareika Hills. So, we go up to Wareika Hills and built up our habitation. By this time, it was I and the sister and my other brethren, three of us together.

Brother Bongo has revealed that a female companion was his close intimate during his identity transformation, and it seems she too was on a
similar path (he said very little about this woman). Yes, by Brother Bongo's account he is playing the "head" role as teacher, but they both were
on an identity journey together. Later in the same conversation, Brother
Bongo offers a different take on women:

> I could see it in you. I could see it coming from you. Immediately, as I
> saw it, you mentioned the women [he anticipated my question because
> he knew I was curious as to his position on women and Rastafari]. Yes,
> I saw the women issue coming up from you. Women have a vital role to
> play because the woman example is Mary, the mother of Jesus. But the
> woman's role is behind the man. Well, I would say beside the man. Not
> in front, but beside. In the administration of government, I do not see
> the woman as an upfront Minister within a theocracy. . . . I resent it. . . .
> Again, I think a woman in the congregation of brethren is supposed to
> cover her locks because the brethren is the head of the woman, and Jah is
> the head of the man, I and I. She must respect I and I, and I must respect
> Jah. But . . . the youth up there now [pointing metaphorically toward
> the Rastafari Federation building], they have a different opinion where
> women are concerned. They see women as equal . . . and they support
> that because they want that, and because I resent that, they see I as a
> woman hater. . . . If you please a woman, you cannot please God.

Brother Bongo has cohabited with a woman, who became versed in the ar-
got and practices of the Rastafari, and whom he spoke of with an affection-
ate tone. He also professes culturally and scripturally defined ideas about
women that he sees as being complementary but which could be construed
by others as subordinating them. He does not see himself as a woman hater.

Rastafari gender relations seem to trouble the non-Rastafari more than
the Rastafari themselves. Observers typically evaluate Rastafari gender relations within the terms of "the western theory of gender equality" rather
than how male and female Rastafari actually live their gender relationships (Rowe, 1985). The Dreadlocks men of the vintage of my narrators
do privilege the masculine over the feminine, and minimized their own
role in the private sphere, just as many Christian men have done (Austin-Broos, 1997). Some male Rastafari, especially the ascetic-oriented
ones, saw women (along with material possessions) as a distraction that
hindered attainment of godliness and asceticism. Some male elders have

spoken of being celibate for up to a decade! I believe, however, that the idealized patriarchal orientation adopted by some of the Rastafari, male and female, is giving way to more fluid understandings of gender based in the realities of the new terrain of the twenty-first century.

My women Rastafari narrators became Rastafari primarily through their own experiences, interests, and pursuits. In this they deviated from the widespread view that women are to become Rastafari through the assistance of men. Sister Mariam, for example, was already in a state of seekership in 1946 when she met the man she called "Brother Ras," who would become her lifelong partner. Laughing to herself as she thought back, Sister Mariam said, "I met Brother Ras in Trenchtown at a Garveyite meeting. I see him there and he see me there. The two a we lock eyes." I asked, "Were you Rastafari then?" She responded, "At that time I had already been listening for God because I wanted to know the true God. That is why I keep company with some Garveyites, because they talk about Black God and King. And that is how I meet Brother Ras." "Was Brother Ras a Rastafari when you first saw him?" I continued. "Yes. He was. The two of we already upon the same path when we meet." In this case Sister Mariam had become Rastafari without the guidance of a man. In the case of my narrators like Sisters Mariam, Pear, and Amme, men populated their stories, but the women gave no indication that men guided them toward Rastafari. Their discoveries and journeying were of their own making. Rasta Ivey and Prophetess rarely mentioned men at all, other than relatives such as brothers or fathers. I do not want to extrapolate too much from the experience of these few women Rastafari, but I do want to emphasize that they were seekers in their own right.

Biographies of Rastafari women would help us grasp why some Rastafari women are independent and resist female subordination while others do not see it as a problem to resolve. We lack a good grasp of the gendered demographic evolution of the Rastafari. It is very likely that some early Rastafari women suffered abuse at the hands of men—Rasta Ivey told me how she had been "lick down" by men, but her militancy probably got her into more difficulties than her gender. That is, if she were a man in Jamaica she would still probably have received many "licks" because of her boldness in professing Rastafari. On the other hand, couples began to become Rastafari by at least the early 1970s, and this route into identity transformation, compared to that of the woman's journey as an individual, appears to have allowed men more influence over women's identity transformation (see also Rowe, 1998; Tafari-Ama, 1998).

Although it is primarily the younger Rastafari that will define the range of gender relations in the coming years, some of the elder male Rastafari have contributed to developing gender equity within a people whose identity revolves around a cluster of justice motifs:

> You see over the years, Rasta man used to put the woman one side and tell her say she must stay in a de house and have baby and stay with the baby. But His Majesty show I and I say that the trouble is for the woman equally as the man. No foundation cannot complete without the woman or by the man alone. So, therefore, we set the woman on a level. . . . So, that is to show how close we work with woman. Some man fight 'gainst it still . . . some man really take a position and tell you say, "You see His Majesty have any woman in a him office?" And him nah look at it [and] say a Queen His Majesty have beside him you know. Him a look 'bout office [while overlooking the Queen]. (Brother Yendis)

Women like Empress Dinah sees the unequal gender relations as something to move past: "No man can really tell me how to worship *my* God. That is fi me and God. A new dispensation is here. We [Rastas] must live up to our own teaching. No oppression is acceptable."

Class, Status, Material Possessions

Contention and conflict between the Rastafari trace to the origins of the people. Early evangelists like Howell, Hinds, Hibbert, and Dunkley cooperated on occasion, even though their views on the fledgling faith and identity differed. Interpretations of ideology and doctrine evolved differently, and these were sources of tension, for example over the nature of Emperor Selassie I's divinity (e.g., Christ returned or living God). During the post-1970s period, however, class manifested as a noticeable marker of intragroup variation and a new source of tension. Those Rastafari who had steady incomes or who were paid salaries, who did not renounce work or education, and who did not interact with the Rastafari sick, aged, infants, and poor, were less likely to bridge the emergent class divides. Elder Rastafari like Ras Brenton acknowledged these new tensions:

> Even you own brother want fight you out because from him have a money, the first thing him no want you to come where him there [to his dwelling or place of income generation]. . . . [T]he second thing him a

keep far from you. You can hardly see him. . . . We call them the society Rastas, who live in a the pocket of society according to the big man them [and] because them live in a de pocket of society so them is like society. We [poor Rastafari] have our own society, but them no agree with it. They hardly want come near we because them say we too down to earth and them is up town stylee [mod].

Some of the Rastafari who have gained financially live in middle-class areas of Kingston, such as the Red Hills, which are not easily accessible to poor Rastafari of the other sections of Kingston (you can sometimes find poor Rastafari living in the bush or fringes of these enclaves). The better-off Rastafari may visit the ghettos and haunts of their poorer brothers and sisters, but outside of these visits and episodic participation in ceremonies, their interaction with other Rastafari is restricted. The monied Rastafari drive new model automobiles, live in modern homes, utilize up-to-the-minute technology, and travel abroad at their own expense. They are criticized, though, by their poor comrades for not sharing their success and for taking on the ways of Babylon. Such behaviors challenge Rastafari identity and tenets of the ideology, such as reciprocity, egalitarianism, and self-sacrifice that Rastafari constructed through the 1970s.

We saw that during the 1950s some people sold all they possessed in order to leave for Africa. By the early 1960s, a significant number of Rastafari had concluded, based on the lessons distilled from the formal and informal Missions to Africa, and from the experience of EWF and UNIA members, that relocation to Africa required preparation and a useful skill set relevant to building a postcolonial Africa governed by Africans. Ras Brenton rhetorically explained to me how attachment to Babylon conflicted with commitment to repatriation and hence a key element of the identity of the elder Rastafari: "If man have big house, big car, payment, and all them things, him is not going to want to leave them for Africa." The obligations and responsibilities attendant to living in a capitalist society—mortgages, car payments, and maintenance of these and other things—compete with the investment, sacrifice, renunciation, mortification, and communion processes vital to sustaining the Rastafari as the elders constructed their identity. Nonetheless, Rastafari like Ras Brenton see material development and spiritual development moving hand-in-hand and that too much of one or the other is not good. A balance is important:

[Rastafari] must have to develop materially and spiritually. And if a man is not spiritually mature as they say, he would not be materially mature either. It is that stage we have reached. So we have to think spiritually, materially, and naturally to be practical about that which we seek. . . . because Rasta says he is king and he wants to be like the King's [Selassie I] son to have everything that the King would have. But that is when we go a yard [Africa]. When we have our land we are not going to have everything abroad, but some man a fight to get everything abroad before he goes home because he says he does not want to go home poor. But I can remember that we did not come here rich neither. So, if we go home poor it is not anything because we came from where the wealth is [Africa]. They brought us [to Jamaica] poor. They took all that we had when they were bringing us. So, we came here with nothing, and we going home back with something. So, whatever we can go with we will go with it, but some of us should start to go from now. (Ras Brenton)

Thus, the idea of a balance between the material and spiritual aspects of living offer a working resolution to the conundrum of living as a Rastafari in a rapidly changing Jamaica. In this rationale, we see that elder Rastafari like Ras Brenton have not renounced or displaced literal repatriation to Africa. Indeed, Rastafari like Brothers Barody and Woks believe that the most militant Dreadlocks were imbalanced in their promotion of fundamentalism and asceticism. These Brothers do not harbor antagonism toward the militant and extremist Rastafari—some are revered precisely for their conviction and commitment—but they know that asceticism is not for them. In this they have perhaps much in common with the majority of Rastafari.

Change and Identity Maintenance

New opportunities, alliances, and interests pose threats to the maintenance of any identity. Groups that make great demands on their members must erect mechanisms that parry intrusions that may lessen the interest of members or lead to defection. As we have seen, the Rastafari have few formalized means of member "protection" against worldly enticements (e.g., guarded compounds). Identity maintenance falls ultimately to each single Rastafari. Thus, the power of investment, sacrifice, and reward are central to internalization and long-term commitment to the identity. After all, few people are born Rastafari; it is an achieved identity.

The main threat to identities like Rastafari is that of weakening loyalty and commitment to the identity and the collectivity. Avoiding centrifugal influences is not easy without a person removing himself literally or symbolically–or both–from the influence of the threats, identities, people, and choices he sought to escape through identity transformation. Having to live among the very people, conditions, and institutions that the person sought to escape can generate anxieties, anger, and problems. As we saw in chapter 5, getting away from the "demons" associated with the pre-Rastafari identity may not be easily accomplished.

Brother Bongo, having been forced to leave the Rastafarian stronghold Back-o-Wall, found himself among the very conditions that many Rastafari loathe. Given some tough personal breaks and the recurrent efforts of law enforcement to disrupt Rastafari communities and squatting, Brother Bongo temporarily lost his capacity to make an independent living, and he had to move into a tenement yard. Tenement yards are sites of (frequently) substandard housing, sometimes densely packed with families and individuals who live under these arrangements because of poverty and a lack of better options. These "yards" may be "home," but are also are known for being chaotic, and the living arrangements contribute to conflict.

> They were going to bulldoze Back-O-Wall to build Tivoli Gardens as it is at present [1966]. So, we were shoved out of Back-o-Wall again. I had to take refuge in the cemetery, Ebenezer Cemetery. That is adjoining Back-O-Wall. From then, I took up residence back to where I started, against the prison wall in Charlotte Street. . . . It was a room in a tenement yard. Knowing that Rasta don't enjoy tenement yard, I could not feel comfortable. Heaps of diversion [distractions, contention] come up, and you have to find yourself sharing with the works of Babylon. You become like an ordinary citizen again until it reach the stage where I said, this is not it still. This is not it.

Brother Bongo was completely uncomfortable among the "Babylonians" who confronted him with the things he had renounced, such as rum and the use of foul language. The identity he had labored to craft and strove to actualize—the person that he told himself he was and should be—was threatened. He began "touching" [drinking] rum and he began losing connection to the things that helped him "know" himself: communion, the quotidian interactions with other Rastafari, the regular engagement with the signs and symbols of Rastafari. Other factors began competing for his attention. He was not as capable as he wanted to be in adhering to the norms and practices expected by the Rastafari and decided he had to leave the yard in order to continue the kind of identity work that helped define who he was. If Brother Bongo had not left, he might be counted among the apostate Rastafari. Given his experience and the lessons we have learned from Black identity theory, it is unsurprising that people revisit their identity commitments as well as wrestle throughout their life course with challenges to their self-concept. For other Rastafari, perhaps even for some of my narrators, the conflicts raised by the new sources of tension may lead to renouncing Rastafari identity.

Change and Cultural Persistence

Many of my oldest narrators have had to fall back on non-Rastafari kin and friends for support as they age. Some of them live among the non-Rastafari but with attenuated social ties. Brother Barody and Brother Dee live in Riverton, just outside of metropolitan Kingston on the Spanish Town Road. Brother Dee, the once militantly aggressive Rastafari, whose experience has been sought by scholars and covered in the Jamaican press, was consigned to irrelevance as he aged. He became dependent upon "baldheads." His daughter, plainly indigent, was generally preoccupied with finding food or money when I visited. The daughter seemed happy to see me most times, though not very interested in my presence. She seemed more pleased that I spent time with her father than with the milk or peas and rice I sometimes brought for Brother Dee (and her family, because she cooked the food). Other Rastafari remembered Brother Dee, told me about him, but did not know exactly where to find him. Some did not know whether he was alive or not. Brother Barody knew he was in the community, but once I explained to him the issue of Brother Dee's isolation, he agreed that finding support for them as they aged was a challenge for the oldest Rastafari. He often returned to his argument about how "the man mash up themself" [their rugged lifestyle and practices] and this "what happen": infirmity; illness; weakness. "Them man say them live forever, but look at them. Man must take care a himself for him live forever." I grasped the irony of Brother Barody's point. The ideology of his generation of Rastafari emphasized "everliving" life, meaning that the Rastafari, like their King, should not die. But all around me, Rasta Ivey, Brother Dee, Sister Coromantee, Ras Sam Brown, they were in failing health or "dropping off."

Thus, another burning issue for the Rastafari will be how the experience and cultural knowledge of those oldest still-living members is recorded, saved, and transmitted to younger members. Certainly, news stories, Rastafari publications, and books like this one will be sources of some information. However, there is much that such media do not and cannot communicate about identity and lived experience. There are a few efforts under way, though, by the Rastafari to build and maintain connections with younger Jamaicans, Rastafari and non-Rastafari, such as the RITA's attempts to encourage the active participation of youth. The experience of elder Rastafari will likely play some role in continued Rastafari ethnogenesis. I hazard to speculate, though, what that role will be or what it might look like because surprise is as likely as demise.

Conclusion

Toward a More Comprehensive Understanding of Racial Identity Formation

When I opened the rickety tin door that served as a gate into Ras General's yard, I saw one of his sons, a teenaged male Rastafari, resting in a hammock. When he saw me, he got out of the hammock and said, "Soon come," disappearing into an open but dark doorway of a very small makeshift of a house. Soon the youth returned with his father, Ras General. Ras General was expecting me because we had agreed a few days earlier that we would make a tape-recorded interview. While I set up the tape recorder, I overheard Ras General tell his son, "I want you to listen to this history so that you will know of the struggles of I n I in this faith." Ras General told us how he gradually "grew" into Rastafari because of his listening to the different messages they were preaching about His Majesty and about righteousness. He also saw how they were mistreated and ridiculed. He was "raise inna the church," but the message of the Rastafari was more appealing to him than those he received in his parents' church. In Ras General's story, both his son and I gained perspective on his motivation to become Rastafari, and his experience during his act of becoming Rastafari.

This book has engaged the words of Rastafari such as Ras General and a reconstruction of ethnogenesis informed by ideas of social complexity to ask and answer new and complicated questions about Black and Rastafari identity. Indeed, I have offered a fresh explanation and approach: a conception of morally configured Blackness based in personal, collective (or social), and historical perspectives on identity formation.

Rasta Ivey, Prophetess, Brother Yendis, and the other Rastafari whose stories inform this book, had particular experiences—encounters—that led them to reconsider and rework their identity and become Rastafari. Their varied experiences revealed themes common to becoming Rastafari:

deep curiosity regarding questions of race and God, questioning of the mistreatment of the Rastafari by other Jamaicans, fascination with the significance of the crowning of Emperor Haile Selassie I, and considering the Rastafari as models of what a person could become. In some cases, the encounter fit into an already present cluster of concerns. Rasta Ivey already had long-standing interest in questions of race and redemption before she became Rastafari. For her, it was her curiosity and the convergence of the various religiously and politically tinged messages of racial redemption and Black culture and history being disseminated in meetings in Kingston, the crowning of Emperor Haile Selassie I, and the proselytizing of fledgling Rastafari evangelists like Leonard Howell and Robert Hinds. These factors constituted her encounter with questions about race and her conclusion, that "the five [versions of Black redemption] is become one." Differently, Prophetess's encounter involved visions, dreams, and hearing voices of "His Majesty" and Jesus Christ talking to her at an early age, delivering at one point an injunction: "'For all my people is taken away from Africa and come here as slaves. So, me want them to come home to me.' So, you see from that, is the two of them. His Majesty Selassie on me left hand. Lord Jesus on me right hand. . . . The two of them talking [to me]." In the case of Brother Yendis, his encounter involved experiential witnessing, and also began at a tender age, when he observed the mistreatment of a Rastafari man. He could not get any satisfactory answers from friends and family that might justify the mistreatment of the man, other than "[it] is Rasta." Brother Yendis never found the evidence that he needed to conclude that something was wrong with the Rastafari people that he began to watch. His young eyes and mind began to pay attention to injustice, and to value righteousness.

In these three cases, we could restrict our focus to the individuals and their personal identities. If we left it at this, however, we would be short-changing ourselves of a broader understanding of Rastafari identity. Rasta Ivey, Prophetess, and Brother Yendis tapped into and embraced an enduring and evolving set of cultural resources, such as those of Ethiopianism and the moral economy of Blackness. What is more, our three elders also chose to affiliate with two stigmatized identifications: Blackness and Rastafari. In order to explain these complex facets of identity and identification, we must situate identity in at least three inseparable but distinctive phenomena: a person's self-concept, collective or social identity, and the relevance of history to both. We must not neglect, though, that identity formation occurs within wider systems of social interaction, and that the complexity of the innumerable interactions involved make the process dynamic, unstable, and unpredictable.

Self-Concept and Rastafari

We learned that becoming Rastafari typically required an identity transformation because both Blackness and Rastafari are socially constructed; people are not born as either. They must achieve the identity. Although the encounter was a fundamental part of the identity transformation of my narrators, the valence of Rastafari identity is tied to Blackness and demands a transformation, catalyzed by people's recognition of how miseducation, deracination, and oppression has shaped, if not defined, their worldview and personal identity. Thus, the encounter and the culture and identity work that follow are the means by which to rework the "old" worldview and identity in light of new ideals. The central task, here, is generating a salient and positive conception of Blackness. This is by no means a self-evident course of action. A person must invest the effort to learn how to live the new identity and beliefs, and in this task he or she must turn to various sources of information such as texts, and most important, other people who are deemed to be exemplars of Rastafari. Inspiration may also come "from within" as with Prophetess, or seekers like Rasta Ivey, but the interior experience will at some point entangle others if identity transformation is to continue. Important personal influences in the experience of my narrators' identity transformation came from kin and friends:

> . . . they [Selassie I and Jesus] continue telling me and telling me say it is the people in slavery they want and they come to take them away from here to take them home, because they are in great difficulty and great suffering. The time is appointed for them to leave Jamaica to go back home to Africa. This continue and continue, but she [Prophetess' mother] wouldn't believe me, and all that I could say to her she wouldn't believe. They [voices] start telling me now that since she won't hear me, they gwine [going] take me away. . . . away from the two of them [her mother and father].

As we saw, Prophetess's mother refused to entertain her incipient identity work, while her father displayed compassion when she talked about her interior conversations with him. For our narrators, personal struggles, engagement in social activities, engagement with history and cultural resources, and the meaning generated in these realms, are inseparable dimensions of their identity as Rastafari.

Nigrescence theory, broadened by the infusion of ideas and questions from religious conversion, provided us with a way to situate and explain how individuals tussled with ideas about Blackness and religion and how to align, however imperfectly, their self-concept with those ideas. There is nothing neat, easy, or quick about the process of Black identity transformation. The only certainty is that it is unlikely to be neat, easy, or quick. It is not only in the hands of the individual to announce, "I am a new person, and here I am!" The convert needs other people to assist him or her in carrying out the transformation and sustaining the new self-concept. This is the inescapably social aspect of identity formation.

Some people balked at the transformation: "A watch how the good boy start to mash himself up" [i.e., damage himself by becoming Rastafari], someone said to Brother Woks, or Brother Yendis's own father saying, "'damn fool turn Rasta.'" While these are disapproving responses delivered by intimate acquaintances, the convert must decide whether to continue on his or her path of transformation and risk alienating family and friends, suffer restricted opportunity, or return to "normal." My narrators kept on the path of identity transformation, and along the way severed many close relationships as a result. They also gained confidence in their identity choice, however, and over time mended many of the torn relationships. They had internalized their identity to the point that they feared no threat to their self-concept and way of life.

One area in which I argued for the elaboration of nigrescence theory concerns religiosity. Theories of religious conversion allowed us to situate a wider range of personal experience and cultural practice within the context of black identity transformation. The idea of a seeker, someone curious about existential questions or the meaning of things, the role of relationships in conversion, and the influence of master frames such as evil, redemption, and the idea of exodus provide a set of symbols and tropes that inform a person's thinking and action. Because of this elaboration of nigrescence theory, we can better situate how the paths to Rastafari differ among converts but share commonalities. Rasta Ivey and Sister Mariam, for example, had been concerned with questions about race and God before the encounters that constituted their initial paths to becoming Rastafari. Brother Yendis and Prophetess both had encounters while they were young, and they continually revisited these encounters as they matured and moved into becoming Rastafari.

The theory of nigrescence aids us in making sense of the problems that the Rastafari, Ethiopianists, and others sought to resolve *before* Fanon, Césaire, Du Bois, Garvey, Woodson, and others formulated their trenchant theoretical and existential critiques of race and White hegemony. Stigma served as a primary challenge. Rastafari treated stigma as a sign of status. They subverted the stigma stamped upon Blackness and valorized Black identity, history, and culture. Black identity theories are of considerable value in understanding this historical, collective resignification of Blackness. Black identity theories such as nigrescence have vast potential to extend our understanding and explanation of Blackness as identification once we solidly position them within the streams of social interaction, history, the cultural production of meaning, and biographical experience, as I have attempted to do.

Complexity, Ethnogenesis, and Social Identity

I drew ideas from theories of complexity and chaos to illustrate how the ethnogenesis of a people involves surprises, disruptions, unintended consequences, and the entwining of an array of cultural resources. I entwined this perspective with another angle on identity formation: collective or social identity. In chapter 2, we saw that, if left alone, the Rastafari might well have been just another new group that eventually drifted off into obscurity or extinction. Instead, we saw cells of adherents, motivated by charismatic leaders, galvanized by repression, encouraged by seeing their own beliefs and prophecies materialize, gradually developed into a recognized people. Along the way, over sociohistorical time, their stigmatized identity shifted status from pariah to exemplar of Black culture and history. These transformations did not happen because the Rastafari themselves made it happen. It involved many complicated interactions and exchanges between the Rastafari and non-Rastafari that led to changes in perception and representation of Rastafari identity by both parties. The coverage of Rastafari in the newspapers, government's suppression of Rastafari public activities like street meetings, the visit of the EWF's Mamie Richardson to Jamaica, the Claudius Henry debacles, the Mission to Africa, the Coral Gardens incident, and the visit of Emperor Selassie I to Jamaica, are a few examples of events that deeply changed how the public perceived and represented the Rastafari and how the Rastafari perceived and represented themselves.

Another value of including the collective aspects of identity formation and ethnogenesis in our analysis is that it brings more plainly into view the influence of other social actors on identity formation. For example, the Rastafari saw themselves as persecuted and chosen people, the non-Rastafari as having to tolerate racial lunatics. Thus, there were complexly different but intersecting logics at work in the formation of collective identity. From the perspective of my narrators, humiliation and persecution bolstered their conviction, and even inspired some of them to change their self-concept and adopt the identity of the Rastafari. From the perspective of the various elites, the Rastafari were nuisances, lunatics, and louts, promoting views that could not possibly appeal to any "normal" person. Thus, they tried to shame and ridicule as a means to tarnish Rastafari identity and dissuade people from adopting it. From the view of the Rastafari, the growth in their numbers pointed to their prescience—a special capacity to see and know what others do not—which nourished their conviction. The internal dynamics of the Rastafari involved factionalism as a younger generation of Rastafari sought to purge some indigenous religious practices of the older Rastafari from their cultural repertoire (e.g., spirit possession). Some fundamentalist cells such as those who came to be called the Dreadlocks gained traction, injecting a new (if not completely welcomed) energy into the evolution of the Rastafari.

The visit of Mamie Richardson was the proverbial stone tossed into the still pool. The disruption and subsequent ripples motivated the Rastafari to push more forcibly for their beliefs. In addition, they asked for rights, the right to become Ethiopian nationals, the right to be recognized by the government as a legitimate religion, the right to be sent to Africa at the expense of the colonial government. Moreover, many external factors swirled in this local vortex. National liberation movements (including the one next door in Cuba); African nations willing to accept their "blood" brothers and sisters from the West; the visit of the God of the Rastafari to the land of the Rastafari themselves. If the metaphor of the stone tossed into the pool functions as a good image of a social perturbation, then the visit of Haile Selassie I to Jamaica generated an avalanche of stones, dropping at the same time. Many of my interlocutors took the visit as evidence of the rightness of the Rastafari, and set out to do the kind of identity and cultural work they needed to do in order to become Rastafari.

> It was when his Majesty come to Jamaica that I come recognize that the
> Rasta them was right all along. I did feel their vibes, but I never did take
> it too deep. Once I see the Emperor, and how the people respond [with
> great adoration], and how the Emperor carry himself [stately], and take in
> the Rasta inna Kings House [the space of political and economic elites], I
> know that Rasta is it. And I know that that is the Man. (Ras Kirk)

It is among these narratives of personal experiences and recollections,
the occurrence of noteworthy events, and the reactions of elites and the
public, that we can plainly make out how a collective identity is manufactured and represented. By conceiving of the evolution of a people and
their social identity as nonlinear complex phenomena, we might better
appreciate the ambiguity and improbabilities that are continually at work
in ethnogenesis.

By including the ethnogenesis of the Rastafari as a part of our focus
on identity, we gained an important perspective on personal identity. Personal identity formation may be shaped within the context of ethnogenesis. For example, we can better appreciate the risks and desires of my
narrators by situating them in the greater arena in which collective identification is worked out over time. We could see how personal conceptions
of Blackness and Rastafari compared to the various social representations,
such as depiction of the Rastafari as dangerous or Afrocentrism as value-
less. Thus, we are able to grasp keenly the shifting dynamics over time
between personal identity and reference group orientation by combing
through the entangled collective (or social) and the personal.

History and Morally Configured Black Identities

> It is the Rasta that keep talking about slavery. Everything was taken from
> us so we forget who we are. The Rasta them say we still live in slavery,
> but [today] there is no chains. No whip. But brutality deh still. . . . We
> Rasta people say through we is Rastafari we move away from the mental
> enslavement, as them woulda say. So we do things different. . . . We re-
> member the past and we see the past in the present. (Ras Brenton)

Ras Brenton, like my other narrators, framed his self-concept in a morally
configured conception of Blackness. These ideas have been refashioned
by the Rastafari, but many of the cultural resources which the Rastafari

utilize are of old vintage, older than themselves. My interlocutors connected themselves to a durable set of ideas about Blackness, justice, and redemption: Ethiopianism. Ethiopianism, a cultural constellation of ideas about Blackness, religion, and politics, and the moral economy of Blackness that it has coexisted with, have provided the fibers for weaving many variations of a morally configured Black identity. Blackness itself had to be constructed by Africans and Europeans which in and of itself is an astonishing outcome (an example of the workings of complexity) because a diversity of African identities gradually was subsumed within a broad, umbrella-like concept of "Black." Black identity, the morally configured filaments in particular, was indelibly etched with the impact of slavery and desire for freedom and liberation. The God of the Christians came to be a central character in this drama. Small groups of Black Jamaicans expressed the ideas that the Christian God was on their side, that they were the modern children of Israel, and that through patience or rebellion they could get to Canaan, the Promised Land. These ideas gained traction and durability over time and through use, girding the fortitude of slaves and other oppressed Blacks to rebel against slavery and exploitation. Again, without the contribution of historical perspective, and the formation of collective identity over time, our grasp of personal identity would be greatly limited.

Moving Forward

Nearly 80 years after their emergence, Jamaica's Rastafari have formed themselves as an unmistakably distinctive people and identity. Their identity and story remain an open project, however. Post-1970s Jamaica has the trappings typical of highly mobile, pluralistic, cosmopolitan capitalist societies. There are many new opportunities and new sources of tension for the Rastafari. These changes, opportunities, and tensions the Rastafari will have to negotiate as they arise.

The contemporary ubiquity of print, audio, and visual media make information about the Rastafari available to more people, allowing people the opportunity to explore the ideas and symbols without ever interacting with the adherents of Rastafari, especially the older ones. It is probable that a growing number of younger Jamaicans will be as likely to become interested in Rastafari identity through consuming reggae music, videos, movies, and scholarly and popular texts, as through a "classic" encounter, of the kind experienced by Rasta Ivey, Prophetess, and Brother Yendis.

As Thomas (2004) has argued, a "modern" Blackness has evolved in post-1960s Jamaica, an expression of Blackness defined by consumerism, individuality, nihilism, the United States and Britain—the antithesis of the morally configured permutation of Blackness expressed by the Rastafari. Internally, the Rastafari now has a fragmented class dynamic in that some adherents have access to and consume some of the trappings of the Babylon that their elders once rejected: homes in middle- and upper-middle-class areas, sporty cars, jet-setting, living a night-club lifestyle associated with reggae music, and so on. Many of the elders see these better-off Rastafari as stingy and standoffish, failing to share their goods with the struggling Rastafari, especially the elders, a growing number of whom are in failing health and need support. Yet, some of the younger Rastafari do identify themselves as a part of the special and chosen people. They, too, interpret persecution within this framework, but in the context of changed times. Rastafarian culture and ideology may be popular, but ironically, it is perhaps in the land of their origin that they still find their greatest obstacles. Ras Desmond was distressed about losing his job because he would not cut off his dreadlocks to suit his employer. He interpreted the employer's action as a threat to his livelihood, an injustice served to a Black man, and an affront to the rights he ought to have as a human being. Desmond, though an individual, should still remind us of the pervasiveness of the moral economy of Blackness, and moral economy in general, and how these ideas and beliefs may slumber, surprising us when they are aroused and openly demonstrated through collective action. How all these new developments will influence the continued evolution of the Rastafari remains for us to see. Our nonlinear perspective counsels us to keep in mind both the predictability and surprise involved in ethnogenesis and identity formation.

I have sought in these pages to offer a novel view on Rastafari identity, and Black identity in general. We know that a person's identity is unquestionably a unique property based in an individual's unique experience. We also know that a person's identity is constructed through interaction with other people, historical imagination and social memory, and the cultural resources used to weave together a self-concept. Our accounts of identity typically focus, however, on one dimension of identity: the individual, the social, or, sometimes, the historical. I have combined the perspectives and applied them to Rastafari identity. In doing so, we have plainly seen how Black Jamaicans utilized their agency to become who they are—Rastafari—and to develop a positive purchase on a stigmatized identity. Not only did the Rastafari apply positive valence to Blackness by subverting its stigma in general, but they also wove a new identity for themselves.

I will close these pages with part of a poem that Ras Sam Brown recited to me. It reminds us of the motivation of so many of my narrators to become Rastafari:

Hail to the lords anointed, Great David's Greater son
hail in this time appointed, his reign on earth begun
he comes to break down oppression, to set all captives free
to take away man's regression and rule in equity
perfect love to the world . . .

Acronyms

Afro-West Indian Welfare League—AWIWL
African Reform Church—ARC
Brothers Solidarity of United Ethiopia—BSUE
Daily Gleaner—DG
Ethiopian Salvation Society—ESS
Ethiopian World Federation—EWF
His Imperial Majesty Haile Selassie I—H.I.M.
Jamaican Labor Party—JLP
People's Nationalist Party—PNP
Rastafari Federation—RF
Rastafari International Theocratic Assembly—RITA
Rastafari Movement Association—RMA
University College of the West Indies—UCWI
United Negro Improvement Association—UNIA

Notes

1. Whiteness develops differently from Blackness in Jamaica. Ethnicity remained salient for Whites far longer than for Blacks because they were able to keep in touch with their homeland or ancestral relations. European ethnicity and nationality continued to coexist with Whiteness, the latter serving as a master identity. As we shall see, Ashanti, Fanti, Ibo and other identities did not survive along with Blackness.

2. I use the term evolution in a nonlinear and adaptive sense: people, identities, and cultures can evolve over time, becoming more complex. There is nothing preordained or teleological in this conception of evolution.

CHAPTER 1

1. I copied the quote from a typed draft of a manuscript written by Ras Sam Brown, which he shared with me. An article authored by Brown with the same title was published in *Caribbean Studies* (1966:39–40).

2. Monica Schuler believes Gordon exploited Blacks as much as anyone else (1980:135).

3. Today Brown is a more inclusive racial category because it can include anyone who is "mixed" with Black. Mulatto, however, is still used in common talk and still signifies offspring of Black and White parents (though not always the first generation). Alleyne offers a different view, explaining "Brown" to be the "'highest shade of mulatto'" (2002:192).

4. A recent census for Jamaica indicated that more than 90 percent of Jamaicans self-reported as "Black" and 6 percent as "mixed" (Statistical Institute of Jamaica, 2003). The Census now uses "Mixed-race" rather than folk terms like Brown or mulatto.

5. Robotham argues the transition to Crown Colony was in the works before the rebellion and that the rebellion provided sufficient justification (1983:60).

6. Coromantine is the name of a slave processing center for Gold Coast Africans. The Coromantines were not a distinct people, although they all spoke Twi.

7. Curtin (1955:25) asserts that a generic Black identity was widely established by the 1830s, while both Craton (1978:157) and Alleyne (1988) believe it was well under way soon after the British took control over slavery in Jamaica 1655.

8. The story of Ham could also be used to argue the inferiority of Blacks as a fallen race.

9. The Maroons developed into two distinct groups, an eastern group situated in the Blue Mountain region, and a western group situated in the Cockpit region.

10. How much Sharpe had planned for violence is uncertain; but the existence of the "Black Regiment" suggests he anticipated the possibility.

11. At least three Afro-Christian sects are a part of Revivalism: Pukumina, Revival, and Revival Zion. Pukumina (like Kumina) has the most obvious African-derived rituals. Revival exhibits African-derived and Christian tendencies. And Revival Zion most closely parallels mainstream Christian rituals.

12. It is possible that Jamaicans developed an indigenous Ethiopianism, which later may have meshed with the ideas of Black American immigrants.

13. Menelik the First is believed by many Rastafari to be the son of King Solomon (of ancient Israel) and Queen Makeda of Sheba (of ancient Ethiopia). Menelik the First is also believed to have taken the Ark of the Covenant from Jerusalem to Ethiopia, where it remains to this day.

14. See Spencer (1999:7), Hill (2001), and Webb's brief tract, *A Black Man Will Be The Coming Universal King Proven By Biblical History*, which can be downloaded through the web address http://kobek.com/universalking.pdf.

CHAPTER 2

1. For thorough but differing historical accounts of the Rastafari, see Chevannes (1994), McPherson (1996), van Dijk (1993), Hill (2001), and Tafari (2001).

2. Even though Philos concocted much of his story, I believe that many Rastafari used the article to bolster their claims to authority and power. I also know that some believe the article is true. On the other hand, some Rastafari probably learned of the Nyabingi independently of Philos, through news reports or seafarers.

3. EWF local 17 did not remain active for long but has periodically revived itself; it was headquartered in St. Ann parish in 2007.

4. For a discussion of what I call "abeyance" or what is described as social movements in "nonreceptive political environments," see Taylor, 1989:761.

5. McPherson locates 1947 as the year of the emergence of the Dreadlocks (1996:23). The Dreadlocks, most of whom identified themselves as Nyabinghis, eventually became the hegemonic group among the Rastafari by the early 1970s. See Chevannes (1978) and Homiak (1998) for thorough treatments of the rise of the Dreadlocks Rastafari.

6. "Raas," or "rass," is a vulgar term for buttocks. Rass is sometimes combined with "clot" or "klaat" (paper, cloth), and used to insult someone (ass or butt cloth).

7. From the mid-1950s, Rastafari from across the island began visiting Kingston to learn the latest about repatriation discussions. Several core groups emerged from these discussions, and their representatives composed the nine-man deputation that negotiated repatriation with the Jamaican Government.

8. Kebede (2001) argues that the longevity of the Rastafari is primarily the result of the flexible "movement culture" that they developed. As I suggest, though, the "movement" aspect of the Rastafari should not be extended to the entire Rastafari. For comparison, consider that the Civil Rights and Black Power movements in the United States did not involve all African (or Black) Americans.

CHAPTER 3

1. Personal communication, 2001.

2. Those analysts who emphasize the fluidity and contingency of identity may be alarmed by language that uses terms such as "stable" and "hierarchically ordered" to talk about identity development and transformation. Stability, how-ever, does not mean rigidity or identifications that remain the same over the life course, and identity hierarchy is more about importance given to particular iden-tifications in various situations than list-like rankings.

3. Cited in James, 1999:71.

4. Janet Helms (1995) made a similar critique and used the term "status" rather than stages to describe racial identity orientations.

5. I have not explained some of the earlier formulations of nigrescence theory due to space constraints. The version of nigrescence that I draw upon (1995, 2001) reflects important advances, though, such as the recognition that even the term "salience" has to allow for multiple variations in order to reflect the diver-sity of Blackness. For example, positive evaluations can be expressed in many ways such as separatism, biculturalism, and multiculturalism (Cross Jr. & Van-diver, 2001).

6. This idea is hinted at but not developed by Cross and his coauthors (Cross Jr., Parham, & Helms, 1991:324).

7. Cross's later revisions of nigrescence more explicitly define types of com-mitment and Black identity orientations (e.g., Cross Jr. & Vandiver, 2001).

8. See Wilmore's *Black Religion and Black Radicalism* (1998) and Cone's *God of the Oppressed* (1975) for classic examples.

9. Published by the Ethiopian World Federation. I have only seen a few issues, all published in 1937.

CHAPTER 4

1. See Pulis (1999a) for a more detailed discussion of "sighting up."

2. "I n I" has other meanings such as "man" in God and God in "man," but these are not discussed here.

3. It also is understood as Rasta-for-I, emphasizing a connection between the individual and the collectivity.

4. The term Babylon was used by the Rastafari primarily in reference to Jamaica, the colonial administration, and the police. Gradually, the concept became more inclusive and is sometimes used generically to refer to Western society and capitalism. The biblical Babylon was once a thriving commercial and cultural center, near modern-day Baghdad, under the rule of King Hammarabi (1728–1686 bc). Babylon was colonized by the Assyrians, who imposed their own king. Other succeeding "foreign" kings assumed the throne, including the son of a Chaldean, Nebuchadnezzar, who exiled the Jews and razed Jerusalem. The Babylonians were polytheistic, and the king also functioned as a priest and leader of a despotic priestly caste. Babylonian gods did not require a moral code of behavior and ethics, unlike the Hebrews, whose singular god required such a code. The Hebrews of that time were worried about their people who were coming under the sway of Babylonian culture. It is this later Babylon that serves as an allegory for Rastafari beliefs.

5. Rasta Ivey could have been born as early as 1906, which would have made her 12 in 1918. Sometimes she talked as if she were around six in 1918; at other times she talked as if she could have been on the verge of her teenage years.

6. Kitzinger was among the first to ask "How does a man become a Rasta?" (1969:246).

7. We saw in chapter 1 how as early as the mid-1860s Black Jamaicans used "heart" as a metaphor to talk about race and morality.

8. Ras Brenton was the only narrator who talked about "reasoning" (discussions that facilitate intellectual and spiritual discovery, illumination) within the context of his encounter experiences. Therefore, I have not emphasized reasoning as one of the primary encounter experiences.

9. My observation should not rule out reading or study as being the primary source of an encounter. This is more likely, I believe, for post-1970s Rastafari who have access to a store of media conveying information on Rastafari, Black culture and history, something largely unavailable to our narrators during early phases of their identity transformation.

10. Some Rastafari see Selassie I as the Christ returned, inaugurating a new era, just as Christ's first "coming" diminished the preeminence of the Old Testament codes. Few Rastafari accept talk about Jesus in the same breath as Selassie, I, unless it is in reference to Selassie, I, as the successor to Christ.

11. The pronunciation "Jeez-us" is typically used when the Rastafari refer to the Blond-haired, blue-eyed Christ. The pronunciation "Jess-us" is typically used when referring to the Christ imagined as sharing the same lineage as Emperor Selassie I (which implies his Blackness).

CHAPTER 5

1. A pipe used for smoking marijuana, commonly used in ritual and ceremonial contexts.

2. Bomba is not an "African," and his exploits were not based in Africa. Bomba, a popular cartoon strip and film character, "lived" in the jungles of South America. Bomba was a low-budget alternative to Tarzan, King of the Apes. Brother Bongo's recalling of Bomba as African may relate to his reading of one particular story in which Bomba visited Africa. Implicated in Brother Bongo's incorrect characterization was the widespread perception in colonial Jamaica that equated jungles with backwardness, primitiveness, and danger—tropes used for Africa and Africans.

3. See Pulis, 1999:377.

4. Among men, Selassie is a common surname adopted after baptism into the Ethiopian Orthodox Church in Jamaica.

CHAPTER 6

1. Twenty years is how I define a generation. However, keep in mind that what defines a generation—the age, ritual, or responsibility set that determines adulthood—varies culturally and across time.

References

PRIMARY

Authored Columns and Articles

Alvaranga, Philmore, Samuel Clayton, and Douglas Mack. 1965. The back to Africa mission. *Daily Gleaner*, March 27.

Alveranga, Philmore, and Douglas Mack. 1961. Experiences among the people. *Daily Gleaner*, July 31.

Carradine, John. 1940. The Ras Tafarites retreat to mountain fastnesses of St. Catherine. *Daily Gleaner*, November 23.

Douglas, M. B. 1961. Most treasured experience of my life. *Daily Gleaner*, July 31.

Evans, Lancelot. 1964. Three cultists build international image for Rastafarians. *Star*, May 1.

Parchment, Clinton. 1960. Rascally Rastafarians. *Daily Gleaner*, April 30.

Reynolds, C. Roy. 2000. Alexander Bedward: The final solution (Part IV). *Daily Gleaner*, October 27.

Spence, Sam. 1959. Back-to-Africa. *Sunday Gleaner*, October 25.

Wright, Thomas. 1960. Candidly yours. . . *Daily Gleaner*, July 9.

News Stories

Daily Gleaner

1930. Presented Scepter to New Emperor, November 3.

1934. Leonard Howell being tried for sedition in St. Thomas, March 14.

1934. Leonard Howell, on trial says Ras Tafari is Messiah returned to earth, March 15.

1934. Ras Tafari disciple found guilty of sedition, March 16.

1934. Howell given 2-year term for sedition, March 17.

1934. Playing with fire, August 20.

1935. Ras Tafari cults excited Portlanders, July 30.

1935. Sequel to Ras-Tafari cult in districts of St. Thomas Parish, August 19.

1937. Ras Tafari cult, March 18.

1939. Ethiopian Salvation Society, April 3.

1939. Society celebration, April 4.

1941. Police Raid "Pinnacle," Ras Tafarian den. Siege sentry, but miss chief, July 15.

1941. Camera record of police raid on Ras Tafaris at "Pinnacle," July 16.

1941. Three tried in Pinnacle camp cases; Pleas taken yesterday. Trials to take place Monday and Tuesday, July 23.

1941. Cult leader held by police in his home, July 26.

1941. Howell before R. M. Court at Spanish town, July 29.

1941. Cult followers sent to prison, July 31.

1941. 'Ras Tafarian' head convicted at Spanish Town, August 25.

1954. Policeman tells court he is now 'Ras Jackson,' April 17.

1955. Large audience hears message from Ethiopia, September 30.

1959. No passports, no bookings; but 'going back to Africa,' October 6.

1959. 'Back-to-Africa' Rastas stranded, October 7.

1960. Weapons seized in raid on church headquarters, April 7.

1960. Rastafarians stone police, May 4.

1960. Letter to Castro in Court, May 6.

1960. Henry and 15 committed, May 11.

1960. 2 more hunted men captured, July 12.

1960. Urges Mission-to-Africa to plan Rasta migration, August 2.

1960. Gov't accepts African mission in principle, August 3.

1960. Migration mission will go to Africa, August 19.

1960. Three more seek appeal to privy council, December 23.

1961. Henry, Gabbidon hanged, March 29.

1961a. Majority report of the mission to Africa, July 31.

1961b. Diverse reactions and behavior within the mission, Dr. L. C. Leslie, reports, July 31.

1961c. The minority report, July 31.

1963. 8 killed after attack on gas station, April 13.

1963. Police net 160 beards, April 13.

1966. When the Emperor spoke in English, April 23.

1974. Armed forces to decide Selassie's future soon, August 27.

1975a. Selassie dies at 83, August 28.

1975b. Manley, Seaga regret, August 28.

Jamaica Times

1963. Rastas and police: An improvement, March 24.

Star

1958. Rastafari convention a nuisance, March 3.

1958. Cultists convention, March 6.

1958. City 'captured'; Cops take it Back, 'Beards' Invade Victoria Park, March 24.

1962. Some Rastas are cavemen, April 9.

1966. Fear Emperor may disown Rastas, n.d.

Sunday Guardian

1960. Photographic essay, May 1.

Sunday Gleaner

1966. Takes dim view of Rastas' behavior, n.d.

Tribune

1958. Bearded Cultists Take Over Old Kings House, June 30.

INTERVIEWS

Formally Interviewed

Women

Prophetess Esther
Rasta Ivey
Sister Amma
Sister Coromanti
Sister Ecila
Sister Mariam
Sister Pear

Men

Bongo J
Brother Barody
Brother Bongo
Brother Dee
Brother Woks
Brother Yendis
Ras Alex
Ras Brenton
Ras Chronicle
Ras General
Ras Sam Brown
Rasta J

Informal Interviews, Conversations

Women

Empress Dinah
Ma Lion
Sister Sersi

Men

Ras Cee

Ras Desmond

Ras Grantly

Ras Jayze

Ras Kirk

Ras Tee

Ras Winston

BIBLIOGRAPHY

Adams, Marianne. 2001. Core processes of racial identity development. In *New perspectives on racial identity development: A theoretical and practical anthology*, eds. C. L. Wijeyesinghe and B. W. Jackson III, 209–242. New York: New York University Press.

Akbar, Maysa, John Chambers Jr., and Vetta L. Sanders Thompson. 2001. Race identity, Afrocentric values, and self-esteem in Jamaican children. *Journal of Black Psychology* 27(3):341–358.

Allen, Richard. 2004. *The concept of self: A study of Black identity and self-esteem*. Detroit, MI: Wayne State University Press.

Alleyne, Mervyn. 1988. *Roots of Jamaican culture*. London: Pluto Press.

———. 2002. *The construction and representation of race and ethnicity in the Caribbean and the world*. Mona, JA: University of the West Indies Press.

Allport, Gordon. 1950. *The individual and his religion: A classic study of the function of religious sentiment in the personality of the individual*. New York: Macmillan.

Atkinson, Robert. 1998. *The life story interview*. Thousand Oaks, CA: Sage Publications.

Austin-Broos, Diane. 1997. *Jamaica genesis: Religion and the politics of moral orders*. Chicago: University of Chicago Press.

———. 2003. The anthropology of conversion: An introduction. In *The anthropology of religious conversion*, eds. A. Huckster & S. Glazier, 1–12. Lanham, MD: Rowman & Littlefield Publishers.

Baker, Lee. 1998. *From savage to Negro: Anthropology and the construction of race, 1896–1954*. Berkeley: University of California Press.

Banks, William. 1999. *Black intellectuals: Race and respectability in American life*. New York: W. W. Norton.

Barrett, Leonard. 1988. *The Rastafarians: Sounds of cultural dissonance*. Boston: Beacon Press.

Bartlett, Lesley, and Dorothy Holland. 2002. Theorizing the space of literacy practices. *Ways of Knowing* 2(1):10–22.

Beckwith, Martha. 1969 [1929]. *Black roadways: A study of Jamaican folk life*. New York: Negro Universities Press.

Bilby, Kenneth. 1996. Ethnogenesis in the Guiana and Jamaica: Two Maroon cases. In *History, power, and identity: Ethnogenesis in the Americas, 1492–1992*, ed. J. Hill, 119–141. Iowa City: University of Iowa Press.

Bogues, Anthony. 1997. Shades of Black and Red: Freedom and Socialism. *Small Axe* 1:65–75.

———. 2003. *Black heretics, Black prophets: Radical political intellectuals*. New York: Routledge.

Boisin, Anton. 1936. *Exploration of the inner world: A study of mental disorder and religious experience*. New York: Harper and Bros.

Bones, Jah. 1986. Language and Rastafari. In *The language of the Black experience*, eds. David Sutcliffe & Ansel Wong, 37–51. New York: Basil Blackwell.

Booth, William. 1994. On the idea of the moral economy. *American Political Science Review* 88(3):653–667.

Bowles, Samuel, and Herbert Gintis. 1998. The moral economy of communities: Structured populations and the evolution of pro-social norms. *Evolution and Human Behavior* 19(1):3–25.

Brathwaite, Edward. 1971. *The development of Creole society in Jamaica, 1770–1820*. Oxford: Oxford University Press.

———. 1981. Rebellion: Anatomy of the slave revolt of 1831/32 on Jamaica. *Jamaican Historical Society Bulletin* 8(4):80–96.

Brooks, A. A. 1917. *The history of Bedwardism, or the Jamaican Native Baptist Free Church, Union Camp, August Town, St. Andrew, JA, B.W.I.* Kingston, JA: The Gleaner Co., Ltd., Printers.

Brown, Beverly. 1975. George Liele: Black Baptist and pan-Africanist, 1750–1826. *Savacou* no. 11/12:58–67.

Brown, Samuel. 1966. Treatise on the Rastafarian movement. *Caribbean Studies* 6(1):39–40.

Bryan, Patrick. 2000. *The Jamaican people, 1880–1902: Race, class, and social control*. Mona, JA: University of the West Indies Press.

Burton, Richard. 1997. *Afro-Creole: Power, opposition, and play in the Caribbean*. Ithaca: Cornell University Press.

Campbell, Horace. 1987. *Rasta and resistance: From Marcus Garvey to Walter Rodney*. Trenton, NJ: Africa World Press.

Carnegie, Charles. 1992. The fate of ethnography: Native social science in the English-speaking Caribbean. *New West Indian Guide* 66(1 and 2):5–25.

———. 1999. Garvey and the Black transnation. *Small Axe* no. 5:48–71.

Cashmore, Ernest E. 1979. More than a version: A study in reality creation. *British Journal of Sociology* 30(3):307–21.

Cassidy, Frederic. 1971. *Jamaica talk: Three hundred years of the English language in Jamaica*. London: Macmillan Educational.

Cattell, Maria, and Jacob Climo. 2002. Introduction: Meaning in social memory and history: Anthropological perspectives. In *Social memory and history:*

Anthropological perspectives, eds. J. Climo and M. Cattell, 1–36. New York: Alta Mira Press.

Césaire, Aimé. 2000. *Discourse on colonialism*. New York: Monthly Review Press.

Cha-Jua, Sundiata K. 1998. C.L.R. James, blackness, and the making of a neo-Marxist diasporan historiography. *Nature, Society, and Thought* 11(1):53–89.

Charles, Christopher. 2003. Skin bleaching, self-hate, and Black identity in Jamaica. *Journal of Black Studies* 33(6):711–728.

Chesters, Graeme, and Ian Welsh. 2006. *Complexity and social movements: Multitudes at the edge of chaos*. New York: Routledge.

Chevannes, Barry. 1971. Revival and Black struggle. *Savacou* no. 5:27–39.

———. 1976. The repairer of the breach: Reverend Claudius Henry and Jamaican society. In *Ethnicity in the Americas*, ed. H. Frances, 263–290. Chicago: Aldine Publishers.

———. 1978. Rastafarianism and the class struggle: The search for a methodology. In *Methodology and change: Problems of applied social science research techniques in the commonwealth Caribbean*. Working paper no. 14, ed. L. Lindsay, 244–251. Mona, Jamaica: Institute of Social and Economic Research, University of the West Indies.

———. 1994. *Rastafari: Roots and ideology*. Syracuse: Syracuse University Press.

———. 2001. Jamaican diasporic identity: the metaphor of yaad. In *Nation Dance: Religion, Identity, and Cultural Difference* in the Caribbean, ed. Patrick Taylor, 129–137. Bloomington: Indiana University Press.

Coe, George. 1917. *Psychology of religion*. Chicago: University of Chicago Press.

Cone, James H. 1975. *God of the oppressed*. New York: Seabury Press.

Cornell, Stephen, and Douglas Hartmann. 1998. *Ethnicity and race: Making identities in a changing world*. Thousand Oaks, CA: Pine Forge Press.

Craton, Michael. 1978. *Searching for the invisible man: Slaves and plantation life in Jamaica*. Cambridge: Harvard University Press.

Cross Jr., William. 1971. The Negro-to-Black conversion experience. *Black World* 20(9):13–27.

———. 1981. Black families and Black identity development: Rediscovering the distinction between self-esteem and reference group orientation. *Journal of Comparative Family Studies* 12(1):19–49.

———. 1991. *Shades of Black: Diversity in African American identity*. Philadelphia: Temple University Press.

———. 1993. In search of blackness and Afrocentricity: The psychology of Black identity change. In *Racial and ethnic identity: Psychological development and creative development*, eds. H. Harris, H. Blue, and E.E.H. Griffith, 53–72. New York: Routledge.

———. 1995. The psychology of nigrescence: Revising the Cross model. In *The handbook of multicultural counseling*, eds. I. Ponterotto, J. Casas, L. Suzuki, and C. Alexander, 93–122. Thousand Oaks, CA: Sage Publications.

———. 1998. The everyday functions of African American identity. In *Prejudice: The target's perspective*, eds. J. Swim & C. Stangor, 267–279. San Diego: Academic Press.

———. 2001. Encountering nigrescence. In *Handbook of multicultural counseling*, 2nd ed., eds. J. Ponterotto, J. Casas, L. Suzuki, & C. Alexander, 30–44. Thousand Oaks, CA: Sage Publications.

Cross Jr., William, Thomas Parham, and Janet Helms. 1991. The stages of Black identity development: Nigrescence models. In *Black psychology*, ed. R. Jones, 319–338. Berkeley: Cobb and Henry Publishers.

Cross Jr., William, and Peony Phagen-Smith. 2001. Patterns of African American identity development: A lifespan perspective. In *New perspectives on racial identity development: A theoretical and practical anthology*, eds. C. L. Wijeyesinghe and B. W. Jackson III, 243–270. New York: New York University Press.

Cross Jr., William, Lakesha Smith, and Yasser Payne. 2002. Black identity: A repertoire of daily enactments. In *Counseling across cultures*, 5th ed., eds. P. Pedersen, J. G. Draguns, W. J. Lonner, and J. E. Trimble, 93–108. Thousand Oaks, CA: Sage Publications.

Cross Jr., William, and Linda Strauss. 1998. The everyday functions of African American identity. In *Prejudice: The target's perspective*, eds. J. Swim and C. Stangor, 267–279. San Diego: Academic Press.

Cross Jr., William, and Beverly J. Vandiver. 2001. Nigrescence theory and measurement: Introducing the Cross Racial Identity Scale (CRIS). In *Handbook of multicultural counseling*, eds. J. G. Ponterotto, J. M. Casas, L. A. Suzuki, and C. M. Alexander, 371–393. Thousand Oaks, CA: Sage Publications.

Crumley, Carole. 2002. Exploring venues of social memory. In *Social memory and history: Anthropological perspectives*, eds. J. Climo and M. Cattell, 39–52. New York: Alta Mira Press.

Curtin, Philip. 1955. *Two Jamaicas: The role of ideas in a tropical colony, 1830–1865*. Westport, CT: Greenwood Press.

———. 1969. *The Atlantic slave trade: A census*. Madison: University of Wisconsin Press.

Dallas, Robert Charles. 1968 [1803]. *History of the Maroons, from their origin to the establishment of their chief at Sierra Leone*. Vol. 1. London: Cass.

De Greene, Kenyon. 1997. Field-theoretic framework for the interpretation of the evolution, instability, structural change, and management of complex systems. In *Chaos theory in the social sciences: Foundations and applications*, eds. L. Kiel & E. Elliot, 273–294. Ann Arbor: University of Michigan Press.

Drake, St. Clair. 1991 [1970]. *The redemption of Africa and Black religion*. Chicago: Third World Press.

DuBois, W.E.B. 1969 [1903]. *The souls of Black folk*. New York: New American Library.

Edelman, Marc. 2005. Bringing the moral economy back in . . . to the study of 21st-century transnational peasant movements. *American Anthropologist* 107(3):331–345.

Edmonds, Ennis. 2003. *From outcasts to culture bearers*. New York: Oxford University Press.

Eisner, Gisela. 1961. *Jamaica, 1830–1930: A study in economic growth*. Manchester: Manchester University Press.

Elkins, W. F. 1977. *Street preachers, faith healers, and herb doctors in Jamaica, 1890–1925*. New York: Revisionist Press.

Erskine, Neol. 2004. *From Garvey to Marley: Rastafari theology*. Gainesville: University of Florida Press.

Escobar, Arturo. 2004. Other worlds are (already) possible: self-organization, complexity, and post-capitalist cultures. In *The World Social Forum: Challenging empires?* eds. J. Sen, A. Anand, A. Escobar, & P. Waterman, 343–359. Delhi, India: Viveka.

Fahim, Hussein, and Katherine Helmer. 1982. Themes and counterthemes: The Berg Wartenstein Symposium. In *Indigenous anthropology in non-Western countries*, ed. H. Fahim, ix–xxxiii. Durham, NC: Carolina Academic Press.

Fanon, Franz. 1963. *The wretched of the earth*. New York: Grove Press.

———. 1967. *Black skins, White masks*. New York: Grove Press.

Fisher, Humphrey. 1973. Conversion reconsidered: Some historical aspects of religious conversion in Black Africa. *Africa* 43(2):27–40.

———. 1985. The juggernaut's apologia: Conversion to Islam in Black Africa. *Africa* 55(2):153–173.

Forsythe, Dennis. 1983. *Rastafari: For the healing of the nation*. Kingston, JA: Zaika Publications.

Fredrickson, George. 1995. *Black liberation: A comparative history of Black ideologies in the United States and South Africa*. New York: Oxford University Press.

Freire, Paulo. 1970. *Pedagogy of the oppressed*. New York: Continuum Publishing Company.

Frey, Sylvia, and Betty Wood. 1998. *Come shouting to Zion: African American Protestantism in the American South and British Caribbean to 1830*. Chapel Hill: University of North Carolina Press.

Galloway, Patricia. 1998. *Choctaw Genesis, 1500–1700*. Lincoln: University of Nebraska Press.

Garvey, Amy Jacques, ed. 1989. *The philosophy and opinions of Marcus Garvey: Or, Africa for the Africans*. Dover, MA: Majority Press.

Garvey, Marcus. 1937. The failure of Haile Selassie as emperor. *The Black Man*, March/April:n.p.

Gayle, Clement. 1982. *George Liele: Pioneer missionary to Jamaica*. Jamaica Baptist Union: Kingston, Jamaica.

Gerlach, Luther, and Virginia Hine. 1970. *People, power, change: Movements of social transformation.* New York: Bobbs-Merrill Company.

Gillespie, V. Bailey. 1979. *Religious conversion and personal identity.* Birmingham, AL: Religious Education Press.

Gilroy, Paul. 1992. *The Black Atlantic: Modernity and double consciousness.* Cambridge: Harvard University Press.

Glazier, Stephen. 2006. Being and becoming a Rastafarian: Notes on the anthropology of religious conversion." Ed. Werner Zips, 256–281. Kingston, JA: Ian Randle Publishers.

Goerner, Sally. 1995. Chaos and deep ecology. In *Chaos theory in psychology,* eds. F. Abraham & A. Gilgen, 3–18. Westport, CT: Praeger Publishers.

Goffman, Erving. 1963. *Stigma: Notes on the management of spoiled identity.* New York: Touchstone.

Gomez, Michael A. 1998. *Exchanging our country marks: The transformation of African identities in the colonial and antebellum South.* Chapel Hill: University of North Carolina Press.

Gosner, Kevin. 1992. *Soldiers of the Virgin: The moral economy of a colonial Maya rebellion.* Tuscon: University of Arizona Press.

Graeber, David. 2004. *Fragments of an anarchist anthropology.* Chicago: Prickly Paradigm Press.

Gray, Obika. 1991. *Radicalism and social change in Jamaica, 1960–1972.* Knoxville: University of Tennessee Press.

Greenbaum, Susan. 2002. *More than Black: Afro-Cubans in Tampa.* Gainesville: University Press of Florida.

Gwaltney, John. 1993. *Drylongso: A self portrait of Black America.* New York: Free Press.

Hall, Stuart. 1995. Negotiating identity. *New Left Review* 209:3–14.

———. 1996. Introduction: Who needs an 'identity?' In *Questions of cultural identity,* eds. S. Hall & P. du Gay, 1–17. Thousand Oaks, CA: Sage.

Hannah, Barbara M. Blake. 2006. The meaning of Rastafari for world critique: Rasta within a universal concept. In *Rastafari: A universal philosophy in the third millennium,* ed. Werner Zips, 1–6. Kingston, JA: Ian Randle Publishers.

Harding, Susan. 1987. Convicted by the Holy Spirit: The rhetoric of fundamentalist Baptist conversion. *American Ethnology* 14(1):167–181.

Harrison, Faye. 1998. Introduction: Expanding the discourse on race. *American Anthropologist* 100(3):609–631.

Hefner, Robert W. 1993. Introduction: World building and the rationality of conversion. In *Conversion to Christianity: Historical and anthropological perspectives on a great transformation,* ed. R. W. Hefner, 3–44. Berkeley: University of California Press.

Heirich, Max. 1977. Change of heart: A test of some widely held theories about religious conversion. *American Journal of Sociology* 83(3):653–680.

Helms, Janet. 1990. Introduction: Review of racial identity terminology. In *Black and White racial identity: Theory, research, and practice*, ed. J. Helms, 3–8. New York: Greenwood Press.

———. 1995. An update of Helms's white and people of color racial identity models. In *The handbook of multicultural counseling*, eds. I. Ponterotto, J. Casas, L. Suzuki, and C. Alexander, 181–198. Thousand Oaks, CA: Sage Publications.

Henderson, Walter. 1910. *The Silver Bluff Church: A history of Negro Baptist churches in America*. Washington, DC: Press of R. L. Pendelton. (electronic edition: http://docsouth.unc.edu/church/brooks/brooks.html).

Henry, Beresford. 1982. *The growth of corporate Black identity among Afro-Caribbean people in Birmingham, England*. Dissertation. University of Warwick.

Heuman, Gad. 1994. *The killing time: The Morant Bay rebellion in Jamaica*. Knoxville: University of Tennessee Press.

Hill, Jonathan. 1996. Introduction: Ethnogenesis in the Americas, 1492–1992. In *History, power, and identity: Ethnogenesis in the Americas, 1492–1992*, ed. J. Hill, 1–19. Iowa City: University of Iowa Press.

Hill, Robert. 2001. *Dread history: Leonard P. Howell and millenarian visions in the early Rastafari religion*. Chicago: Research Associates School Times Publications Publications/Frontline Distribution International Inc.

Hobson, Fred. 1999. *But now I see: The White southern racial conversion narrative*. Baton Rouge: Louisiana State University Press.

Holland, Dorothy, and William Lachicotte. 2007. Vygotsky, Mead and the new sociocultural studies of identity. In *The Cambridge companion to Vygotsky*, eds. H. Daniels, M. Cole, and J. Wertsch, 101–135. New York: Cambridge University Press.

Holland, Dorothy, William Lachicotte, Deborah Skinner, and Carole Cain. 1998. *Identity and agency in cultural worlds*. Cambridge: Harvard University Press.

Holland, Dorothy, and Jean Lave. 2001. *History in person: Enduring struggles, contentious practice, intimate identities*. Santa Fe, NM: School of American Research.

Holt, Thomas C. 1992. *The problem of freedom: Race, labor, and politics in Jamaica and Britain, 1832–1938*. Baltimore: Johns Hopkins University Press.

———. 2000. *The Problem of race in the twenty-first century*. Cambridge: Harvard University Press.

Homiak, John. 1987. The mystic revelation of Rasta Far-Eye: Visionary communication in a prophetic movement. In *Dreaming: Anthropological and psychological interpretations*, ed. Barbara Tedlock, 220–245. Santa Fe, NM: School of American Research Press.

———. 1998. Dub history: Soundings on Rastafari livity and language. In *Rastafari and other African-Caribbean worldviews*, ed. B. Chevannes, 127–181. New Brunswick, NJ: Rutgers University Press.

———. 1999. Movements of Jah people: From sounds capes to media scape. In *Religion, diaspora, and cultural identity: A reader in the Anglophone Caribbean*, ed. J. Pulis, 87–123. New York: Gordon & Breach.

Hopkins, Elizabeth. 1971. The Nyabinghi cult of southwestern Uganda. In *Rebellion in Black Africa*, ed. R. Rotberg, 60–132. New York: Oxford University Press.

Hornstein, Donald. 2005. Complexity theory, adaptation, and administrative law. *Duke Law Journal* 54(4):913–960.

Horton, Robin. 1971. African conversion. *Africa* 41(2)85–108.

———. 1975. On the rationality of conversion. *Africa* 45(3):219–235.

Horton, R., and J.D.Y. Peel. 1976. Conversion and confusion: A rejoinder on Christianity in eastern Nigeria. *Canadian Journal of African Studies* 10(3):481–498.

Jackson, III, Bailey W. 2001. Black identity development: Further analysis and elaboration. In *New perspectives on racial identity development: A theoretical and practical anthology*, eds. C. L. Wijeyesinghe and B. W. Jackson III, 8–31. New York: New York University Press.

James, William. 1929. *Varieties of religious experience*. New York: Random House.

James, Winston. 1999. *Holding aloft the banner of Ethiopia: Caribbean radicalism in early twentieth century America*. New York: Verso Press.

Jasper, James. 1997. *The art of moral protest: Culture, biography, and creativity in social movements*. Chicago: University of Chicago Press.

Jones, Delmos. 1973. Toward a native anthropology. In *Explorations in anthropology*, ed. M. Fried, 448–458. New York: Thomas Crowell.

———. 1994. Anthropology and the oppressed: Reflections on 'native' anthropology. Working paper. Discussed at the annual meeting of the *Society for Applied Anthropology*, Cancun, Mexico, April 13.

Kanter, Rosabeth. 1972. *Commitment and community: Communes and utopians in sociological perspective*. Cambridge: Harvard University Press.

Kebede, AlemSeghed. 2001. Decentered movements: The case of the structural and perceptual versatility of the Rastafari. *Sociological Spectrum* 21(2):175–205.

Kebede, AlemSeghed, and J. Knottnerus. 1998. Beyond the pales of Babylon: The ideational components and social psychological foundations of Rastafari. *Sociological Perspectives* 41(3):499–517.

Kebede, AlemSeghed, T. Shriver, and J. Knottnerus. 2000. Social movement endurance: Collective identity and the Rastafari. *Sociological Inquiry* 70(3):313–337.

Keith, Nelson, and Novella Keith. 1992. *The social origins of democratic socialism in Jamaica*. Philadelphia: Temple University Press

Kilbourne, Brock, and James Richardson. 1988. Paradigm conflict, types of conversion, and conversion theories. *Sociological Analysis* 50(1):1–21.

Kitzinger, Sheila. 1966. The Rastafarian Brethren of Jamaica. *Comparative Studies in Society and History* 9(1):34–39.

———. 1969. Protest and mysticism: The Rastafari cult of Jamaica. *Journal for the Scientific Study of Religion* 8(2):240–262.

Klein, Herbert. 1978. *The middle passage: Comparative studies in the Atlantic slave trade.* Princeton: Princeton University Press.

Knox, Arbuthnot John G. 1962. Race relations in Jamaica, 1833–1958: With special reference to British colonial policy. Dissertation: University of Florida, Gainesville.

Lake, Obiagele. 1994. The many voices of Rastafarian women: Sexual subordination in the midst of liberation. *New West Indian Guide* 68(3–4):235–258.

———. 1998. *Rastafari women: Subordination in the midst of liberation theology.* Durham, NC: Carolina Academic Press.

Lansing, J. S. 2003. Complex adaptive systems. *Annual Review in Anthropology* 32:183–204.

Lewis, Rupert. 1987. Garvey's forerunners: Love and Bedward. *Race and Class* 28(3):29–40.

Lewis, William F. 1993. *Soul rebels: The Rastafari.* Long Grove, IL: Waveland Press.

Lichtenstein, Alex. 1995. Theft, moral economy, and the transition from slavery to freedom in the American South. In *Slave cultures and cultures of slavery*, ed. S. Palmié, 176–186. Knoxville: University of Tennessee Press.

Lincoln, C. Eric. 1993. Black religion and racial identity. In *Racial and ethnic identity: Psychological development and creative development*, eds. H. Harris, H. Blue, and E.E.H. Griffith, 209–221. New York: Routledge.

Linebaugh, Peter, and Marcus Rediker. 1990. The many-headed hydra: Sailors, slaves, and the Atlantic working class in the eighteenth century. *Journal of Historical Sociology* 3(3):226–252.

Lofland, John, and Rodney Stark. 1965. On becoming a world-saver: A theory of conversion to a deviant perspective. *American Sociological Review* 30:862–875.

Mack, Douglas. 1999. *From Babylon to Rastafari: Origin and history of the Rastafari movement.* Research Associates School Times Publication.

McClure, Bud. 2005. *Putting a new spin on groups: The science of chaos.* Mahwah, NJ: Lawrence Erlbaum.

McGuire, Meredith. 1992. *Religion: The social context.* Belmont, CA: Wadsworth.

McPherson, E.S.P. 1996. *The culture-history and universal spread of Rastafari: Two essays.* Bronx, NY: Black International Iyabinghi Press.

Meeks, Brian. 2000. *Narratives of resistance: Jamaica, Trinidad, the Caribbean.* Mona, JA: University of the West Indies Press.

Memmi, Albert. 1965. *The colonizer and the colonized.* Boston: Beacon Press.

Mills, C. Wright. 2000 [1959]. *The sociological imagination.* New York: Oxford University Press.

Moses, Wilson Jeremiah. 1978. *The golden age of Black nationalism, 1850–1925.* New York: Oxford University Press.

———. 1996. *Classical Black nationalism: From the American Revolution to Marcus Garvey*. New York: New York University Press.

Mosko, Mark, and Frederick Damon, eds. 2005. *On the order of chaos: Social anthropology and the science of chaos*. New York: Berghahn Books.

Mostern, Kenneth. 1999. *Autobiography and black identity politics*. New York: Cambridge University Press.

Murrell, Nathaniel S. 1998. Introduction: The Rastafari phenomenon. In *Chanting down Babylon: The Rastafari reader*, eds. N. Murrell, D. Spencer, and A. MacFarlane, 1–19. Philadelphia: Temple University Press.

Mutabaruka. 2006. Rasta from experience. In *Rastafari: A universal philosophy in the third millennium*, ed. Werner Zips, 21–41. Kingston, JA: Ian Randle Publishers.

Narayan, Kirin. 1993. How native is a "native" anthropologist? *American Anthropologist* 95(3):671–686.

Nettleford, Rex. 1972. *Identity, race and protest in Jamaica*. New York: William Morrow.

Omi, Michael, and Howard Winant. 1986. *Racial formation in the United States: From the 1960s to the 1980s*. New York: Routledge.

Owens, Joseph. 1976. *Dread: The Rastafarians of Jamaica*. London: Heinemann Educational Books.

Parham, Thomas. 1989. Nigrescence: The transformation of Black consciousness across the life cycle. In *Black adult development and aging*, ed. R. Jones, 151–166. Berkeley, CA: Cobb and Henry.

Payne, Anthony. 1994. *Politics in Jamaica*. New York: St. Martin's Press.

Peacock, James L., and Dorothy C. Holland. 1993. The narrated self: Life stories in process. *Ethos* 21(4):367–383.

Phillippo, James. 1971 [1843]. *Jamaica: Its past and present state*. Freeport, NY: Books for Libraries Press.

Pierson, Roscoe. 1969. Alexander Bedward and the Jamaica native Baptist Free Church. *Lexington Theological Quarterly* 4(3):65–76.

Piven, Frances Fox. 2006. *Challenging authority: How ordinary people change America*. Lanham, MD: Rowman & Littlefield.

Piven, Frances Fox, and Richard Cloward. 1979. *Poor people's movements: How they succeed and why they fail*. New York: Vintage Books.

Poletta, Franscesca. 2002. *Freedom is an endless meeting: Democracy in American social movements*. Chicago: University of Chicago Press.

Post, Ken. 1978. *Arise ye starvelings: The Jamaican labour rebellion of 1938 and its aftermath*. Boston: Martinus Nijhoff.

Price, Charles. 2001. Political and radical aspects of the Rastafarian Movement in Jamaica. *Nature, Society & Thought* 13(2):155–180.

———. 2003. 'Cleave to the Black': Expressions of Ethiopianism in Jamaica. *New West Indian Guide* 77(1 and 2):31–64.

Price, Charles, D. Nonini, and E. Foxtree. 2008. Grounded utopian movements: Subjects of neglect. *Anthropological Quarterly* 81(1):127–159.

Pruitt, Deborah, and Suzanne LaFont. 1995. For Love and Money: Romance Tourism in Jamaica. *Annals of Tourism Research* 22(2):422–440.

Pulis, John. 1999. Bridging troubled waters: Moses Baker, George Liele, and the African American diaspora to Jamaica. In *Moving on: Black loyalists in the Afro-Atlantic World*, ed. J. Pulis, 183–221. New York: Garland.

———. 1999a. Citing [Sighting]-up: Words, sounds, and reading scripture in Jamaica. In *Religion, diaspora, and cultural identity: A reader in the Anglophone Caribbean*, ed. J. Pulis, 311–335. New York: Gordon & Breach.

Pullen-Burry, Bessie. 1971 [1905]. *Ethiopia revisited: Jamaica in exile*. London: T. F. Unwin.

Purcell, Trevor. 1993. *Banana fallout: Class, color, and culture among West Indians in Costa Rica*. Los Angeles: Center for Afro-American Studies, University of California, Los Angeles.

Rambo, Lewis. 1993. *Understanding religious conversion*. New Haven: Yale University Press.

———. 2003. Anthropology and the study of conversion. In *The anthropology of religious conversion*, eds. A. Huckster & S. Glazier, 211–222. Lanham, MD: Rowman & Littlefield.

Randal, Adrian, and Andrew Charlesworth. 2000. The moral economy: Riot, markets, and social conflict. In *Moral economy and popular protest: Crowds, conflict, and authority*, eds. A. Randall and A. Charlesworth, 1–32. New York: St. Martin's Press.

Reckord, Mary. 1968. The Jamaican slave rebellion of 1831. *Past and Present* no. 40:108–125.

Robbins, Thomas. 1988. *Cults, converts, and charisma: The sociology of new religious movements*. Newbury Park, CA: Sage Publications.

Robinson, Cedric. 1985. The African Diaspora and the Italo-Ethiopian Crisis. *Race & Class* 27(2):51–65.

Robotham, Don. 1983. The Notorious Riot: The socio-economic and political bases of Paul Bogle's Revolt. *Anales Del Caribe* 3:51–111.

———. 1994. The development of a Black ethnicity in Jamaica. In *Garvey: His work and impact*, eds. R. Lewis and P. Bryan, 23–38. Trenton, NJ: Africa World Press.

Rodney, Walter. 1996 [1969]. *The Groundings with my brothers*. Chicago: Research Associates School Times Publications.

Rowe, Maureen. 1985. The woman in Rastafari. In *Caribbean Quarterly Monograph: Rastafari*, ed. R. Nettleford, 13–21. Kingston, JA: Caribbean Quarterly, University of West Indies.

———. 1998. Gender and family relationships in RastafarI: A personal perspective. In *Chanting down Babylon: The Rastafari reader*, eds. N. Murrell, D. Spencer, and A. MacFarlane, 72–88. Philadelphia: Temple University Press.

Rowe, Wayne, J. Behrens, and M. Leach. 1995. Racial/ethnic identity and racial consciousness. In *The handbook of multicultural counseling*, eds. I. Ponterotto, J. Casas, L. Suzuki, and C. Alexander, 95–122. Thousand Oaks, CA: Sage Publications.

Sattler, Richard. 1996. Remnants, renegades, and runaways: Seminole ethnogenesis reconsidered. In *History, power, and identity: Ethnogenesis in the Americas, 1492–1992*, ed. J. Hill, 36–69. Iowa City: University of Iowa Press.

Savishinsky, Neil. 1994. Rastafari in the Promised Land: The spread of a Jamaican socioreligious movement among the youth of West Africa. *African Studies Review* 37(3):19–50.

Sayer, Andrew. 2000. Moral economy and political economy. *Studies in Political Economy* no. 61:79–103.

Schuler, Monica. 1980. *Alas, alas, Kongo: A social history of indentured African immigration into Jamaica, 1841–1865*. Baltimore: Johns Hopkins University Press.

Scott, David. 1999. The archaeology of Black memory: An interview with Robert A. Hill. *Small Axe* 5:80–150.

Scott, James. 1976. *The moral economy of the peasant: Rebellion and subsistence in Southeast Asia*. New Haven: Yale University Press.

———. 2000. The moral economy as an argument and as a fight. In *Moral economy and popular protest: Crowds, conflict and authority*, eds. A. Randall and A. Charlesworth, 187–208. New York: St. Martin's Press.

Scott, William. 1978. And Ethiopia shall stretch forth its hands: The origins of Ethiopianism in Afro-American thought, 1767–1896. *Umoja* 2(1):1–13.

———. 1993. *The sons of Sheba's race: African Americans and the Italo-Ethiopian War, 1935–1941*. Bloomington: Indiana University Press.

Sellers, Robert M., M. A. Smith, J. N. Shelton, S. A. Rowley, and T. M. Chavous. 1998. Multidimensional model of racial identity: A reconceptualization of African American racial identity. *Personality and Social Psychology Review* 2(1):18–39.

Semaj, Leachim. 1980. Race and identity and children of the African Diaspora. *Caribe* (n.v.):14–18.

Shepperson, George. 1968. Ethiopianism: Past and present. In *Christianity in tropical Africa: Studies presented and discussed at the Seventh International Seminar, University of Ghana, April 1965*, ed. C. G. Baeta, 249–264. New York: Oxford University Press.

Sherlock, Philip, and Hazel Bennett. 1998. *The Story of the Jamaican People*. Princeton, NJ: Markus Wiener.

Simpson, George Eaton. 1955. The Ras Tafari movement in Jamaica: A study of race and class conflict. *Social Forces* 34(2):167–171.

Smith, M. G., R. Augier, and R. Nettleford. 1960. *The Rastafari in Kingston, Jamaica*. Mona, Jamaica: Institute of Social and Economic Research, University of the West Indies.

Smith, R. T. 1997. Foreword to *Jamaica genesis: Religion and the politics of moral orders*. Chicago: University of Chicago Press.

Snow, Davis, and Richard Machalek. 1984. The sociology of conversion. *Annual Review in Sociology* 10:167–190.

Sorokin, Pitirim. 1954. *The ways of power and love: Types, factors and techniques of moral transformation*. Boston: Beacon Press.

Spencer, David. 1999. *Dread Jesus*. London: SPCK.

Statistical Institute of Jamaica. 2003. *Population Census 2001: Jamaica* (Volume 1). Kingston, JA: Statistical Institute of Jamaica.

Strauss, Claudia, and Naomi Quinn. 1997. *A cognitive theory of cultural meaning*. New York: Cambridge University Press.

Stromberg, Peter. 1985. The impression point: Synthesis of symbol and self. *Ethos* 13(1):56–74.

Sturtevant, William. 1971. From Creek into Seminole: North American Indians. In *Historical perspective*, ed. E. Leacock and N. Lurie, 92–128. New York: Random House.

Sundkler, Bengt. 1964 [1948]. *Bantu prophets in South Africa*. New York: Oxford University Press.

Tafari-Ama, Imani. 1998. Rastawoman as rebel: Case studies in Jamaica. In *Chanting down Babylon: The Rastafari reader*, eds. N. Murrell, D. Spencer, and A. MacFarlane, 89–106. Philadelphia: Temple University Press.

Tafari, Ikael. 2001. *Rastafari in transition: The politics of cultural confrontation in Africa and the Caribbean, 1966-1988*. Chicago: Research Associates School Times Publications.

Tatum, Beverly. 2003 [1997]. *Why are all the Black kids sitting together in the cafeteria? And other conversations about race*. New York: Basic Books.

Taylor, Patrick. 1990. Perspectives on history in Rastafari thought. *Studies in Religion* 19(2):191–205.

Taylor, Ronald. 1979. Black ethnicity and the persistence of ethnogenesis. *American Journal of Sociology* 84(6):1401–1422.

Taylor, Verta. 1989. Social movement continuity: The women's movement in abeyance. *American Sociological Review* 54:761–775.

Thomas, Deborah. 2004. *Modern blackness: Nationalism, globalization, and the politics of culture in Jamaica*. Durham: Duke University Press.

Thomas, Herbert. 1927. *The story of a West Indian policeman or forty-seven years in the Jamaica Constabulary*. Kingston, JA: The Gleaner Co., Ltd.

Thompson, E. P. 1971. The moral economy of the English crowd in the eighteenth century. *Past and Present: Journal of Historical Studies* 50:76–136.

Thwaite, Daniel. 1936. *The seething African pot: A study of Black nationalism, 1882-1935*. London: Constable and Co., Ltd.

Toch, Hans. 1965. *The social psychology of social movements*. Indianapolis: Bobbs-Merrill Co.

Tucker, Jeremy. 1991. *The role of cosmology in societal change: The development of indigenous agricultural technology within the Rastafari movement in Jamaica.* Master's thesis. Ontario, Canada. York University.

Turner, Mary. 1982. *Slaves and missionaries: The disintegration of Jamaican slave society, 1787–1834.* Urbana: University of Illinois Press.

van Dijk, Frank. 1993. *JAHmaica: Rastafari and Jamaican society, 1930–1990.* Utrecht, The Netherlands: ISOR.

———. 1995. Sociological means: Colonial reactions to the radicalization of Rastafari in Jamaica, 1956–1959. *New West Indian Guide* 69(1–2):67–101.

Wallace, Anthony. 1957. Revitalization movements. *American Anthropologist* 58:264–281.

Walzer, Michael. 1985. *Exodus and revolution.* New York: Basic Books.

Waters, Anita. 1989. *Race, class, and political symbols: Rastafari and reggae in Jamaican politics.* New Brunswick, NJ: Transaction Publishers.

Weisbord, Robert. 1970. British West Indian Reaction to the Italian-Ethiopian War: An Episode in Pan-Africanism. *Caribbean Studies* 10(1):34–51.

Whitten Jr., Norman. 1996. The Equidorian Levantamiento Indigena of 1990 and the epitomizing symbols of 1992: Reflections on nationalism, ethnic-bloc formation, and racialist ideologies. In *History, power, and identity: Ethnogenesis in the Americas, 1492–1992,* ed. J. Hill, 193–217. Iowa City: University of Iowa Press.

Wilmore, Gayraud. 1998. *Black religion and Black radicalism: An interpretation of the religious history of African Americans.* Maryknoll, NY: Orbis Books.

Wilmot, Swithin. 1997. *Freedom in Jamaica: Challenges and opportunities, 1838–1865.* Kingston, Jamaica: Jamaica Information Service (July).

Woodson, Carter G. 1933. *The miseducation of the Negro.* Elmont, NY: African Tree Press.

Yawney, Carole. 1994. Moving with the dawtas of Rastafari: From myth to reality. In *Arise ye mighty people! Gender, class and race in popular struggles,* ed. T. Turner, 65–73. Trenton, NJ: Africa World Press.

———. 1999. Only visitors here: Representing Rastafari into the 21st century. In *Religion, diaspora, and cultural identity: A reader in the Anglophone Caribbean,* ed. J. Pulis, 153–181. New York: Gordon & Breach.

Yelvington, Kevin. 1999. The War in Ethiopia and Trinidad 1935–1936. In *The colonial Caribbean in transition: Essays on postemancipation social and cultural history,* eds. B. Brereton & K. Yelvington, 189–225. Gainesville: University Press of Florida.

Index

Abyssinia. *See* Ethiopia

Africa, 70, 71; learning about, 164, 169; Mission to, 78–84. *See also* Repatriation

African Methodist Episcopal (AME) Church, 41

African Reform Church (ARC), 74. *See also* Henry, Claudius

Africans, race, xii. *See also* Jamaica

Afro-Athlyican Constructive Gaathlyans, 48–49. *See also Holy Piby*; Rogers, Robert

Alvaranga, Philmore, 79–80, 87

Amharic, 71, 91, 170–71, 214

Appeal to the Colored Citizens of the World, 40

Austin-Broos, D., 214

Babylon, 67, 139, 174, 231, 238n4

Back-O-Wall, 86–87, 220

Back-to-Africa movement, 73, 82. *See also* Repatriation

Baldheads, 192, 221

Baptist: Ethiopian Baptist Church, 33; Jamaica Native Baptist Free Church, 44; Rowe, John, 34. *See also* Native Baptist

Bayen, Malaku, 63

Bedward, Alexander, 40, 43–46. *See also* Native Baptist; Racial rhetoric

Bedwardites, 43–44, 58

Bible, 49, 171–72; Egypt in, 26; Ethiopia in, 26, 38–39; Hebrews in, 26;

King James version, 38, 49, 173; New Testament, ix; Old Testament, ix; Revelations, ix, x

Black identity theory, 8, 9, 110–11, 99, 104; contemporary studies, 113; early studies, 111–12. *See also* Blackness; Cross, William, Jr.; Identity; Nigrescence theory; Sellers, Robert, et al.

Black Nationalism, 1, 47, 172

Blackness, 1, 8, 116, 117, 230, 231–32; capitalization of, xv–xvi; compared with Whiteness, 235n1; content of, 110; cultural dimensions of, 4; ideas of proper, 139; as identification, 4, 113, 225; in Jamaica, 3, 21–22, 191, 205, 226; moral economy of, 26–29; morally configured, 3–4, 99, 230 (*see* Ethiopianism; Justice motifs); as pathology, 110; purposes of, 8, 105; Rastafari view of, 137; and religiosity, 4, 100 (*see* Ethiopianism; Justice motifs); stigmatized, 106, 112, 117. *See also* Identity; Nigrescence theory; Rastafari; Stigmatization

Black Power, 92–93; Michael Manley on, 94–95

Black redemption, 194; and Black king, 46–47; and return of Messiah, 50–53

Black Skins, White Masks, 104. *See also* Fanon, Frantz

Bogle, Paul, 22, 24, 26, 62. *See also* Gordon, George; Morant Bay; Native Baptist; Rebellion
Bones, Jah, 98
Bongo J, 24, 25, 118, 209, 212; on education, 207; on fear of Rastafari, 24; identity transformation, 128–29; photo, 25
Brother Alex, 89
Brother Bags, 177, 187
Brother Barody, 7, 187, 221; on becoming Rastafari, 118, 159–60; learning Amharic, 170–71
Brother Bongo, 129–30, 214–15, 220; on Christianity, 174; on his name, 100; on imprisonment, 190; on Jesus Christ, 158; learning about Africa, 169–70; on organizing Rastafari, 86–87; on politics, 84; on renouncing Jamaican nationality, 180–81; on scorn of Rastafari, 189; and relationship stress, 178–79, 184; on Selassie I, 54, 89–91; on women, 214–215; visions, 147
Brother Dee, 55–56, 68, 72–73, 221; on becoming Rastafari, 53, 106, 163; photo, 69; and Rasta Ivey, 55–56, 68, 72–73
Brothers Solidarity of United Ethiopia (BSUE), 70
Brother Woks, 13, 177, 188, 197, 226; on the Bible, 51, 171–72; on the Dreadlocks, 65; on Garvey, Marcus, 47, 51, 172–73; on growth of Rastafari, 206–7; on markers of Rastafari, 135
Brother Yendis, 1, 65, 72, 98, 191; on authenticity, 198–99, 212; becoming Rastafari, 182–83; and communion, 193; experiential witnessing, 161–62, 224; on inborn conception, 144; on *National Geographic*, 50; on

race and governance, 140; on Rastafari prophecy, 200; on redemption, 38–39; on relationship stress, 182; on Selassie I, 92; suppression of Rastafari, 65, 189; on violence against Rastafari, 196–97; on Walter Rodney, 93
Brown (racial identity), 25, 235n3
Brown, Bishop, 53–54
Bustamante, Alexander, 86

Campbell, Trevor, 91, 100
Cannabis. *See* Ganja
Caribbean, map of, 37
Carmichael, Stokely, 112, 123
Cashmore, E., 134
Césaire, Aimé, xii–xiii
Chalice, 193
Chants (Rastafari), xvii, 12, 88, 195
Chevannes, Barry, 14
Chosen people, 108, 168, 185, 188, 197; and peculiar, 71, 107–8, 158
Christianity, 126, 230; Christ, 136, 238n10, 239n10; Christians, 95, 173–74; Rastafari conversion to, 185; and slaves, 31–32
Class (social), 217–219, 231
Clayton, Sam, 87
Combsomes, 65–66, 109, 168
Communion. *See* Identity
Complexity (theory), 5, 57–58; disruption, 5, 57, 58, 228; initial conditions, 58; perturbation, 5, 92, 96; self-organization, 5, 58, 77; surprise, 57, 58. *See also* Ethnogenesis
Conquests (Rastafari): of Kings House, 73; of Victoria Square, 73
Conversion: as identity transformation, 9, 124; and potent ideas, 129; religious and racial, 100, 124; and seekership, 126–27; and social networks, 129; and sociocultural

context, 128–29; theories of religious, 100, 123, 124–25, 226; and turning points, 127. *See also* Identity transformation

Coral Gardens, 85–86

Cross Jr., William, 8, 114, 121, 124, 125; on change in referents, 125; on social movements, 112. *See also* Black identity theory; Nigrescence theory

Cultural: dissonance, 133–34; resources, 20–21; work, 10, 134

Daily Gleaner (*DG*), 60; announces death of Selassie, 203; coronation of Ras Tafari, ix; coverage of Pinnacle raid and trial, 64–65; coverage of trial of Howell and Hinds, 60; on deposing Selassie, 203

Dangerous Drugs Act, 64

Deracination, 21, 30, 117, 119

Douglas, M. B., 80–81

Dreadlocks, 168, 171; faction of Rastafari, 65–67, 71, 108–9, 168, 177, 215, 236n5; locks and, 65, 108, 171, 187; popularity of, 188

Dreams, 146. *See also* Visions

Du Bois, W.E.B, 109, 114, 118, 122

Dunkley, Archibald, 53–54

Elders, definition of, 15

Elites, 56, 79, 90, 203, 228; efforts to ruin Rastafari, 60, 65, 84, 88, 92

Empress Dinah, 19, 213, 217

Erlington, Paul, 63

Ethiopia, 39, 62, 70, 71, 172; Mission to, 80–81; Shashemene land grant, 71

Ethiopia Calls, 91

Ethiopian Baptist Church, 33

Ethiopianism, 38–42, 101, 230; and Black God, 45; and Black intellectuals, 40; connection to Black people, 38; and Haile Selassie I, 41; language of, 45, 60; messianic and millenarian, 38; secular, 40; spiritual, 40. *See also* Blackness; Justice motifs; Religion

Ethiopian Manifesto (Young), 40

Ethiopian Orthodox Church, 8–9, 202

Ethiopian Salvation Society (ESS), 63. *See also* Pinnacle

Ethiopian World Federation (EWF): on Blackness, 63; Local 17, 63, 236n3; Local 37, 70–71, 78. *See also* Richardson, Mamie

Ethnogenesis, 6, 20, 57, 124, 202, 222; evolution of new groups, 2, 20, 57, 227–29. *See also* Complexity (theory)

Existential questions, 9, 130, 124, 156

Experiential witnessing, 160–61, 163

Fanon, Franz, xiv; Blackness, xi, xii, xiii; internalization of oppression, 104–5

Fire, as symbol, 208

"Fire bu'n" (Fire burn), 72, 175, 177

Fisher, Edna, 74

Freedom: emancipation, 35; ideas about, 28

Freire, Paulo, 105

Gad, 73

Ganja, 64, 205, 211; "licking" chalice, 193–94

Garvey, Marcus, 46–48, 63, 76, 194; in Edelweiss Park, 163–64; Ethiopianist, 47; prophecy, 51, 172–73; race leader, 114. *See also* United Negro Improvement Association

Garveyites, 128–29

Gender, 16–17, 214, 215. *See also* Men, and signs of Rastafari identity, 65; Women, and Rastafari

Generation, definition of, 239n1. *See also* Rastafari, generational issues
Ghana, 82
Glazier, Stephen, 128
Gleaner. See Daily Gleaner
God (Black), 47, 103, 158, 159, 172–74
Gordon, George, 24–25, Native Baptist, 25. *See also* Bogle, Paul

Hannah, Barbara, xiv
Heart, 11, 24, 142; Blackheart, 24, 107
Henry, Claudius, 74–75, 78; letter to Fidel Castro, 75; and Michael Manley, 95. *See also* African Reform Church; Repatriation
Henry, Reynold, 75–76
Hibbert, Joseph, 53, 70
Hinds, Robert, 44, 54, 58–62, 71; on being Ethiopian, 38; trial, 59–60
Holy Piby, 48–49
Howell, Leonard, 5, 27, 58–64, 71, 163; trial, 1934, 59–60. *See also* Pinnacle; *Promise Key*

Identity: communion and, 192–94, 197–99; investment in, 191; mortification and, 179–80; personal, ix, 101, 114; petition for Ethiopian, 70, 87; purposes of, 101–4, 105, 113; Rastafari, 132, 143, 165; renunciation and, 168, 180–81; rewards of, 185, 191–93, 197–99; sacrifice for, 190; seeds, 134–35; self-concept, 101, 103; stigmatized, ix, 106–9; western, 109; work, 10, 168, 175. *See also* Black identity theory; Blackness; Nigrescence theory
Identity transformation, 6–7, 8, 10, 102–3, 104; 123; becoming Rastafari, 8, 10, 103; and name change, 68, 100, 181; and recycling, 122;

and relationship tension, 129, 131, 155, 178–80, 181–84, 226; and re-socialization, 120; as solution, xi, xiv, 102, 131, 132, 167. *See also* Blackness; Black identity theory; Conversion; Identity; Stigmatization
Immigrants to Jamaica, 36
Inborn conception, 142–45, 163; "anciency" and "latency," 141
I n I, 71, 136, 238n2
Internalization. *See* Nigrescence theory
Internalized oppression, 137–40, 166; transcending, 142
Investment. *See* Identity

Jackson III, Bailey, 112
Jackson, C. A., 68
Jah Bones, 98
Jamaica, 87, 191; early Rastafari in Portland parish, 61; early Rastafari in St. Thomas parish, 59, 61–62; indentured Africans in, 70, 141, 159; map of, 23; settlement of, especially African, 29–30; slave trade, 29–30. *See also* Africans, race; Kingston
Jamaica Native Baptist Free Church, 44
Jamaican Ethiopian Orthodox Church, 181
Jesus, 103; and Prophetess, 152, 153, 154
Johnson, Millard, 84, 85
Jones, Delmos, 13
Joshua, 95. *See also* Manley, Michael
Justice motifs, 21, 45, 132, 153. *See also* Ethiopianism; Moral economy, of Blackness

Kenya, mission to, 87
Kenyatta, Jomo, 87
Kilbourne, B., and J. Richardson, 124
King David, 41

King James Bible, 38, 173. *See also*
　Bible
King of Lagos, 81
King Ras Tafari. *See* Selasie I, Haile
Kingston, 61–63
Kumina, 33

Lake, O., 214
Language used by Rastafari, 7, 68, 71
Leslie, L. C., 79
Lewis, George, 33
Liberia, 82–83
Life stories, 10–11
Lisle, George, 33
Lyall, Sir Robert, 59–60

Mack, Douglas, 79–80, 91, 163
Majority Report, 80. See also *Minority
　Report*
Malcolm X, 114
Ma Lion, 51
Manley, Michael, 94–96, 203. *See also*
　Joshua
Manley, Norman, 76, 78–79; Mission
　to Africa, 83; on slavery, 81–82
Margai, Sir Milton, 83
Marley, Bob, 94, 96, 185, 191
Maroons, 26, 57, 83, 236n9; and free-
　dom, 31; Peace Treaty, 31
Mau Mau movement, 67–68
McNeil, Roy, 87, 93
Men, and signs of Rastafari identity, 65
Menen, Empress, 198
Mental slavery, emancipation from,
　174
Millenarian groups, 72, 144
Minority Report, 81. See also *Majority
　Report*
Miseducation, 21, 105, 117, 119, 168–
　69; explanation of, 39–40. *See also*
　Nigrescence theory
Mission to Africa, 78–85

Monroe–Scarlett, Z., 80
Moral community, 192
Moral economy, 27–28; and Bedward-
　ites, 44–45; of Blackness, 26–29;
　racialized, 21; Rastafari and, 54. *See
　also* Ethiopianism; Justice motifs
Morant Bay, 22, 26; rebellion, 22–24,
　59, 62. *See also* Bogle, Paul
Mortification. *See* Identity
Muhammed, Elijah, 112
Mussolini, Benito, 62
Mutabaruka, 1, 160
Myalism, 32–33; Myalist War 34–35

Narayan, Kirin, 13
National Geographic, 49–50
Native Baptist, 24, 25; and Myalism,
　33. *See also* Bedward, Alexander;
　Bogle, Paul; Sam Sharpe Rebellion
Native researcher issue, 11, 13–14
Nettleford, Rex, 77, 85, 87
Nigeria, 81–82
Nigrescence theory, 7, 8, 9, 100, 226,
　227, 237n5; critique of, 123; en-
　counter, 104, 116, 118–19, 130, 146,
　167, 223–24; explanation of, 100,
　113–16, 237n5; extending 104, 119,
　122–23, 146; immersion–emersion,
　116, 120–21, 170, 213; internaliza-
　tion, 116, 121–22; internalization-
　commitment, 116, 122, 184–92, 199,
　220; pre-encounter, 116–17; refer-
　ence group orientation, 114–15, 120;
　states and processes in, 115–16, 123.
　See also Black identity theory; Black-
　ness; Cross Jr., William; Identity
Nkrumah, Kwame, 82
Nyabingi (African), 62; vs. Nyabinghi,
　62
Nyabinghi, 62, 140, 157, 195, 200;
　"universal convention (Grounda-
　tion)," 73

Order of Melchisidec, 44, 154
Organic intellect, 163–65
Organizations (Rastafari), 63, 68, 195–96. *See also* Brothers Solidarity of United Ethiopia; Ethiopian Salvation Society; Rastafari Federation; Rastafari International Theocratic Assembly; Rastafari Movement Association
Owens, J., 14

Parchment, Clinton, 75–76
Peculiar people. *See* Chosen people
People's National Party (PNP), 7, 96
Pettersburgh, Reverend Fitz, 49
Phillippo, James, 26
Philos, Frederico, 62
Pinnacle, 63–64, 69; *See also* Ethiopian Salvation Society; Howell, Leonard
Planner (also Planno), Mortimer, 50, 77, 80, 142, 166
Price, Charles (of Morant Bay), 23–24
Prince Emmanuel (Charles Edwards), 73
Prince Hall, 40
Promise Key, 49
Prophetess, 147–56, 224–26; photo, 149, 150

Queen Victoria of England, 73

Race, 21, 25, 138; construction of, ix, 8; formation, 3
Racial rhetoric, 22, 24, 45, 61, 62, 138
Rambo, L., 9, 124, 125
Ras Brenton, 77, 100, 142, 179, 183; on becoming Rastafari, 165, 167, 238n8; on Christ, 197–98; on class, 217–19; on Ethiopia, 39; fire bu'n, 176; on inborn conception, 143; on learning, 122, 171; on the Messiah, 50; on race and governance, 137–38; on Rastafari youth, 206; and relationship stress, 178, 183; on repatriation, 195; on technology, 208–9; on time, 229
Ras Burrell, 120, 126–27; on becoming Rastafari, 160
Ras Cee, 201–2
Ras Chronicle, 102, 122, 202, 209–10; on education, 207; on King David, 41; on nations, 210–12; on stigma, 107
Ras Desmond, 175–76, 231
Ras General, 223
Ras Grantly, 175, 185, 193, 203–4
Ras Jayze, 5, 67, 177
Ras Kirk, 229
Ras Sam Brown, 6, 55, 182, 199, 232; on becoming Rastafari, 145, 163–65; on church, 133–34; on Dreadlocks, 65–66; on meeting Marcus Garvey, 163–64; photo, 66; on politics, 84–85, 96; about Rastafari, 19; on repatriating, 194; on reward, 199; on White oppression, 110, 138
Rastafari, x, 1, 174; authentic, 198; becoming, 103, 130–31, 142; and Black liberation, 20; class tension, 217–18; commitment, 184–89, 220; and education, 207–8; emerging, 132; experimental, 212; gender, 16–17, 213–17; generational issues, 6, 175–76, 202; ideal of "peace and love," 72–73; identification with past, xv, 3, 19, 35, 143, 144, 145; international dimensions of, 203, 205, 210–12; language, xvi, 7, 68, 71, 181; people, x, 6; popularity, 191–92; reaction to Selassie's "death," 204; seeing, 132, 136, 157, 228; stigma, 106–07; suppression of, 62, 188; symbols of, 65; use of Selassie's speeches, 175; and technology, 208–10; titles of address,

xvi, 181; violence, symbolic, 62, 72, 105, 131; women, 54, 66–68, 203, 213–17; youth, 201–2. *See also* Blackness; Chosen people; Dreadlocks; Identity; Identity transformation; Nyabinghi; "Sight up"

Rastafari Federation (RF), 192, 202, 204, 210; women and, 15, 147, 215

Rastafari International Theocratic Assembly (RITA), 196, 222

Rastafari Movement Association (RMA), 85, 196, 203

Rasta Ivey, 1, 12–13, 54, 163, 238n5; on becoming Rastafari, 158–59, 224; and Brother Dee, 55–56, 68, 72–73; on harshness of Brown and Black authorities, 68–69, 138–39; on persecution, 188; photo, 43; and Rastafari diversity, 210; on righteousness, 18; on Salvation Army, 52–53; on Sam Sharpe rebellion, 35; on time, 141, 144–45; view of Haile Selassie I, 145, 154

Rasta J, 78–79

Rebellion: and moral economy, 29; Morant Bay, 22–24, 26–27, and religion, 33; Sam Sharpe (or Myalist), 34–35; Tacky, 32

Redemption, 27

Reference group orientation, 114–15, 173–74, 180

Reggae, 205, 211

Reid, Altamont, 78

Relative deprivation, 133

Religion: purposes, 124, 126; and race, 2, 3, 8, 9, 100–101, 123–24. *See also* Conversion; Ethiopianism

Renunciation. *See* Identity

Repatriation, 61, 74, 194–95, 218; Mission to Africa, 78–84; Rastafari organizing for, 70–71, 86–87. *See also* Back-to-Africa movement

Report (Smith et al.), 14, 77–78

Reward. *See* Identity

Richardson, Mamie, 70–71, 73, 78. *See also* Ethiopian World Federation

Rodney Riot, 92 94

Rodney, Walter, 92–94

Rogers, Robert, 48–49. *See also* Afro-Athlyican Constructive Gaathlyans; *Holy Piby*

Royal Parchment Scroll of Black Supremacy, 48–49

Sacrifice. *See* Identity

Salvation Army, 51–52, 53

Sam Sharpe Rebellion, 34–35

Scott, James, 27

Seaga, Edward, 95, 203

Seekership, 126–27, 226. *See also* Conversion; Nigrescence theory

Selassie I, Haile, 1, 70–71, 145, 198; celebrations of, 194; coronation of, ix; "death" of, 96 97, 203; the elect of, 107; and Menelik, 39, 236n13; Messiah, 59; and Mission to Ethiopia, 80–81; in *National Geographic*, 50; the Redeemer, 59, 71, 154; removed from power, 203; visit to Jamaica, 88–92. *See also* Ethiopia; Rastafari; Mission to Africa

Self-elevation, 107–8, 136

Sellers, Robert, et al., 113

Sharpe, Sam, 34–35; Rebellion, 34—35

Shashemene, 71

Shearer, Hugh, 86, 112

Sierra Leone, 83

"Sight up," 99, 136, 142. *See also* Identity transformation; Rastafari

Sister Amme, 111, 156–58

Sister Coromantee, 17

Sister Ecila, 8–9

Sister Mariam, 4, 47–48, 216

Sister Pear, 103, 130–31

Slavery: acts, 31–32; slave ethnicity, 30; trade and, 29–30

Smith, M. G., 77

Social movement, 5, 6, 92, 112, 237n8; decentralization, 7; grievances, 132; prefigurative, 7

South Africa, 40–42, 200

Stigmatization, 106, 107; of Blackness, 106, 112, 227; of Rastafari, 106, 107, 182; and self-elevation, 107, 108; and voluntary disclosure, 109. *See also* Blackness; Identity

Sturtevant, William, 57

Subversion of identity, race, xi-xii, 102, 181

Tacky Rebellion, 32

Tainos, 29

Thomas, D., 205, 231

Thompson, E. P., 28, 34

Tubman, William, 82

Turner, Henry, 41–42

Turner, Nat, 114, 122

Turning point, 127–29. *See also* Conversion

United Negro Improvement Association (UNIA), 46–47, 130, 172; Liberty Hall, 63. *See also* Garvey, Marcus

University College of the West Indies (UCWI), 77, 92, 94

Vestry, 22, 26

Visions, 146–47

Voices of Ethiopia, 130

Walker, David, 40

Wallace, Anthony, 124

Walters, Herben, 102

White (racial identity), 25, 235n1; hegemony, x

Women, and Rastafari, 54, 66–68, 203, 213–17; markers of, 65; presence among Rastafari, 66–67. *See also* Gender; Rastafari

Woodson, Carter, 105

"Word, sound and power," theory of, 71–72, 78–79

Yard, 195–96; tenement, 220

Young, Robert, 40; on Black Messiah, 51

About the Author

CHARLES PRICE is Associate Professor of Anthropology at the University of North Carolina at Chapel Hill.